D1518035

God *in* Everyday Life

Life

The Book of Ruth for Expositors and Biblical Counselors

Brad Brandt & Eric Kress

Kress Christian
PUBLICATIONS

God in Everyday Life
The Book of Ruth for Expositors and Biblical Counselors

© 2007 Brad Brandt and Eric Kress

All Rights Reserved
No part of this publication may be reproduced, stored in a retrieval system, or transmitted in any form or by any means—electronic, mechanical, photocopy, recording, or any other—except for brief quotations embodied in critical articles or printed reviews, without prior written permission of the publisher.

Published by:

Kress Christian
PUBLICATIONS

P.O. Box 132228
The Woodlands, TX 77393
www.kresschristianpublications.com

Unless otherwise indicated, Scripture in Brad's expository sermon taken from the *HOLY BIBLE, NEW INTERNATIONAL VERSION* ® Copyright © 1973, 1978, 1984 by International Bible Society. Used by permission of Zondervan Publishing House. All rights reserved.

Unless otherwise indicated, Scripture in Rick's expositional commentary taken from the *NEW AMERICAN STANDARD BIBLE* ® Copyright © 1960, 1962, 1963, 1968, 1971, 1972, 1973, 1975, 1977, 1995 by The Lockman Foundation. Used by permission. (www.Lockman.org)

Scripture quotations marked (NLT) are from the NEW LIVING TRANSLATION. Copyright © 1996. Used by permission of Tyndale House Publishers.

Scripture quotations marked (YLT) are from the YOUNG'S LITERAL TRANSLATION.

Front Cover Image courtesy of Pitts Theology Library, Candler School of Theology, Emory University.

ISBN 0-9772262-5-5
Cover Design: Paul Lewis
Text Design: Valerie Moreno
Editorial Consultants: Kevin McAteer; Valerie Moreno; Margaret Randall; Diana Severance; Traci Stephenson

To Sherry, my beloved wife.

I am eternally grateful that in His providence God blessed me
with a wife like you, a woman who selflessly lives out Ruth's vow…

*"Where you go I will go, and where you stay I will stay.
Your people will be my people and your God my God."*
Ruth 1:16

Brad

To Elizabeth and David, who God used to plant the seed-idea for this project.
And to Raymond, my co-laborer, who shares a God-implanted passion for the
Scriptures.

Rick

Contents

Introduction

"He didn't parse any Hebrew verbs," Bob muttered as the student body filed out of seminary chapel. "Yea, and he didn't even mention the chiasm in the text," Eric chimed in. "I'd bet you five bucks he doesn't even know Hebrew."

"What are you guys mumbling about?" It was Jim, a second year student in the Master of Religious Education program. "I don't care what you say, *now* that was a sermon! That man hit me right *here*," countered Jim as he pumped his fist into his chest. "I wish we had a few more chapel speakers that preached like we lived in the twentieth century."

That conversation occurred twenty-four years ago during my first year in seminary. Well, sort of. I'm not sure those were the actual words or names, but the tension was real. Within the sacred halls of higher learning there were a couple of distinct types of men preparing for ministry. There were the 'scholarly' sorts and then there were the 'practical' sorts. There were students who measured a sermon's success based on the preacher's ability to connect with the biblical world and others who considered a good sermon one that hit a home run tapping into the real world of the present.

Then I became a pastor. At the age of twenty-six and fresh out of seminary, I moved to the Appalachian foothills of southern Ohio and began shepherding an established church, one that had been around one hundred and ten years. After four years of theological education I was now in the *real world*. Surely the scholarship/relevance rivalry was past. Unfortunately, it didn't take me long to discover otherwise.

I am committed to expository preaching, predominantly preaching through books of the Bible line-by-line, word-by-word. I believe God's Word is not only inspired and inerrant, but also sufficient for the needs of the precious saints entrusted to my care.

My approach in preparing a message begins with careful exegesis of the text. "What was the intent of the author?" is the question that drives this initial study. My people will need to know the authorial intent, too. They will need to see that the source of the instruction they are receiving is not *me*, but *God Himself* speaking through a divinely chosen biblical author. But I know as I prepare the sermon that the flock needs more than a mere history lesson from their shepherd. They need fresh food. "How does this apply to my life?" is the question they are asking and I too must ask. And seek to answer.

Yet here is where the rivalry remains. Commentaries are a pastor's friend. At least that is what I assumed they *should* be when I became a pastor. However, after nearly two decades of working through biblical texts and calling upon dozens and dozens of commentaries for assistance, I have come to a conclusion. Commentaries are like seminarians. Some provide a tedious examination of the biblical text but apparently assume that the bridge to the world of the present either is not necessary or will just take care of itself. Others offer quite down to earth biblical 'application' but leave the pastor scratching his head wondering just how *biblical* the application really is.

Why does it have to be either/or? Is it not possible to write a commentary that takes seriously the biblical world *and* the contemporary world? Is that not why our gracious, revealing God gave the world His Word in the first place, so we could both understand it *and* live it? I believe it is.

That is why the book you are holding came to be. This is an expositional commentary on the book of Ruth. It is also a commentary on how the book of Ruth speaks to the people with whom we live and minister today. What you are about to read (I realize this is an assumption but I hope you will continue to read!) is the fruit of local church ministry. What began as exegesis in my study resulted in proclamation from the church pulpit. Understanding the message of the book of Ruth was a life and death matter for me because entrusted to my care are the lives of men and women, boys and girls, who desperately need to hear the speech of God. Getting it right exegetically was essential. But so was getting it (the message of Ruth) into the lives of nurses, businessmen, teachers, elementary school children, and all the rest of God's image-bearers who come to hear God's Word.

In the providence of God I received a phone call last month from a pastor in Texas. "I've been reading your Ruth manuscripts online," he shared. "Would you be interested in writing a commentary for pastors?" he asked. And so God brought Rick Kress into my life. "Perhaps we could do it together," Rick added. "I taught the book of Ruth here recently. I'll send you my manuscripts if you're interested." And that's what happened.

This book is a joint effort. Although Rick and I share a mutual commitment to sound biblical exposition, you will quickly note our differences in perspective and approach (Rick used six messages to work through Ruth, while I used five). We hope the variety will encourage you.

Each chapter also includes a *Getting Intentional about Application* section. In addition to serving as a pastor, I am also a Fellow with the National

Association of Nouthetic Counselors. I believe that God has given us in His sufficient Word real answers for the real problems of life. That is why I engage in biblical counseling as well as in training biblical counselors. The *Getting Intentional about Application* section seeks to put tools in your hands (such as case studies, discussion questions, and counseling assignments) that you can use to implement the message of Ruth in local church ministry.

Must scholarship and application remain at odds? No. Our aim is to put them together as friends, in one book no less. Our prayer is that God will use this resource to encourage and equip our fellow-soldiers in the trenches, all to the glory of our worthy King!

Brad Brandt
May 2007

Some may ask, "Why write another expositional commentary on the book of Ruth?" "Hasn't that been done before?" Countless times. But the Bible is an infinite book, as it is the Word of an infinite God. Its riches cannot be fully exhausted. Our glorious Lord and Savior is worthy of our worship as we seek to understand His Word and apply it to our lives. This book is meant to be a tool to aid Bible teachers and individuals in their quest to worship Him with their lives and proclaim His excellencies to others.

As a pastor-teacher, I buy many books dealing with Bible exposition. Some I buy for the nuts and bolts of exegesis. Some I buy simply because the outline is detailed and suggestive as it follows the flow of thought throughout the biblical book. Some I buy because the writer is very quotable, or because the book is helpful for application. This book is an attempt to combine a few of the varied elements and styles of different types of study aids into one resource, in order to facilitate the biblical exposition and application of the book of Ruth. What follows is not a detailed exegetical work, but rather an expositional commentary, and expository sermon, and some tools to help apply the biblical text.

We have chosen to leave many of our grammatical, stylistic and literary idiosyncrasies in our respective sermon notes. We hope that the variety (i.e., lack of uniformity) will be more helpful than distracting. We've also included a bibliography of resources we found helpful on the book of Ruth with brief annotations to give you a reference for further study.

May God and His glorious redemption through Christ be magnified as you read this book!

Rick Kress
June 2007

CHAPTER

1

Seeing God in Our Losses

Ruth 1:1-22

Expositional Commentary and Outline:
The Pain of Covenant Faithlessness (1:1-5)

Expositional Commentary and Outline:
The Pity/Kindness of God That Leads to Repentance (1:6-22)

Expository Sermon: Seeing God in Our Losses (1:1-22)

Getting Intentional About Application

Tool #1: A Teaching Outline
Tool #2: "Digging Deeper" Discussion Questions
Tool #3: A Counseling Case Study
Tool #4: Counseling Assignments

Expositional Outline:

Ruth 1:1-5

by Rick Kress

Introductory Matters

I. **The author**
   A. The human author
   B. The divine Author (2 Tim. 3:16; 2 Pet. 1:20-21; cf. Heb. 1:1)

II. **The audience**
   A. The first audience
   B. The current audience (Rom. 15:4; 1 Cor. 10:11)

III. **The aim**
   A. To reveal God's grace and loyal love to the believing remnant in spite of Israel's covenant unfaithfulness (1:1-6; 2:20)
   B. To reveal God's sovereignty in furthering His purposes in spite of His people's covenant unfaithfulness (1:22b; 2:1-3; 4:13)
   C. To reveal the character of true faith and love in light of Yahweh's sovereign grace (1:16-17; 2:11-12, 15-17; 3:1, 10-11)
   D. To reveal a portrait of redemption (2:12; 3:12-13; 4:9-10, 14)
   E. To reveal that even a Gentile can receive God's sovereign redemption through faith (1:4, 22; 2:2, 6, 21; 4:5, 10; cf. 2:12)
   F. To reveal that there is always a remnant of those who believe, even in times of great apostasy (1:16-17; 2:4, 11-12, 20; 3:10; see especially 4:11-14)
   G. To reveal that God's sovereign plan of redemption continues on—through the Seed of the woman/Messiah—no matter the apparent state of the world (1:1-2; cf. 4:17-22; Judges 17:1; 19:1; 21:25; see also Rom. 8:28)

The Book of Ruth—A Portrait of God's Loyal Love, Sovereign Redemption, and the Faith of His Believing Remnant

I. **The pain of covenant faithlessness [an empty profession] (1:1-5)**
   A. **Famine and faithlessness in the land (1:1-2)**
      1. Covenant faithlessness as a nation (v. 1a)
      2. Covenant faithlessness as a family (v. 1b-2)
   B. **Funerals and weddings in Moab (1:3-5)**
      1. Naomi's husband died (1:3)
      2. Naomi's sons married Moabite women (1:4)
      3. Naomi's sons died but she was left as a remnant out of her two children and her husband (1:5)

Expositional Commentary:
The Pain of Covenant Faithlessness

Ruth 1:1-5

by Rick Kress

All of us have made decisions in our lives that seemed logical and expedient, but were in reality faithless. We may have not questioned God's goodness verbally, but we decided to take matters in our own hands. A job change—a marriage—a divorce—a move—a change of churches—you name it. Sometimes our decisions have had devastating consequences in our lives. And sometimes we're tempted to believe that because of our unfaithfulness in the past, we've lost any opportunity to participate in God's plan and program in the future. Today in introducing the book of Ruth, we will begin to see the grace of God against the backdrop of such pain and devastating consequences.

Let's begin looking at the introductory material that sets the stage for our study of the book of Ruth.

I. The author
A. The human author
The Scriptures do not explicitly identify the human author of the book of Ruth. Jewish tradition held that Samuel was the author. Ruth 1:1 sets the context for the events of the story of Naomi, Ruth and Boaz "in the days when the judges governed". Thus, we can assume that the book was actually written down after the days of the judges (see also the explanation of 4:7 indicating some time lapse between the customs of those days and the era concurrent with the actual writing down of Ruth). Samuel was the last of the judges and actually inaugurated the monarchy in Israel by anointing Saul as King over Israel (1 Sam. 10:1ff), and later David (1 Sam. 16:6-13). As well, the mention of "David" in 4:17 and the genealogy of 4:18-22 may give a clue as to the time period that the book was written. It would seem that it was written when "David" was prominent in Israel—thus sometime during or after his reign. Yet the absence of Solomon in the genealogy may indicate that it was written before Solomon came to power. David reigned in Israel from 1011-971 B.C.

Since God did not see fit to reveal the human author of the book of Ruth, He evidently didn't deem it as necessary for understanding its contents. But He did give us clues as to its historical context and its purposes, as we shall see.

B. The divine Author (2 Tim. 3:16; 2 Pet. 1:20-21; cf. Heb. 1:1)
We must never forget that the book of Ruth is more than just an interesting story. It is God's Word—written to reveal His glory, and His unfolding plan of redemption.

II. The audience
A. The first audience
It is clear, from 1:1 and the many references to Yahweh, that the book of Ruth was written for a Jewish audience. And as just discussed, it was an audience who lived in a different era than that of when the judges judged in Israel (1:1; 4:7). The audience was familiar with "David" (4:17) and concerned with his lineage (4:18-22)—and the "Seed" promise (4:12; cf. Gen. 3:15; 49:10).

In summary, Ruth was written for a believing remnant in Israel, perhaps during David's reign and preserved for subsequent generations of God's people.

B. The current audience (Rom. 15:4; 1 Cor. 10:11)
The book of Ruth was written for our instruction as New Testament believers as well. The truths contained in this precious gem will also reprove, rebuke, correct and train us in righteousness.

III. The aim
A. To reveal God's grace and loyal love to the believing remnant in spite of Israel's covenant unfaithfulness (1:1-6; 2:20)
B. To reveal God's sovereignty in furthering His purposes in spite of His people's covenant unfaithfulness (1:22b; 2:1-3; 4:13)
C. To reveal the character of true faith and love in light of Yahweh's sovereign grace (1:16-17; 2:11-12, 15-17; 3:1, 10-11)
D. To reveal a portrait of redemption (2:12; 3:12-13; 4:9-10, 14)
E. To reveal that even a Gentile can receive God's sovereign redemption through faith (1:4, 22; 2:2, 6, 21; 4:5, 10; cf. 2:12)
F. To reveal that there is always a remnant of those who believe, even in times of great apostasy (1:16-17; 2:4, 11-12, 20; 3:10; see especially 4:11-14)
G. To reveal that God's sovereign plan of redemption continues on— through the Seed of the woman/Messiah—no matter the apparent state of the world (1:1-2; cf. 4:17-22; Judges 17:1; 19:1; 21:25; see also Rom. 8:28)

The Book of Ruth—A Portrait of God's Loyal Love, Sovereign Redemption, and the Faith of His Believing Remnant
I. The pain of covenant faithlessness [an empty profession] (1:1-5)
A. Famine and faithlessness in the land (1:1-2)
1. Covenant faithlessness as a nation (v. 1a)
"Now it came about in the days when the judges governed, that there was a famine in the land"
The Hebrew phrase, "The days of the judging of the judges", would immediately signal to the believing Israelite that the historical context that surround-

ed this narrative was one of apostasy, chaos, disobedience and sin. Judges 17:6 and 21:25 both provide a summary of the rather dismal theme of the days of the judges—they both say, "In those days there was no king in Israel; everyone did what was right in his own eyes" (cf. 18:1; 19:1).

The mention of "a famine in the land" would also alert the believer to the fact that God was being faithful to His promise of covenant curses as contained in Deuteronomy 28 and Leviticus 26 (see specifically Lev. 26:19-20, 26; Deut. 28:15, 17, 23-24, 38-40, 42; cf. Deut. 11:16-17).

"And a certain man of Bethlehem in Judah . . . Ephrathites of Bethlehem in Judah"
The mention of "Bethlehem in Judah" here in verse 1, and "Ephrathites of Bethlehem in Judah" in verse two, would also serve to create a mental picture for the believing Israelite as he heard the teaching of the book of Ruth. Judges 17:7ff reveals the bleak account of a Levite (Moses' grandson) who lived in "Bethlehem", and who actually became an idolatrous priest for the Danites (see Judges 17-18; esp. 17:7-10; 18:27-31). It was a place where the faith of Yahweh had become more than a little corrupted. In addition, the second appendix of the book of Judges involves "Bethlehem in Judah". According to Judges 19:1ff, a civil war actually arose in Israel over the rape and murder of a woman who hailed from "Bethlehem in Judah" (cf. Josh. 19:15 for "Bethlehem" in the territory of Zebulun in northern Israel).

The term "Ephrathites" would have been a clue, however, that the story of Ruth might in some way be connected to David, as 1 Samuel 17:12 says that "David was the son of the Ephrathite of Bethlehem in Judah, whose name was Jesse" (cf. Gen. 35:19; 48:7; Micah 5:2). Likely "Ephrathites" designates a founding or notable family in Bethlehem.

Everything mentioned in this introduction to the book of Ruth smacked of national covenant unfaithfulness. It was "in the days when the judges governed", and "there was a famine in the land", and the notorious town of "Bethlehem in Judah" was involved.

2. Covenant faithlessness as a family (v. 1b-2)
"And a certain man of Bethlehem in Judah went to sojourn in the land of Moab with his wife and his two sons"
"Bethlehem" literally means, "house of bread". It was no doubt a fertile area within Israel and Judah. But the famine in the land had reached the point that a resident of "Bethlehem in Judah went to sojourn in the land of Moab with his wife and his two sons". In Gideon's day during the period of the judges, there was a famine according to the evidence in Judges 6:3-6. But the exact time period of this famine cannot be determined.

It is quite interesting to note that the first two uses in Scripture of the word "sojourn" are found in Genesis 12:10 and Genesis 19:9—Abraham's disobedient "sojourn" in Egypt during famine and Lot's stay as an alien in Sodom. It is also used of Israel's sanctioned stay in Egypt in Genesis 47:4—but only after reluctant Jacob received divine permission to leave the Promised Land (Gen. 46:3-4). Thus, though it is not specifically stated here, it would seem that this "certain man of Bethlehem in Judah" who left the Promised Land for "the land of Moab" was not acting in faith. The more appropriate response would have been repentance and a turning to Yahweh with all of one's heart (Deut. 30:1ff). Instead, he "went to sojourn in the land of Moab with his wife and two sons". The act very well may have been a practical questioning of God's goodness. If God would not provide for them in the land He had promised to them, then they would go elsewhere to provide for themselves.

"Moab" was the nation east of Israel on the other side of the Jordan and Dead Sea area (Deut. 32:48). The nation originated from the incestuous episode of Lot and his oldest daughter recorded in Genesis 19:30-37 (cf. Deut. 2:9). The name "Moab" literally means "from father". Later, the Moabites would hire Balaam to curse Israel (Num. 22-24) and seek to destroy Israel through immorality and idolatry (Num. 25:1-9). The book of Judges says that the nation of Moab also oppressed Israel during the days of the judges (Judges 3:12-30). See also Judges 10:6 for a further mention of their idolatrous influence on Israel. And finally, Deuteronomy 23:3-6 says that a Moabite was forbidden to enter the assembly of Yahweh, even "to the tenth generation" (see also Neh. 13:1; cf. Is. 56:1-8; Ruth 1:16; 2:12).

All of these factors suggest strongly that this "certain man" who left Israel to "sojourn" in "Moab"—indeed acted faithlessly. The phrase "certain man", by the way, indicates that this was an individual choice and not a mass migration of Israelites at this time. The grammar suggests that he was responsible for the move, and "his wife and two sons" followed as tagalongs so to speak (Block, p. 626). As family leader he led them in familial covenant faithlessness.

"The name of the man was Elimelech, and the name of his wife, Naomi"
Ironically in light of the aforementioned context, the "certain man's" name was "Elimelech", "And Elimelech", which means "my God is King". Yet by his actions, he was denying the very truth that his name proclaimed. "Naomi" in Hebrew, means "delightful/sweet/pleasant" (cf. 1:20).

"And the names of his two sons were Mahlon and Chilion, Ephrathites of Bethlehem in Judah"
"Mahlon and Chilion" are names that are debated as to their meaning. Many believe "Mahlon" to mean "weak" or "sick"; and "Chilion" to mean "to come to an end", or "mortality" (Block, p. 625; Morris, p. 249).

As previously mentioned, the phrase, "Ephrathites of Bethlehem in Judah" likely sets apart this family as from a distinguished or notable clan. So the move to Moab may have been even a bit more scandalous.

"Now they entered the land of Moab and remained there"
The word "land" here is not the normal Hebrew term for "land". It is more often translated "field". "Now they went to the field of Moab and lived there." Elimelech left his own "field" in the Promised Land (4:3, 5—same Hebrew word—*sadeh*) for "the field of Moab". It became more than a temporary stay—for they "remained there".

So the initial context is one of *famine and faithlessness in the land*.

B. Funerals and weddings in Moab (1:3-5)
1. Naomi's husband died (1:3)
"Then Elimelech, Naomi's husband, died; and she was left with her two sons"
Using a great economy of words, we're told that "Elimelech . . . died". The designation "Naomi's husband" seems to indicate that she is of greater importance to the story than "Elimelech" himself. The author chose not to discuss the manner of his death, but only that he "died". "Elimelech" had left with his family to find relief from the famine—i.e., the divine consequence of national covenant unfaithfulness. But instead of relief, he found death. As Amos 7:17 would reveal in a later era, to die upon unclean soil was not an honor to the Israelite.

Naomi was now "left with her two sons". Interestingly, the term "left" is often used for a "remnant" who survives the judgment of God (Block, p. 628). Almost every phrase is tinged with the pain of covenant unfaithfulness, yet even in Naomi's widowhood she was left as a remnant—i.e., implying that she had survived the judgment of God—revealing the grace of God. Sadly, the text does not say that Naomi and her sons repented and went back to Bethlehem, but rather verse four tells us they actually dug deeper roots in Moab's soil.

2. Naomi's sons married Moabite women (1:4)
"They took for themselves Moabite women as wives"
After the brief respite of Naomi being left as a remnant, again the writer records the painful events that followed. The phrase, "they took for themselves," reveals that Mahlon and Chilion chose their own wives, and they were "Moabite women". Literally, the word "took" means to "lift" or "carry". When used in contexts of marriage, it always has negative connotations in the Scriptures (Judges 21:23; Ruth 1:4; 2 Chron. 11:21; 13:21; 24:3; Ezra 9:2, 12; 10:44; Neh. 13:25; cf. Block, p. 628-39).

Moabites worshipped the false god, Chemosh (Num. 21:29; Judges 11:24), which evidently at least sometimes involved child sacrifice (cf. 2 Kings 3:26-

27). The principle of Deuteronomy 7:3-4 prohibiting Israelites from marrying pagans could well be applied here, even if Moabites were not specifically mentioned (cf. Ex. 34:11-16; 1 Kings 11:1-11; Ezra 9:1ff; Neh. 13:23-27). ["It is obvious from the study of Deuteronomy 7 that not every nation is mentioned, only the outstanding political enemies that controlled Canaan at that time" (Davis, p. 159).] As previously mentioned, Deuteronomy 23:3-6 cast the Moabites in an entirely negative light. According to Deuteronomy 28:32, one of God's covenant curses was that "Your sons and your daughters shall be given to another people, while your eyes look on and yearn for them continually, but there will be nothing you can do" (though likely speaking of captivity and exile, the principle seems to be relevant here).

Thus here we're confronted with the context of the pain of marriage outside of covenant faithfulness and faith. Yet even this, as we will see, is not beyond God's grace.

"The name of the one was Orpah and the name of the other was Ruth"
The meanings of the names "Orpah" and "Ruth" are disputed, but some have suggested that "Orpah" meant "stubborn"—from the root "neck" or "turn the neck"; and "Ruth" meaning "friendship". Ruth 4:10 reveals that "Ruth" was married to Mahlon, and thus "Orpah" was evidently Chilion's wife. They are mentioned by name here, however, for the sake of the narrative in the rest of chapter one.

"And they lived there about ten years"
Though some believe that the "ten years" here would include the total time of the family's stay in Moab, the sequence of the narrative is more naturally understood to mean that they "dwelled" in Moab for approximately 10 years after their marriage. If this was indeed the case, then it is noteworthy to mention that barrenness could also be considered one of God's covenant curses according to Deuteronomy 28:18 (cf. Deut. 7:13).

What began as a "sojourn" in verse 1 had become a dwelling place for a decade (Luter, p. 28). There was famine, faithlessness, a funeral and then a foreboding statement concerning marriage and a decade of life in Moab. This was the tragic and excruciating scene that introduced the book of Ruth. But the pain does not end there.

3. Naomi's sons died but she was left as a remnant out of her two children and her husband (1:5)
"Then both Mahlon and Chilion also died, and the woman was bereft of her two children and her husband"
Again here, the Hebrew could read—"the woman was left a remnant out of her two children and her husband". And again with an economy of words, the

text says, "both Mahlon and Chilion also died". Naomi had just lost her livelihood and her hope from a human standpoint. There was no social security system in those days. She was truly in dire straights now. Though there is the devastating pain of yet another loss—very likely due to the judgment of God because of covenant unfaithfulness—yet there was hope. "The woman was left a remnant out of her two children and her husband". Though she no doubt felt like it, God had not abandoned her, but rather she was a remnant. In spite of her sin and her family's sin, she was still alive and still had the opportunity to turn to God for refuge.

These verses are wrought with pain from beginning to end. The audience would recognize the ominous and painful setting. Yet behind the surface there was a glimmer of hope. Naomi was still alive. What would happen to her, and her daughters-in-law? The rest of the text reveals the answer. The next verse—1:6—becomes more explicit as it reveals Yahweh's pity upon his wandering people: "she heard that Yahweh had visited His people in giving them food".

Conclusion
The lessons that the book of Ruth was inspired to teach are set against a backdrop of national turmoil within Israel. Apostasy, sin and covenant unfaithfulness were rampant. Perversion and heinous, sickening depravity marked the territory where the narrative would take place. The personal compromise and covenant faithlessness of Elimelech as he led his family was implied—even though his name meant "my God is King". This is the pitch-black curtain against which the light of God's sovereign grace, loyal love, and the faith of a remnant would shine.

The remnant of believers throughout Israel's history must have wondered if God could overcome all of Israel's sin and apostasy. They must have wondered if they had lost their place in His plan and program for redemption. Ruth would teach that God's plan and purposes can never be thwarted in an ultimate sense. His grace shines even in the bleakest of circumstances.

Elimelech and his family are more like us than we may think. How often have we acted prudently according to so-called logical standards, or the current culture's standards, but not consulted God and His Word? He was likely just trying to provide for his family. He intended to be a sojourner, but ended up being buried in Moab. Then his sons took wives from the Moabites. Many of us have taken worldly shortcuts and have found ourselves suffering the painful consequences. But Ruth was written to remind us that for those who will return to God, His grace and loyal love can shine beautifully and brightly in spite of the darkness of our sin and failure—and *not only in spite of our sin*, but amazingly—even *through it*. He can cause even our sin to somehow turn out for the greater good and advance His glorious and good plan and purposes in the world (cf. Rom. 8:28).

We need to ask ourselves, however, are we like Elimelech? Do we have a name, but in practice take the expedient road rather than the road of faith? Husbands and fathers—are you leading your family down a road of tragedy? You call yourself a Christian, but do you have a true and abiding faith in Christ? God is calling you to turn and embrace living by faith in His Son.
Will the trials of life push us toward God, or will we question God's goodness and seek worldly-wise solutions? Will the pain of life and the decisions we've made, push us toward God or solidify us in our distance from Him?

We are all bearing the pain and consequences of the unfaithfulness of those who profess to be believers but do not live for Christ. Yet there is hope for those who will return to the Lord. He can use even our sinful past to bring about His glorious future. We ought to marvel at the grace of God and honor Him who is steadfast in His loyal love.

Expositional Outline:

Ruth 1:6-22

by Rick Kress

I. **The pain of covenant faithlessness [an empty profession] (1:1-5)**

II. **The pity of God and the initial glimmers of faith (1:6-22)**

    A. **The report of Yahweh's pity/mercy (1:6)**

        1. The return introduced (v. 6a)

        2. The reason for the return—the report of Yahweh's mercy/pity (v. 6b)

    B. **The "realism" of Naomi on the return to the Promised Land (1:7-15)**

        1. The road back to the land of Judah (1:7)

        2. The "realism" of Naomi (1:8-15)

            a. It was well meaning and included the terminology of faith (v. 8-10)

                i. Go, return each of you to your mother's house (v. 8a)

                ii. God [Yahweh] bless (v. 8b)

                iii. God [Yahweh] grant you husbands (v. 9)

                iv. The girls were attached to Naomi (v. 10)

            b. It was worldly-wise and actually exposed a measure of bitterness toward God (v. 11-15)

                i. Only hopelessness awaits you with me (v. 11-13a)

                ii. Only hardship awaits you with me (v. 13b)

                iii. Orpah has acted "sensibly" and returned to her people and gods (v. 14-15)

    C. **The reality of Ruth's love and glimmers of true faith (1:16-18)**

        1. Ruth's protestation against Naomi's pressure (1:16a)

        2. Ruth's pledge of loyalty (1:16b-17)

        3. Ruth's perseverance and Naomi's silence (1:18)

    D. **The report of Yahweh's chastening (1:19-21)**

        1. Bethlehem was stirred because of "them", but spoke only to Naomi (1:19)

        2. Bitterness, emptiness and affliction was Naomi's testimony (1:20-21)

            a. Bitterness (v. 20)

            b. Emptiness (v. 21a)

            c. Affliction (v. 21b)

    E. **The revelation of Yahweh's pity/mercy (1:22)**

        1. Naomi returned (1:22a)

        2. Naomi returned with Ruth

        3. Naomi and Ruth came to Bethlehem at the beginning of barley harvest

Expositional Commentary:
The Pity/Kindness of God that Leads to Repentance

Ruth 1:6-22

by Rick Kress

Have you ever known bitterness, emptiness, affliction and pain? Have you ever known it because of your own foolish choices? The book of Ruth reveals that God's loyal love, sovereignty, and redeeming grace cannot be thwarted for His elect, but He will actually use those foolish choices to bring about His perfect plan of redemption—to the praise of the glory of His grace.

Let's begin looking at the first scene that reveals God's mercy here in Ruth chapter one.

The Book of Ruth—A Portrait of God's Loyal Love, Sovereign Redemption, and the Faith of His Believing Remnant

I. The pain of covenant faithlessness [an empty profession] (1:1-5)

II. The pity of God and the initial glimmers of faith (1:6-22)

A. The report of Yahweh's pity/mercy (1:6)

1. The return introduced (v. 6a)

"Then she arose with her daughters-in-law that she might return from the land of Moab"

After coming to "the field of Moab" because of famine, at least a decade before if not longer, now Naomi "arose with her daughters-in-law that she might return from the field of Moab". She had known famine and the funerals of her husband and sons. The singular—"*she* might return"—signals that it was Naomi's plan to return alone, rather than "with her daughters-in-law". The word "return" often conveys the idea of repentance in the Scriptures. But the rest of the context gives a bit of a mixed view of her attitude. If indeed there was a measure of repentance, it was mixed with self-pity and bitterness as the rest of the chapter makes clear.

The reason for her return is revealed in the next phrase—the report of Yahweh's mercy/pity upon His people.

2. The reason for the return—the report of Yahweh's mercy/pity (v. 6b)

"For she had heard in the land of Moab that the LORD had visited His people in giving them food"

Naomi "heard *in the land of Moab*" this report of Yahweh's mercy. That the report reached her in Moab is the beginning of the revelation of the LORD's mercy to Naomi. What she "heard" was that "Yahweh had come to the aid of His people in giving them food". The term "visited", when used in the context of God's mercy toward "His people", is variously translated—"took note"

Chapter 1: Seeing God in Our Losses ■

(Gen. 21:1); "take care" (Gen. 50:24, 25); "concerned" (Ex. 3:16; 4:31). See also 1 Samuel 2:21.

That the famine had ended is evidence of Yahweh's mercy upon "His people"—i.e., Israel. Or to state it another way, His pity, compassion, mercy, and grace were evidenced in that He had gifted "His people" with *lechem*—bread. This was *the report that Naomi heard from the field of Moab.*

B. The "realism" of Naomi on the return to the Promised Land (1:7-15)
1. The road back to the land of Judah (1:7)
Again, the grammar indicates that Naomi was the one leaving the place where she was—and her daughters-in-law were "with her". They evidently had traveled some distance on "the road to return to the land of Judah" together before Naomi began the conversation of verses 8-15. Perhaps she was contemplating the plight of two Moabite women in Judah. Maybe she was thinking of the added stigma she would bear in bringing the women with her. Whatever the case, the setting of her belabored attempt to get Orpah and Ruth to return to their homes happened some distance "on the way" to Judah.

2. The "realism" of Naomi (1:8-15)
a. It was well meaning and included the terminology of faith (v. 8-10)
i. Go, return each of you to your mother's house (v. 8a)
"And Naomi said to her two daughters-in-law, 'Go, return each of you to her mother's house'"
"Naomi" gave her "two daughters-in-law" a double command—"Go, return". Basically, she was commanding them to walk away and repent from following her to Judah. It is obvious from the next several verses that she had affection for them both, but here she would act according to hard "realism" so to speak. The world at that time was no place for widows, but especially, Judah was no place for Moabite widows.

It is quite interesting to note that Naomi told them to "return each of you *to her mother's house*" (emphasis added). Normally a widow would return to her father's house (Gen. 38:11; Lev. 22:12; cf. Deut. 22:21; Judges 19:2-3). The phrase "mother's house" is used in Genesis 24:28 and Song of Songs 3:4 and 8:2—all in contexts of love and marriage (Block, p. 632). It seems likely here, that Naomi was implying that her two daughters-in-law should go home and get remarried—something she will make explicit in verse 9.

In and of itself, such a suggestion could be construed as noble and wise. But God has a way of overthrowing the world's wisdom. It may be, as suggested earlier, that Naomi did not want to face Bethlehem with two Moabite widows—the women her sons had married and left bereaved after their deaths.

Taken at face value, however, it would appear that Naomi was at least well intentioned in her command to Orpah and Ruth.

ii. God [Yahweh] bless (v. 8b)

"May the LORD deal kindly with you as you have dealt with the dead and with me"
The word "kindly" here is the Hebrew term *hesed*—normally translated "loyal love"; "unfailing love"; "tender mercies"; "lovingkindness". It speaks of grace, love, mercy and loyalty all in one term. Orpah and Ruth had dealt graciously, in loyal love to Naomi and her two sons—i.e., "the dead".

Now she was invoking "Yahweh's" blessing upon these women. She desired Israel's covenant-keeping God, the One who is steadfast in loyal love, grace, kindness and mercy—to deal with the two Moabite women with covenant type love.

Here then, Naomi reveals that she could still talk the talk at least. She could use the name "Yahweh" in a context of sovereign love. The latter part of the chapter will reveal bitterness concerning Yahweh's sovereign chastening.

Verse 9 also reveals Naomi's "realism"—as well as her good intentions and talk of God.

iii. God [Yahweh] grant you husbands (v. 9)

"May the LORD grant that you may find rest, each in the house of her husband"
It was a fairly realistic assessment in that era that a widowed woman could only find "rest...in the house of her husband". The word "rest" includes the idea of permanence (cf. 1 Chron. 28:2). As widows from a foreign land, they would have no stability and permanence. But Naomi's prayer/wish was that "Yahweh" would "give" as a gift of grace, such permanence, "each in the house of her man". Naomi was praying/desiring that the two women go and remarry. And again, she invokes "Yahweh" as the One able to bless even these Moabite women.

"Then she kissed them, and they lifted up their voices and wept"
The "kiss" here would signal an affectionate parting (cf. 1:14). The expression "they lifted up their voices and wept" conveys the idea of loud weeping at the attempted parting.

iv. The girls were attached to Naomi (v. 10)

"And they said to her, 'No, but we will surely return with you to your people'"
It is amazing that these two women display such loyalty to Naomi in spite of the devastation that they had all been through. Perhaps Naomi had been a vessel of God's love and truth to the girls. They would rather "return" with her "to [her] people" than remain in Moab—though natives.

Naomi's "realism" was perhaps well intentioned, and included the terminology of faith, but verses 11-15 reveal the bitterness attached to her "realism".

b. It was worldly-wise and actually exposed a measure of bitterness toward God (v. 11-15)

i. Only hopelessness awaits you with me (v. 11-13a)

It is evident in verse 11 that Naomi, Ruth and Orpah were aware—either culturally, or biblically (and perhaps both)—of the provision of levirate marriage recorded in Deuteronomy 25:5-10 (see also Gen. 38:8-10). Naomi's argument was that they would have no hope of husbands coming from Naomi's "womb"—literally, "inward parts", "intestines", or "belly". It would seem from the vocabulary that Naomi was speaking rather curtly to prove a point— "Do I have any more sons in my 'guts' that they could become your husbands?" (Block, p. 635).

Again, there was at least a measure of concern for the welfare of her two daughters-in-law. Their only hope from a human-wisdom standpoint would be marriage. And they would have a much better chance of marrying in Moab, than Israel—save sons from Naomi herself. That prospect was ridiculous, as Naomi made clear here.

Note Naomi's repetition of the phrase of verse 11—"return, my daughters" (see also "my daughters" in v. 13). There was a familial relationship there. There was affection and connection. But Naomi was trying to do what seemed best. Here in verses 12-13, she answered her own rhetorical question posed in verse 11. She had no more sons in her guts.

Naomi's first argument is that she's basically too old to remarry. It would seem likely that Naomi was approaching 50 years old (i.e., marriage at 15; two sons by 20; if they are 20 when they marry, that puts Naomi at 40; then 10 years of marriage for her sons before their deaths). Then, even if she had a husband "tonight and also bear sons" it would be 15 to 20 years before they would be ready to marry.

Would Orpah and Ruth realistically wait for them? They themselves would be at least 40, if not older by that time. Would they literally "shut themselves in" instead of marrying? Naomi was trying to get them to see the absurdity of it all. They were being emotional and shortsighted in their decision to follow her to Israel—at least from the worldly-wise perspective. They had a better hope of remarriage in Moab. Again, from a cultural perspective, life was hopeless apart from a husband. Naomi wanted them to see that only hopelessness awaited them if they remained with her.

ii. Only hardship awaits you with me (v. 13b)

"For it is harder for me than for you, for the hand of the LORD has gone forth against me"

The expression, "it is harder for me than for you" could be rendered, "I am much too bitter for you" or "my bitterness is greater than yours" (Block, p. 637). The reason this is so, however, is seen in the next phrase—"for the hand of Yahweh has gone forth against me". Naomi, at this point in her life, viewed herself as under God's curse. If the two younger women accompanied her, only hardship/bitterness would await them.

It is interesting to note the mixture of apparent faith and faithlessness in Naomi's words. She knew that Yahweh is sovereign over all the events of life. His "hand" is an anthropomorphism that speaks of His power. Yet, according to the narrator in verses three and five, Naomi was in reality a "remnant" left after the deaths of her husband and sons. She was actually a recipient of God's grace and mercy, but for now, she saw only the judgment of God. She could not see past her own bitterness, and she blamed Yahweh for it.

iii. Orpah has acted "sensibly" and returned to her people and gods (v. 14-15)

"And they lifted up their voices and wept again"
Again, the women all wept loudly (cf. v. 9). But this time, Naomi's speech has convinced at least one of her daughters-in-law, as the next phrase reveals.

"And Orpah kissed her mother-in-law, but Ruth clung to her"
"Orpah" had seen the apparent wisdom in Naomi's impassioned plea. Thus, she "kissed her mother-in-law" and went back the way they had come—to find security/rest in Moab. "Ruth" however "clung" to Naomi. The Hebrew term, "clung", was used in Genesis 2:24 of the "cleaving" of the husband and wife relationship. Ruth was attached to Naomi, and would not leave.

"Then she said, 'Behold, your sister-in-law has gone back to her people and her gods; return after your sister-in-law'"
Naomi even tried to dissuade Ruth through the sensible example of Orpah. She told Ruth to "look" or pay attention to Orpah's submissive wisdom. She repented/turned from the folly of following the cursed Naomi, and had turned back "to her people and her god[s]". Moab worshipped many gods, but supremely Chemosh (Num. 21:29; Jer. 48:46). From the human perspective, Orpah made the wise decision.

Yet it was the same humanistic logic that led Elimelech and Naomi to Moab—and that certainly was a mistake. It was wisdom devoid of faith in Yahweh's Person and promises. Orpah is never heard from again in the Scriptures.

Then for a fourth time (cf. 1:8, 11, 12), Naomi commanded Ruth to "return"—but this time with the added incentive that her "sister-in-law" had already done so. Ruth would not, however, repent from her loyal love for Naomi, or evidently her fledgling faith in Yahweh, as verses 16-17 reveal.

Naomi's "realism" was likely well intentioned and cloaked in the terminology of faith. It convinced Orpah, but in God's pity upon Naomi, Israel, and the whole world—it could not destroy Ruth's love and fledgling faith.

C. The reality of Ruth's love and glimmers of true faith (1:16-18)
1. Ruth's protestation against Naomi's pressure (1:16a)
"Ruth said, 'Do not urge me to leave you or turn back from following you'"
The same root word here translated "urge" is used in 2:22, there translated, "fall upon"—i.e., attack. Here it carries the idea of "pressure" (cf. Jer. 7:16; 27:18; Job 21:15; cf. Block, p. 641). Ruth's response to Naomi's impassioned and repeated command to "return" was to say, "Stop pressuring me to forsake you in regard to repenting/turning from following after you". Ruth refused to "abandon" Naomi. This was again confirmation of the *hesed*—the loyal love, grace, and faithful kindness—of this young woman from Moab.

2. Ruth's pledge of loyalty (1:16b-17)
"For where you go, I will go, and where you lodge, I will lodge"
"Because unto which you walk—I walk; and among which you spend the night—I spend the night" was the first stanza of Ruth's pledge. She was going to travel with Naomi no matter what. But the next stanza heightens the commitment from merely a journey to national and religious identity.

"Your people, my people; and your God, my God"
Ruth was pledging to forsake her own heritage and the gods of Moab, rather than forsake Naomi. She was vowing to turn her back on her kinsmen and the religion of her culture. Though primarily a pledge of loyalty to Naomi, in the next verse Ruth invokes the name "Yahweh", as the One who could, would, and should judge her if she did not keep her vow. This indicates that she indeed had at least a fledgling faith in Israel's covenant God—the One true and living God (see also 2:12). And notably, she here directly answered Naomi's final charge to return like Orpah to her people and gods. She would not. She would identify with Naomi's people and Naomi's God. "With radical self-sacrifice she abandons every base of security that any person, let alone a poor widow, in that cultural context would have clung to" (Block, p. 641).

"Where you die, I will die, and there I will be buried"
Ruth's words here indicate a pledge of familial solidarity with Naomi. She will be buried in the family tomb (Block, p. 641). "The place of a person's grave in ancient Near Eastern life was very significant (cf. Gen. 23; 25:9-10; 50:1-14, 23-25; Josh. 24:32). It identified the area he or she considered his or her true home" (*Constable's Expository Notes on the Bible*).

"Thus may the LORD do to me, and worse, if anything but death parts you and me"
This final stanza of Ruth's pledge serves as an oath before Yahweh. The actual curse invoked is left unstated. Perhaps Ruth used a hand gesture, something

akin to slitting the throat. Perhaps the curses were culturally understood or based on the national curses of Leviticus 26 and Deuteronomy 28. Whatever the specific judgment, it is obvious that Ruth placed herself under an oath to be bound to Naomi unto death, even in the place of burial. For emphasis, she added the phrase, "and worse"—literally, "and may He add".

Ruth's faith in some senses parallel's Abraham's as he was called out of his own country and people to follow Yahweh (Gen. 12:1ff; cf. Josh. 24:2). But here, Ruth only had Naomi's character and life as testimony to Yahweh, which makes her vow even more incredible. Though Naomi is pictured in the chapter as having the language of faith, yet filled with bitterness, she was a woman who had evidently endeared herself to this young Moabitess. Perhaps Naomi had demonstrated true love and faith over the years.

Clearly, God had gifted Ruth with a heart of sacrificial love for Naomi.

3. Ruth's perseverance and Naomi's silence (1:18)
"When she saw that she was determined to go with her, she said no more to her"
Naomi "saw" that Ruth had "strengthened herself to go with her". It was obvious by her vow that Ruth was committed to following Naomi. Thus Naomi literally, "ceased speaking to her". We are left to wonder whether her silence was in admiration and acceptance, or rather irritation and agitation because she would now be strapped with a Moabite daughter-in-law in a land not accepting of her. The latter seems more likely in light of Naomi's statements in verses 20-21, and the lack of any introduction of her beloved daughter-in-law upon their arrival in Bethlehem.

Yet in this scene *the reality of Ruth's love and glimmers of true faith* emerged.

D. The report of Yahweh's chastening (1:19-21)
1. Bethlehem was stirred because of "them", but spoke only to Naomi (1:19)
"So they both went until they came to Bethlehem"
The trip from Moab to Bethlehem was approximately 60 to 75 miles and involved a descent of 4,500 feet to the Jordan, then a climb through the hills of Judah of 3,500 feet. But with brevity, the author simply states that "they both went until they came to Bethlehem".

The Hebrew emphasizes that the "two" went—"they *both* went" until they came to Bethlehem. The next phrases use the plural pronouns "they" and "them". This becomes important as the dialogue is revealed in verses 19-21.

"And it came about when they had come to Bethlehem, that all the city was stirred because of them"
After they came to Bethlehem, "all the city was agitated/buzzing on account

of them". Naomi and Ruth caused "all the city" to hum with talk of their arrival. Their arrival was big news in town. Again, the plural pronoun "them" is used, but the conversation that follows is only with Naomi—about Naomi.

"And the women said, 'Is this Naomi?'"
Notably, "the women said" (literally, "they [feminine plural] said",) "Is this [singular] Naomi?" There is no mention of Ruth or dialogue about Ruth. Naomi's words that follow do not mention Ruth either. There is an uncomfortable silence in regard to this Moabitess (cf. Duguid, p. 144).

No doubt 10—possibly 20—years of a foreign culture, the funeral of a husband, the marriage of sons to foreign women, the funerals of the two sons, and the infertility of the two daughters-in-law had taken its toll on Naomi physically. She was no longer the same woman—physically as is implied here, and emotionally as she will make explicit in the next two verses.

2. Bitterness, emptiness and affliction was Naomi's testimony (1:20-21)
a. Bitterness (v. 20)
"She said to them, 'Do not call me Naomi; call me Mara, for the Almighty has dealt very bitterly with me'"
Perhaps sensing the loaded nature of their questioning (Naomi had surprised them by her arrival, but likely surprised them by her appearance as well), Naomi used the meaning of her name to create a word picture for the women of Bethlehem. "Naomi" means "delightful" or "pleasant". "Mara" means "bitterness". In her estimation, she is the exact opposite of her name. Thus the essence of what she said was—"Do not call me delightful, call me Mara, for the Almighty has marred me greatly/exceedingly" (cf. Morris, p. 262).

"Mara" to the Jewish people would have brought to mind the sad episode of bitterness and complaining in Exodus 15:23 where just a few days after the deliverance through the Red Sea, the people were complaining because of their circumstances—a lack of drinkable water. They came to "Marah," the place of bitter waters, and they complained. But the Lord in His grace, made the bitter waters sweet. Little did Naomi know that she too would experience the sweetness of God's grace in days to come. She evidently didn't remember the episode at the time of this confession, since she was not compelled to stop her complaining at this time.

The reference to "the Almighty"—*shaddai*—is used in poetic or prophetic contexts. The book of Job uses it quite frequently as well. Scholars place its etymology in connection with the Ugaritic term for "mountain". Power and majesty seem to be conveyed by the term. The powerful and majestic One had done bitterly toward Naomi, in her estimation. More accurately Yahweh had shown pity on Naomi, but she was blind to it and stood in her own bitterness.

b. Emptiness (v. 21a)

"I went out full, but the LORD has brought me back empty"

Interestingly she said, "I myself full walked out, but emptily Yahweh brought me back". Ruth had testified to her loyal love and commitment to Naomi, her people, and her God. Naomi, upon arriving back in Bethlehem, evidently said very little—if not anything about Ruth—but testified to *her* pain and Yahweh's sovereign judgment. She went out "full"—though strictly speaking, it was during a famine in Israel. Evidently she meant "full" as far as having a husband and two sons.

Sadly, Naomi's bitterness at the moment was a backhanded insult to Ruth. Was she really empty? She had the mercy of God in that her daughter-in-law had bound herself to her unto death. She had love—the love of God and the love of Ruth—but she did not recognize either.

By self-confession at that moment, Naomi was filled with bitterness, emptiness, and . . .

c. Affliction (v. 21b)

"Why do you call me Naomi, since the LORD has witnessed against me"

Again Naomi used the meaning of her name to make a point—"why do you call me delightful, since Yahweh has testified against me". The construction carries a judicial sense. Naomi is not pleasant, she is convicted and held guilty before Yahweh's court. Perhaps again there are the seeds of faith in her words, but they are marred by bitterness and self—rather than crowned with contrition and humility.

"And the Almighty has afflicted me?"

The word "afflicted" here can speak of "evil" in the sense of "calamity". It refers to God's powerful judgment against Naomi. This was her testimony—bitterness, emptiness and affliction. She acknowledges God's sovereign hand in all of her circumstances, but she will not see His sovereign pity, compassion and mercy (note the contrast with Ezra's prayer in Ezra 9).

What a picture Naomi would be here of many subsequent generations in Israel. They had survived as a remnant from God's chastening in exile, only to miss His grace and see only the bitterness, emptiness and affliction. Yet the narrator, in verse 22, will indeed subtly remind the audience of Yahweh's pity/mercy to complete the section that began with news that He had "visited" His people with food.

E. The revelation of Yahweh's pity/mercy (1:22)
1. Naomi returned (1:22a)

"So Naomi returned"

That Naomi was back in Israel is a clear signal that God had mercy, pity and compassion upon her regardless of her outlook at the time. She was a remnant preserved through the judgment, and now "returned" to the land.

2. Naomi returned with Ruth (1:22b)

"And with her Ruth the Moabitess, her daughter-in-law, who returned from the land of Moab"

The second reminder of God's mercy/pity in spite of and through the pain of covenant faithlessness was that Naomi had not only returned to God's people and the Promised Land but she was also accompanied by "Ruth the Moabitess, her daughter-in-law, who returned from the land of Moab". Although she may have seemed like something of a liability in the highly ethnocentric land of Judah, she was actually an evidence of God's pity/mercy and grace.

The fact that the term "returned" is used here of Ruth, who had never been to Bethlehem, may have been a subtle technique of the narrator to communicate that though a "Moabitess", she too was a remnant of God's people now "returning" to the land—much as generations later, Israelites born in captivity would "return"; or Israel in Moses' day returned to the Promised Land, though they were born and lived in Egypt.

Yahweh's pity is seen in the fact that Naomi returned; and she returned with Ruth—she had one who loved her with a Yahweh-like love. And the final testimony of Yahweh's pity/mercy is seen in the last phrase of 1:22.

3. Naomi and Ruth came to Bethlehem at the beginning of barley harvest (1:22c)

"And they came to Bethlehem at the beginning of barley harvest"

Naomi and Ruth "came to [the house of bread] at the beginning of the harvest of barley". In God's sovereign mercy, they arrived in late April when there would be fields to glean in—even if one was destitute. God had seen to that in the national law of Israel (cf. Lev. 19:9-10; 23:22; Deut. 24:19-22).

Naomi's return, in actuality, testified to God's mercy, though she didn't see it. That Naomi returned with this Moabitess who loved her testified to God's mercy though she didn't seem to acknowledge it. That they returned at the beginning of barley harvest testified to God's mercy. In a day or so Naomi would come to her senses and her profession would seem more filled with faith than bitterness (2:20), but for now only the narrator's brief statements testify to God's mercy.

Conclusion

The book of Ruth is meant to reveal God's loyal love and sovereign redemption, and encourage the faith of His remnant. *God's love and sovereign redemption are on display even in the midst of and through the pain and consequences of sin.* We often overlook it, however, and are instead filled with bitterness, emptiness and affliction. We need to understand that even though we have sinned and chastening has come (even if devastating in their consequences)—He is still merciful and is working out His plan and purposes. He is good and His lovingkindness is everlasting.

Naomi used the language of faith, but she still looked at her circumstances from a worldly perspective. Ruth, however, chose to deny herself, look out for the needs of Naomi, and identify with Yahweh—even if it meant death. See Matthew 10:28-29; 16:24-26; Mark 8:34-38; Luke 9:23ff; 14:27.

Again, Naomi would see things in a different light just a few days later (2:20). For now we can learn from her pain, bitterness, emptiness, and calamity. God is merciful no matter the circumstances, consequences or pain. We can learn from Ruth's sacrificial love, devotion and rather simple yet radical faith.

Romans 2:4b says, do you not know "that the kindness of God leads you to repentance?" Even when afflicted and chastened we ought to kiss the hand of mercy that is at that very moment—no matter the pain—being kind to us. We should also not be too quick to judge Naomi for her bitterness—as Job has said, "Do you intend to reprove my words, when the words of one in despair belong to the wind?" (Job 6:26). Though this should not justify our bitterness, it should cause us to be gracious to those who are in the midst of their pain.

Let's ask God to help us see His wondrous mercy, especially when we're tempted in our flesh to see bitterness, emptiness and calamity. When we see His mercy and compassion in spite of and because of the pain, we can praise Him and thus know the delight for which we were created and redeemed.

Expository Sermon:
Seeing God in Our Losses

Ruth 1:6-22

by Brad Brandt

"It was different back then." Sometimes I get the feeling that's the conclusion that's stuck in the back of our minds as we read God's Word.

"Back in Bible days, it was easier to live for God because He was always doing miracles to help out His people in times of need. You know, manna falling out of the sky, killing a giant with a stone and a slingshot, getting a taxi-ride inside of a giant fish, marching around a city and watching the walls fall down, blind men receiving sight, dead people being raised from the grave, that's what I mean, *those* kind of things, *miracles.* They happened all the time in Bible times, but they don't happen today. It was easier to live for God *then. It was different then."*

But wait. Was it really so different? For starters, sure the miracles just mentioned happened in the Bible, but were they commonplace even in the Bible? God took approximately 1,500 years (from Moses who wrote Genesis around 1400 B.C. to John who wrote Revelation around 100 A.D.) and used around forty human authors to record His inspired Scriptures. Did all the people living during those 1,500 years see a miracle occur? No. Granted, they all saw God at work, but few saw the kinds of spectacular miracles just mentioned. *It was different back then?* That assertion doesn't hold.

In fact, God specifically included certain books in the Bible that challenge such a notion. We're beginning a study of one of them, the fascinating Old Testament book of Ruth.

Ruth is only four chapters long. You can easily read it in a sitting. And if you do you'll notice something by its absence—nobody's raised from the dead, no sick child is healed, and no bread falls from the sky. To the contrary, in this book people die and *are not* raised from the dead. Sick children are not made well, but they too die. If people get hungry, they go out in fields, harvest grain, and make their own bread.

Ruth is a book about ordinary people facing ordinary challenges in ordinary life. In some ways it's like the story of Joseph in Genesis 37-50, and the story of Esther, and many other stories in the Bible, about real people who confronted real problems, overwhelming problems, and never saw a single miracle.

As we read the book of Ruth, we discover something vital, something you and I need to know as we live our lives. Ruth makes it clear that God is a God who is always at work behind the scenes. Granted, He sometimes does the miraculous, then and now, but He is *always* working out His sovereign and perfect plan in the background.

There's a good word for this, a word we need to use more often. It's called providence. According to the Miriam Webster online dictionary, providence means "divine guidance or care." But sometimes a definition just doesn't cut it. Sometimes if you want to understand the real meaning of a word only a story will do. And I can't think of a better story to illustrate what God's *providence* means any better than Ruth.

Notice the setting of our story in verse 1, "In the days when the judges ruled." To appreciate the story we must appreciate the backdrop. Who were the judges? In your Bible you'll find a book called *Judges.* The story of Ruth took place toward the end of the period of the Judges, in the thirteenth century B.C. David's birth can be dated around 1040 B.C. at the earliest. Obed must have been born near the end of the twelfth century since Ruth 4:17 says that Obed was the grandfather of David. Just who were these judges?

Around the year 2000 B.C. the Creator God revealed Himself to and entered into a relationship with a man named Abraham. In Genesis 12:1-4, as well as in subsequent passages in Genesis, God promised to bless Abraham, to give him a son and through that son a great family of sons and daughters. He also promised to give his descendants a special land. What's more, God said that through Abraham He was going to bring blessing and hope to the world.

And that's what we see when we read the first six books of the Bible. The first five books tell the story of how God through Abraham formed a nation called Israel and how He entered into a covenantal relationship with Israel. In the sixth book of the Bible, Joshua, we read how God kept His promise and gave Israel the promised land. Then we come to the seventh book, *Judges.* In Judges we discover that the Lord's people did not keep their promise to the Lord, but time and time again turned away from Him to serve false gods. Time and time again the Lord chastened His wayward people until they cried out to Him, and in His covenant mercy time and time again He raised up *judges* to deliver them.

Our story took place during that roller-coaster phase in Israel's history. In the book of Ruth, the author (and we don't know who he is; some feel Samuel) puts the spotlight on what happened to one particular family in that dismal time period.

Here's what we're going to see in the opening chapter. There are three scenes in the first chapter of Ruth. The first scene occurs in Moab (1-5), the second involves Naomi's decision to return to the promised land (6-18), and the third scene occurs in Bethlehem (19-22). In these three scenes we learn three truths about the Lord and how He works in the lives of His people, particularly how He works through suffering.

I. Truth #1: The Lord does not exempt His people from suffering (1-5).
Let me reiterate. There is no exemption clause when it comes to suffering.

We're introduced to the characters of the story in verses 1-2. "In the days when the judges ruled, there was a famine in the land, and a man from Bethlehem in Judah [to distinguish from another Bethlehem in Zebulun], together with his wife and two sons, went to live for a while in the country of Moab. The man's name was Elimelech, his wife's name Naomi, and the names of his two sons were Mahlon and Kilion. They were Ephrathites from Bethlehem, Judah. And they went to Moab and lived there."

Our story begins in Judah, in southern Israel. There was a famine, we're told. Was that coincidental? No. There are no coincidences in God's universe. There is no room for a coincidence when there's providence.

Providence is different from a miracle. A miracle is a non-repeatable contradiction of an otherwise demonstrable law of nature, such as giving instant sight to a blind man. When God works through providence, He doesn't change the laws of nature. Providence points to God's behind-the-scenes activity. In providence God works *through* the laws of nature (laws He Himself established in the first place).

In verse 1 it stops raining. Is that a miracle? No. Is God behind that cessation of rain? Yes. Does He have a reason for causing the rain to stop? Yes, a providential reason, in this case a reason He spelled out ahead of time.

Turn to Deuteronomy 28:15 and see the warning God gave Israel before they entered the promised land: "If you do not obey the LORD your God and do not carefully follow all his commands and decrees I am giving you today, all these curses will come upon you and overtake you."

Included in the list of curses we find this specific curse in verses 23-24, "The sky over your head will be bronze, the ground beneath you iron. The LORD will turn the rain of your country into dust and powder; it will come down from the skies until you are destroyed."

God said He would make life miserable for His people if they disobeyed Him. Why? Because He is mean? No! It's because He knows that it is in the best interest of His people if they seek and obey Him. Indeed, the curses He would send were intended to shake them so they would turn back to Him.

How did Elimelech respond to the famine? He took his family to Moab. Moab was some 50 miles to the southeast, across the Dead Sea. Let that sink in. He *left the promised land and went to the country of Moab.* Elimelech's name meant "My God is king," yet there's a conflict between the meaning of his name and his actions. We'll come back to that thought in a moment. First, let's notice what happened subsequent to his choice. A series of losses occurred. Since the story is told with the spotlight on Naomi, I'll identify the losses as they relate to Naomi.

A. Naomi lost her home (1-2).
The choice to move to Moab meant that Naomi, her husband, and their two sons were parting from the inheritance the Lord had given their ancestors. They left Bethlehem, which in Hebrew means "house of bread," to go to Moab, a land of a people under curse.

B. Naomi lost her spouse (3-4a).
Verse 3—"Now Elimelech, Naomi's husband, died, and she was left with her two sons." Put yourself in Naomi's shoes.

1. She experienced the challenge of being a single parent.
She's in a strange place and now her husband is gone. She alone is left to raise two sons, two teenage sons it would appear based on time indicators we'll see shortly.

We're told Naomi experienced something else in the next verse.

2. She watched her children make painful decisions.
Note what her sons did in verse 4—"They married Moabite women, one named Orpah and the other Ruth." According to 4:10 we're told that Mahlon married Ruth which means Orpah was Kilion's wife. There's no mention that Naomi had anything to do with these marriages, perhaps indicating her sons acted without her input.

The sons married non-Israelite women, Moabite women. Although this wasn't forbidden in the letter of the law, it certainly was in violation of the spirit of the law. The Moabites were a people that began in incest, as the result of Lot's daughters getting him drunk and having sex with him (Gen. 19). The Moabites refused to help the Israelites on their journey to the promised land and even hired Balaam to curse them. What's more, the people of Moab worshiped the pagan god, Chemosh, to whom human sacrifices were offered.

Naomi's suffering continued. She lost her home and her spouse. Then…

C. Naomi lost her children (4b-5).
"After they had lived there about ten years, both Mahlon and Kilion also died, and Naomi was left without her two sons and her husband." How the young men died we're not told. But they died, and they left behind two widows and

a widowed, broken-hearted mother.

This raises a question. What were they doing in Moab in the first place? You say, "Well, there was a famine. They had to leave to find food." Did they? Apparently, others didn't leave as we'll see at the end of the chapter.

You say, "But real estate is real estate. One piece of ground is as good as another." That's not true. God gave the Israelites the promised land. He also gave them promises that He would provide for them if they would seek and obey Him.

So, was it right for Elimelech to leave Israel and to live in Moab? The book of Ruth does not explicitly say Elimelech was *wrong* for leaving Israel, but was it a *wise* thing to do?

This family found food alright, but at what expense?! There is something worse than going hungry, even worse than starving to death. And that is choosing a course that takes us outside the will of God.

Matthew Henry commented, "It is evidence of a discontented, distrustful, unstable spirit to be weary of the place in which God has set us, and to be leaving it immediately, whenever we meet with any uneasiness or inconvenience in it."

It's never right to disobey God's will. Never. Specifically, it's never right to go against God's revealed will in His Word. Never. No matter how viable an option may seem to our human eyes, if that option violates God's Word, it is not an option.

The fact of the matter is, we too have our Moabs. We, too, have gone our own way. How many times have we made decisions without consulting God and without seeking His will in the matter?

The good news is that even after we've blown it by making foolish decisions, there is hope. God is gracious. He even works providentially through the consequences of the sinful choices we make to bring about glory for Himself and good to those who will seek Him. That's certainly what we're going to see in the book of Ruth.

So ends scene one. There's truth #1. The Lord does not exempt His people from suffering. Perhaps you know that firsthand. This will encourage you...

II. Truth #2: The Lord sustains His people in their suffering (6-18).
The narrative progresses with four episodes involving Naomi.
A. Naomi decided to return home (6-7).
"When she heard in Moab that the LORD had come to the aid of his people by providing food for them, Naomi and her daughters-in-law prepared to

return home from there. With her two daughters-in-law she left the place where she had been living and set out on the road that would take them back to the land of Judah."

Notice that...

1. The Lord had provided food.

Verse 6 is very clear that *the LORD* provided the food. The LORD shut off the rain that caused the famine, and now He "gives bread," as the KJV puts it.

Sadly, we miss God's hand in the little things. We attribute good crops to changing weather patterns and fertilizer, instead of seeing the hand of God. We've lost the truth contained in Maltlie Babcock's poem (Gardiner, *The Romance of Ruth*, p. 23):

> *Back of the loaf is the snowy flour,*
> *And back of the flour the mill,*
> *And back of the mill is the wheat, and the shower,*
> *And the sun, and the Father's will.*

Beloved, God is at work. Even when we don't understand His ways, He is still at work. And here is why...

2. The Lord is faithful to His covenant promises.

He does what He promised to do. The famine was no accident, no glitch of global warming. God said He would send famines if His people turned away from Him, and He did. And now in His mercy He sends relief.

We're told that Naomi heard the report and decided to head back home. Somewhat surprisingly, her two daughters-in-law decided to leave their own blood relatives and go with her.

B. Naomi tried to send her daughters-in-law back to their mothers (8-9).

"Then Naomi said to her two daughters-in-law, 'Go back, each of you, to your mother's home. May the LORD show kindness to you, as you have shown to your dead and to me. May the LORD grant that each of you will find rest in the home of another husband.' Then she kissed them and they wept aloud..."

Apparently, once the three widows started down the road, reality set in for Naomi. She told Orpah and Ruth to go back to their mothers—perhaps she was thinking that the challenge of caring for herself would be overwhelming, let alone feeding two more mouths. But she doesn't mention that. More likely, she thought life would be better *for them* if they stayed in Moab. Notice her two verbalized prayer requests.

1. She asked the Lord to show them kindness (8).

And...

2. She asked the Lord to give them husbands (9).

Does it surprise you to hear Naomi using the name of the LORD? For starters, many women who endured the tragedy of losing a home, a husband, and two adult sons wouldn't even mention the name of the Lord, let alone ask for Him to show kindness to another. "How can I believe in the Lord after all that's happened in my life?" Yet Naomi believes in Him. She may not understand His ways, but she affirms His presence in her life.

Something else strikes me about Naomi's use of the name of the LORD. We might expect her to use the more general name "God" since Orpah and Ruth are Moabites, and Moabites believed in a different god. But for Naomi there is only one true God and it's not Chemosh, even if she is in Moab. She specifically asks *the LORD* (Yahweh) to show kindness and give husbands to her daughters-in-law.

But the young ladies objected, not to her use of the LORD's name, but to her command that they go back to their mothers. Note the last words of verse 9 and the first words of verse 10—"They wept aloud and said to her, 'We will go back with you to your people.'" Note the words, *your people.* They admit that they will be outsiders in Israel, yet such is their love for Naomi that they insist they go with her.

C. Naomi insisted her daughters-in-law go home (10-14).

Verses 10-11—"But Naomi said, 'Return home, my daughters. Why would you come with me? Am I going to have any more sons, who could become your husbands?'" She's talking about the law concerning levirate marriage, a law in Israel (Deut 25:5-6) that was given to protect widows and insure the continuance of the family line.

Verses 12-13—"Return home, my daughters; I am too old to have another husband. Even if I thought there was still hope for me—even if I had a husband tonight and then gave birth to sons—would you wait until they grew up? Would you remain unmarried for them? No, my daughters. It is more bitter for me than for you, because the LORD's hand has gone out against me!"

Don't miss Naomi's view of God. He is the one who helps His people (verse 6). He's also in charge of the things that hurt His people (verse 13)—"the LORD's hand has gone out against me!" she says.

Note the effect her words had on her daughters-in-law. Verse 14—"At this they wept again. Then Orpah kissed her mother-in-law good-by, but Ruth clung to her."

1. Orpah went back.

She said goodbye and headed down the road. But Ruth was a different story…

2. Ruth clung to her mother-in-law.

The verb "clung" is a powerful word. In Genesis 2:24 it refers to a man cleaving to his wife in the bond of marriage. In Deuteronomy 10:20 it depicts the committed faithfulness that God desires from His covenant people in response to His gracious salvation. Ruth *clung* to Naomi.

Some might see that word and suppose Ruth to be an insecure and frightened little girl who just can't let mama go, but that's certainly not the case, as will soon be evident.

D. Naomi could not shake Ruth's resolve (15-18).

Verse 15—"'Look,' said Naomi, 'your sister-in-law is going back to her people and her gods. Go back with her.'" Don't miss those words, *and her gods.*

1. Orpah went back to her gods.

What does that tell us about Orpah? She was a nice person, kind to her mother-in-law, loyal and even willing to leave her own country to show her care. But she doesn't believe in the LORD. Because of common grace, even people who don't know the LORD can love, show compassion, and make great sacrifices. But they're still lost. They're still enslaved to their false gods.

Orpah was a polytheist. She worshipped many gods. That means that Kilion, a man who professed to believe in the One true God, married a woman who did not believe in the One true God but who indeed believed in many gods.

Young people, please take note. Make sure you marry a person who loves the Lord you know. God is very clear when he says in 2 Corinthians 6:14, "Do not be yoked together with unbelievers. For what do righteousness and wickedness have in common? Or what fellowship can light have with darkness?"

Ruth, too, had been a polytheist. But somewhere along the way, God in His mercy opened her eyes to her folly and granted her saving faith in Himself. How do I know that? By her answer to Naomi.

Verse 16—"But Ruth replied, 'Don't urge me to leave you or to turn back from you. Where you go I will go, and where you stay I will stay. Your people will be my people and your God my God.'" These words are often used in wedding services, but realize this originally was a promise a woman made to her mother-in-law. Now we see why Ruth won't remain in Moab. It's not just about her love for Naomi—Orpah had that.

2. Ruth made a choice for Naomi's people and Naomi's God.

What would cause a person to turn from the traditions of her people, including those of her own parents and including the very gods they had worshipped for centuries? And what would cause that same woman to give up the security of her homeland, her friends, and everything she has ever known? What would cause her to do this knowing her father and mother would never approve and indeed, would probably never speak to her again? There's only one answer. It's a one-word answer. *Grace.*

Ephesians 2:8-9: "For it is by grace you have been saved, through faith—and this not from yourselves, it is the gift of God—not by works, so that no one can boast."

For Ruth, this decision wasn't just about Naomi. It was also about Naomi's God. Lest there be any doubt, listen to Ruth's next words…

Verse 17—"Where you die I will die, and there I will be buried. May **the LORD** deal with me, be it ever so severely, if anything but death separates you and me." Did you catch that? Ruth uses the name of Naomi's God. Her devotion is no longer to Chemosh, but to *the God of Israel, the LORD.*

Verse 18—"When Naomi realized that Ruth was determined to go with her, she stopped urging her." End of discussion.

Now go back to verse 16. I want you to notice again something Ruth said. *Your people will be my people and your God my God.* The order is significant. Ruth mentions Naomi's people first, then her God. Why? Because she understands that she cannot enter a relationship with God apart from His people, the Jews. All gods are not the same. All religions do not lead to the same place. God chose one people, the Jews, to whom He gave His Word and through whom He would eventually send the Messiah. Jesus would later say, "Salvation is from the Jews" (John 4:22).

Ruth affirms that. Ruth is turning her back on everything she has known since childhood. She has known only the worship of Chemosh all her life, but now she is breaking religious ties. And family ties, too. According to 2:11, her father and mother are still living, but Ruth willingly makes a costly choice. She is saying that something is more important to her than family honor and family tradition. She is choosing to turn away from what she's always known to something else, to Someone else.

Yes, Ruth and Orpah both made a decision on that road in Moab. Each of us today are faced with the same decision, and the consequences of that decision last for eternity. Are we going to go back to what we've always known, or are we going to move forward? Are we going to remain the same or go to the One who alone is the way, the truth, and the life?

What happened to Orpah? We never hear about her again. All we know is that she went back, back to Moab, back to her mother, and back to her idolatry. On the other hand, Ruth went forward, and as Ruth heads to Bethlehem she's heading into history.

We've seen two truths thus far in Ruth 1. First, the Lord does not exempt His people from suffering (1-5). Secondly, the Lord sustains His people in their suffering (6-18). Here's the third…

III. Truth #3: The Lord is real to His people even while they are suffering (19-22).

Verse 19—"So the two women went on until they came to Bethlehem. When they arrived in Bethlehem, the whole town was stirred because of them, and the women exclaimed, 'Can this be Naomi?'" The term "women" isn't in the original, but since the verbal form is feminine plural the sense is there. The men were out in the fields harvesting the barley, as we'll see later in the story.

It's been 10 years since Naomi's peers have seen her. Her losses have taken a toll on her. They hardly recognize her.

Naomi responds in verses 20-21, "'Don't call me Naomi,' she told them. 'Call me Mara, because the Almighty has made my life very bitter. I went away full, but the LORD has brought me back empty. Why call me Naomi? The LORD has afflicted me; the Almighty has brought misfortune upon me.'"

She requested a name change. The Hebrew word *Mara* means "bitter." There's a word play here. "Call me *Mara, for* God Almighty has *marred* me."

"The LORD brought me back *empty,*" she says. That's how she felt. *Empty.* That's how she estimated her God-given possessions as she returned home. *Empty.* But was she empty? C. J. Goslinga observes, "Naomi's bitter words underestimated the treasure that God had given to her in the love of her daughter-in-law Ruth" (Goslinga, *Joshua, Judges, Ruth*, p. 528).

Isn't Naomi's perspective typical of us? We get easily preoccupied with what the Lord *hasn't* given us that we miss the treasure of what He *has* given us.

"If I only had a wife!" "If only I had better parents!" "If only I had a better job!" "My life is so empty. Why doesn't God do something to fill this void?" But He has. He has given us so much already, far more than we deserve. He's given us Christ. He's given us everything we need for life and godliness in Christ (2 Pet 1:3). A better plea would be, "Oh Lord! Give me eyes to see what You've already given me!"

Having said that, please notice two things about Naomi…

A. Naomi affirmed that God was in control of her losses (20-21).

Don't miss her repeated references here to the LORD. *"The Almighty has made my life very bitter. I went away full, but the LORD has brought me back empty. Why call me Naomi? The LORD has afflicted me; the Almighty has brought misfortune upon me."*

She may not understand what God is up to, but she affirms His control over her life, even over her losses. She attributes *everything* to God, both the pleasant and unpleasant.

B. Naomi would eventually learn that God is filling the void left by her losses (22).

"So Naomi returned from Moab accompanied by Ruth the Moabitess, her daughter-in-law, arriving in Bethlehem as the barley harvest was beginning."

So ends chapter one. Chapter one tells what happened in ten years. Chapter two will cover the events of one day.

Chapter one ends telling us it was barley harvest time, meaning it's towards the end of April. Why that detail? It shows that God's timing is perfect. It shows that the famine that prompted Naomi to leave Bethlehem in the first place is indeed over. Although Naomi doesn't know it yet, things are about to change for her. God is at work.

We can see the providence of God illustrated in two ways in Ruth 1, both of which will be illustrated more fully for us in the rest of the book.

1. He provided Naomi with a devoted daughter-in-law.

Naomi has a jewel, and she will soon discover just how precious this God-given jewel really is! What an amazing thing God did in the life of Ruth...

George Gardner writes, "Ruth was the product of a degraded race, the children of Moab. The race began with the incestuous episode between drunken Lot and his daughters in a cave outside the smoking ruins of Sodom. Moab was the child of Lot's oldest daughter...Could any good or noble person come out of such a background? We say no. It is too much to expect. The hereditary and environmental factors are too powerful, and humanly speaking, such conclusions are possibly correct. 'But God...' Two little words that make a large difference" (Gardiner, p. 30).

Oh, what a difference providence makes! The world says, "You can't change human nature!" But God does it all the time. God took a pagan woman, an outsider, and saved her soul and blessed Naomi. But the blessing wasn't just for Naomi...

2. He provided His people with a link to the Messiah.

In chapter two Ruth is going to meet a man. There will be romance and a proposal in chapter three, a wedding and a son born in chapter four. This special son is Obed, the father of Jesse, the father of David, and the royal ancestor to Jesus the Messiah.

God knew what He was doing, even in Naomi's losses. He was preparing to give the world His Son, the One who would give His life on the cross and then rise again, securing salvation from sin for all who would believe in Him.

My friend, this same God knows what He is doing in *your life,* too. Was it really easier to live for God back then? I don't think so. I don't know what you are facing today, but I urge you to take to heart the message of the book of Ruth…

Make It Personal: Resolve to affirm the goodness and wisdom of God in every situation.

Getting Intentional About Application

by Brad Brandt

Our goal isn't merely for the people of God to *hear* God's Word but to *live* it. Far too often as a pastor I have settled for less. I have assumed that it was a good message if the presentation went well and if the congregation responded well on the day of delivery. I should know better. Jesus made it clear in the parable of the four soils (Matt. 13:1-9, 18-23) that *hearing* God's Word is insufficient (all four types of people in the illustration *hear* the Word). The desired outcome, as represented by the fourth soil, is to see people not only hear the Word, but also understand it and then bear lasting fruit because of it. The longer I pastor the more I realize that the progression from *hearing* to *living* is where the rubber meets the road. How does this occur? Fundamentally, of course, it is a work that God alone can accomplish (James 1:18, 22). Due to the depraved condition of the human heart, proclaiming God's Word to descendants of Adam would be like shining a spotlight into the eyes of a blind person. There would be no response, not because the light is deficient but because blind eyes simply cannot see. Thankfully, God is in the business of making spiritually blind eyes see (2 Cor. 4:6). He uses His Word to regenerate dead hearts (1 Pet. 1:23) and transform once tarnished lives into the glorious likeness of His Son (2 Cor. 3:18; Eph. 4:20-24).

"If God does this, then I'm off the hook, right? If I don't see my people changing, there's nothing I can do about it, is there?" Of course, we know better. We know that God often works through *means*. That's why Paul exhorted Timothy, "Do your best to present yourself to God as one approved, a workman who does not need to be ashamed and who *correctly handles* the word of truth" (2 Tim. 2:15, emphasis added).

That's what *Getting Intentional About Application* is all about. Our goal in communicating God's Word is to do so with a view towards life change to the glory of God. We want to see the Scriptures become woven into the very fabric of our people's lives. The following tools are attempts to facilitate this ambition, to help those who listen to Word move from *hearing* to *living*.

Tool #1: A Teaching Outline

There are various ways to utilize a teaching outline. For starters, we use them as bulletin inserts, with key words removed from each point, to encourage active participation in the learning process by sermon hearers.

The outline can also be used in a small group setting designed to achieve more intensive follow-up of the Sunday morning message. For instance, our congregation has at times used the Sunday evening or Wednesday evening service as an opportunity to "go deeper" into the Sunday morning text. The leader can begin by taking the first ten minutes of the service to reread the text, then walk through the main points of the message using the outline, followed by a discussion time. Both prepared and spontaneous questions are utilized for the purposes of both *clarification* and *application.*

Sermonic outlines can also be utilized as part of a counseling homework assignment. For instance, when working with a person who is struggling with significant losses in life, a pastor-counselor might ask the counselee to listen to the message from Ruth chapter 1, fill in the outline-blanks, and be prepared to discuss the three most meaningful points in the next counseling session.

Here is my outline from Ruth chapter one.

Brad's exposition
Main Idea: In Ruth 1 we learn three truths about the Lord and how He works in the lives of His people, particularly in times of suffering.
I.   **The Lord does not exempt His people from suffering (1-5).**
    A. **Naomi lost her home (1-2).**
    B. **Naomi lost her spouse (3-4a).**
        1. She experienced the challenge of being a single parent.
        2. She watched her children make painful decisions.
    C. **Naomi lost her children (4b-5).**
II. **The Lord sustains His people in their suffering (6-18).**
    A. **Naomi decided to return home (6-7).**
        1. The Lord had provided food.
        2. The Lord is faithful to His covenant promises.
    B. **Naomi tried to send her daughters-in-law back to their mothers (8-9).**
        1. She asked the Lord to show them kindness (8).
        2. She asked the Lord to give them husbands (9).
    C. **Naomi insisted her daughters-in-law go home (10-14).**
        1. Orpah went back.
        2. Ruth clung to her mother-in-law.
    D. **Naomi could not shake Ruth's resolve (15-18).**
        1. Orpah went back to her gods.
        2. Ruth made a choice for Naomi's people and Naomi's God.
III. **The Lord is real to His people even while they are suffering (19-22).**
    A. **Naomi affirmed that God was in control of her losses (20-21).**
    B. **Naomi would eventually learn that God is filling the void left by her losses (22).**
        1. He provided her with a devoted daughter-in-law.
        2. He provided His people with a link to the Messiah.
Make It Personal: Resolve to affirm the goodness and wisdom of God in every situation.

Tool #2: "Digging Deeper" Discussion Questions
These questions could be utilized in a variety of ways. Parents could use them to facilitate family discussion of the Sunday sermon. Sunday evening small groups in homes could utilize them. I have found it helpful at times to use the

mid-week service as an opportunity to revisit the Sunday morning message with the people of God, asking prepared discussion questions as well as allowing the people to interact with spontaneous questions.

Questions for Clarification:
1. In your own words, what does *providence* mean?
2. How does the book of Ruth illustrate the doctrine of providence?
3. How is the faithfulness of God demonstrated in the first chapter of Ruth? The sovereignty of God? The wisdom of God? The mercy of God?
4. In what ways are Orpah and Ruth similar? In what ways do they differ?
5. What questions do the events of Ruth one raise in your mind?

Questions for Application:
1. What do we learn about true godliness from this chapter?
2. What does it mean to say that God is *real* in someone's life?
3. God gave Naomi a great blessing in the person of Ruth, but at this point in the story Naomi doesn't recognize it. Think of a time in your own life when God blessed you but you didn't recognize it immediately (have several share their 'blessing in disguise' with the group). What do we learn about ourselves from this?
4. Naomi lost her husband and sons in this chapter. Think about what that meant for her. Now think about widows in need that you know. What insights does God's Word give us, both in this passage and in other passages, about ministering to widows?
5. What is something you believe God would want you to do in light of what you have learned in Ruth one?

Tool #3: A Counseling Case Study
The use of case studies can be a helpful piece of leadership training for God's shepherds. The following scenario could be read and discussed at an elders' (or deacons', or small group leaders', etc.) meeting. As you will see, the case study attempts to help us see how the principles learned from the book of Ruth might apply in a present-day ministry opportunity. An appendix is provided at the end of this book, which gives suggested answers for the counseling case studies.

Scenario: Bob is a fifty-five year old member of your church. He and his wife, Sally, raised three children, all college graduates with honors. The children are now living, working, and raising their own families in other parts of the country. When the children were younger and at home Bob and Sally never missed any of their school functions (Bob coached their Little League teams, Sally was a den-mother, and so on). The couple team-taught a teen Sunday School class for the past eight years.

Nine months ago Sally died suddenly of a stroke and Bob understandably hasn't been the same since. He continues to attend church regularly but sits by himself, often cries as the hymns are sung, and leaves quickly once the service ends. He asked for a break from his Sunday School teaching the week after the funeral, and hasn't shown any desire to resume since.

You approach him after the service one Sunday, affirm your love and express your desire to help Bob. He breaks down and begins to sob, saying, "I just can't live without Sally. I need her. We did everything together. Why does God seem so distant from me?"

Case Study Discussion Questions: (see Appendix for suggested answers)
1. What insights from Ruth chapter one should affect the way we view and seek to help Bob?

2. In light of these biblical principles from the book of Ruth, what can the church do to help Bob?

3. Suppose you offer to meet with Bob for counseling and he agrees…

a. What would you want to accomplish in the *first session*? What passages of Scripture might you share with him that would give him hope?

b. What practical homework assignment(s) might you give Bob to help him?

c. Suppose you meet weekly with Bob to pray with him and provide biblical encouragement and counsel, yet in the *fifth* session he is still saying, "I *must* have Sally back. I just can't live without her." What biblical truth might you share with Bob to help him think differently? What homework might you give Bob at this point to transform his thinking?

Tool #4: Counseling Assignments Utilizing Ruth 1:1-22
In biblical counseling the use of relevant, targeted homework is vital in order to encourage and facilitate necessary change in the thinking and life of a counselee. Supposing that "Bob" (from the previous scenario) agreed to meet with you for biblical counseling, the book of Ruth could provide a very helpful platform from which to minister hope. If Bob agreed to meet weekly for one month, you might take him through the book of Ruth one chapter a week.

Week One Reading Assignment:
1. Read Ruth chapter one three times this week. Each time you read write down your answer to the following questions:

a. What do I learn about God from this passage?

b. What do I learn about God's plan for His people from this passage?

c. What do I learn about living for God from this passage?

2. Write out Ruth 1:16 on a 3x5 card and seek to memorize it by reading it out loud three times every day. Each time think about the significance of Ruth's bold profession.

3. Do this assignment after the others, towards the end of the week. In light of what you have learned from Ruth chapter one this week, make a list of three ways you might honor God, even though you are hurting, in the coming week. We'll discuss those at our next meeting.

A Word about Biblical Counseling Training:
Biblical counseling certainly involves more than reading Bible stories and applying principles to people's problems. The use of counseling scenarios in the "Getting Intentional about Application" sections of this book is not meant to promote a flippant use of the Scriptures in people-helping. Rather it is to encourage individuals to see the practical effect the Scriptures are intended to have when rightly understood and applied. Biblical theology should lead to practical theology. The fruit of solid exegesis ought to be seen in the lives of God's people. I am indebted to the ministry of the National Association of Nouthetic Counselors in this regard. The Lord has used this ministry to give me practical assistance in how to cross the bridge from the text of God's Word to the specific needs in the lives of people. For those interested in obtaining further training in Biblical Counseling, I highly recommend contacting NANC for information regarding counseling training centers, training seminars, and other resources, at www.nanc.org. In addition, I encourage you to consider the Certificate Program in Biblical Counseling offered by Dr. Jay Adams through the *Institute for Nouthetic Studies*. For information concerning this distance learning option, go to www.nouthetic.org.

CHAPTER

2

"God in a Barley Field"

Ruth 2:1-23

Expositional Commentary and Outline:
Providential Provision and Protection for the Destitute who Live By Faith

Expository Sermon:
God in a Barley Field

Getting Intentional About Application

Tool #1: A Teaching Outline
Tool #2: "Digging Deeper" Discussion Questions
Tool #3: A Counseling Case Study
Tool #4: Counseling Assignments

Expositional Outline:

Ruth 2:1-23

by Rick Kress

The Book of Ruth—A Portrait of God's Loyal Love, Sovereign Redemption, and the Faith of His Believing Remnant

I. The pain of covenant faithlessness [an empty profession] (1:1-5)

II. The pity of God and the initial glimmers of faith (1:6-22)

III. The providential provision and protection of God for the destitute who live by faith (2:1-23)

    A. The family of Elimelech—Naomi had a wealthy kinsman named Boaz (2:1)

    B. The field of Boaz—Ruth "happened" to glean in Boaz's field (2:2-3)

        1. The perspective of Ruth and Naomi (2:2)

        2. The providence of God (2:3)

    C. The favor of Boaz—he heard of Ruth's love, and faith in Yahweh (2:4-17)

        1. His concern (2:4-7)

            a. Piety/Love for Yahweh (v. 4)

            b. Perceptiveness/Love for people (v. 5-7)

                i. The question (v. 5)

                ii. The explanation (v. 6-7)

        2. His compassion and continued provision in light of Ruth's faith and love (2:8-13)

            a. He offered provision and protection to Ruth (v. 8-9)

                i. Her responsibility (v. 8)

                ii. Her reassurance (v. 9)

            b. He offered prayer for Ruth's blessings because of her faith in Yahweh's mercies (v. 10-13)

                i. The recognition of favor/grace (v. 10)

                ii. The request for Yahweh's blessing in light of Ruth's faith (v. 11-12)

                iii. The recognition of favor/grace (v. 13)

        3. His communion and gracious protection (2:14-17)

            a. The fellowship with Boaz and his people (v. 14)

            b. The further favor extended (v. 15-17)

                i. Grace gave her privilege, though undeserved (v. 15)

                ii. Grace gave her purposed blessing (v. 16)

                iii. Grace gave her plenty (v. 17)

    D. The favor of Yahweh recognized through the faith of Naomi (2:18-23)

        1. The favor of Yahweh recognized by faith (2:18-22)

            a. The report of Boaz's provision (v. 18-19)

            b. The request for Yahweh's blessing upon him (v. 20a)

            c. The recognition that Boaz is a kinsman redeemer (v. 20b)

            d. The report of Boaz's protection and continued provision (v. 21)

            e. The recognition of goodness (v. 22)

        2. The favor of Yahweh remained upon the women (2:23)

Expositional Commentary:
Providential Provision and Protection for the Destitute who Live by Faith

Ruth 2:1-23

by Rick Kress

Does anything really happen by chance? Or is God providentially moving in all circumstances of life and history to bring about His good and perfect plan, for His people's good and His own glory? If the latter is the case, what role do we play in this sovereign drama we call life? It wouldn't appear that we are merely automatons that cannot be held responsible for our choices. But rather we are morally responsible beings who are accountable for the choices we make. This is the mystery never fully explained in the Scriptures, but revealed to be true throughout God's Word. Our responsibility as believers is not only to trust in God's good sovereignty, but also to pursue the inseparable triumvirate of love, faith and obedience as we walk through this life.

Let's begin looking at the first indicator in Ruth chapter two, of God's sovereign mercy in providentially leading of the destitute, who turn to Him in faith.

III. The providential provision and protection of God for the destitute who live by faith (2:1-23)
A. The family of Elimelech—Naomi had a wealthy kinsman named Boaz (2:1)
"Now Naomi had a kinsman of her husband"
The word here translated "kinsman" means literally, "one who is known"—i.e., a friend or companion (cf. Prov. 7:4b). It will be revealed in the next phrase that he was of the same "clan/family" as Elimelech, and 2:20 says that he was a "close relative" (goel—kinsman redeemer; see also 3:9, 12). Here, however, the narrator introduces his audience to the fact that "Naomi had a friend of her husband". This again highlights God's mercy upon her, though she was as yet unaware of it.

"A man of great wealth, of the family of Elimelech, whose name was Boaz"
This friend of her husband is described here as "a man of great wealth". The expression "great wealth" is used of Gideon in Judges 6:12 and Jephthah in Judges 11:1, both translated, "valiant warrior". It carries the idea of a man of great power, and influence—militarily, politically, and economically, depending on the context. "Boaz", living in the days of the judges, would have likely been a man who was indeed a "valiant warrior". The following context indicates that he was a man of economic influence and power as well. This powerful "friend" of Naomi's husband was also from the same "clan" or "family"

as Elimelech. He was a relative of some sort to him. His name, "Boaz", though somewhat disputed, is reported to mean "strength".

Though admittedly his approach is subtle, the narrator has begun to focus on the hidden providence of God in this chapter. He began actually in the previous verse—1:22, where he matter-of-factly states that Naomi and Ruth returned at the beginning of barley harvest. In God's providential timing, these two destitute women returned to a place at the perfect time, so as to offer them some relief and hope in their poverty.

Then as we read verse one here, we are told that Naomi's husband had a close friend and relative that was a man of power, wealth and influence. Some would write such things off to "chance" or "coincidence". But verse three will serve to undergird the truth that God's hidden hand of providence was at work in Naomi's world.

B. The field of Boaz—Ruth "happened" to glean in Boaz's field (2:2-3)
1. The perspective of Ruth and Naomi (2:2)
"And Ruth the Moabitess said to Naomi, 'Please let me go to the field . . .'"
Once again we are reminded of Ruth's nationality/ethnicity. She was "Ruth the Moabitess"—an outsider and foreigner in Israel. Many people in the Israelite culture would have despised her. Yet she was loyal to Naomi, and here submissively asked permission from her mother-in-law to "go to the field and glean".

"And glean among the ears of grain after one in whose sight I may find favor"
The term, "glean", speaks of gathering up scraps and leftovers that remained after the harvesters had harvested the grain (see Is. 17:4-5 for the meager results of gleaning). Ruth evidently possessed some knowledge of the Israelite law recorded in Leviticus 19:9-10; 23:22; and Deuteronomy 24:19—that the leftovers were to be left for the aliens and needy in Israel.

The phrase, "after one in whose sight I may find favor/grace", indicates that Ruth suspected that not all would extend grace to a poor Moabite widow. And it also indicates that she saw her destitution and need for "favor/grace".

"And she said to her, 'Go, my daughter'"
Likely only a day or two after arriving in Bethlehem, Naomi was back to speaking to Ruth—and that, with the endearing term, "my daughter". As we shall see, Naomi had evidently come to the place where she faithfully reported Ruth's love and faith to others in Bethlehem (cf. 2:11-12). Perhaps Naomi was unfit for the work physically, but here she gave Ruth permission to "go".

Ruth and Naomi both knew their need. Ruth would go in search of the scraps left over from following behind someone who would show her grace.

2. The providence of God (2:3)

"So she departed and went and gleaned in the field after the reapers"
With the hope of finding someone gracious who would allow her to take advantage of the provision in the levitical law, Ruth "went and came and gathered in the field behind the harvesters".

"And she happened to come to the portion of the field belonging to Boaz, who was of the family of Elimelech"
Here now we see another subtle clue given by the narrator meant to point his audience to God's sovereign control over even the seemingly chance happenings of life. As Ruth walked and went forth to glean, "she *happened* to come to the portion of the field belonging to Boaz, who was of the family of Elimelech" (emphasis added)—that is, the same influential friend and relative mentioned in verse one.

Evidently there were not separate fields in this area near Bethlehem, but one large "field" that was apportioned in sections to various owners. As it "happened", or "quite by accident" is the thought, Ruth found herself in Boaz's portion of the field. The term "happened" is used in 1 Samuel 6:9 of the Philistines speaking of "chance" or "luck". But the believing Israelite understood that there is no such thing as "chance" or "happenstance"—only God's providence and sovereign control of history. As Proverbs 16:33 says, "The lot is cast into the lap, but its every decision is from the LORD" (cf. Prov. 3:6; 16:9; 19:21; 20:24; 21:1; Jer. 10:23).

Here then are the first two indicators of God's sovereign/providential protection and provision for those who are destitute, but walk by faith. One is the *family of Elimelech*: Naomi had a wealthy and influential relative on her husband's side; and the other is the *field of Boaz*: Ruth just "happened" to find herself in the portion of the field belonging to that wealthy and influential relative of Naomi's deceased husband.

C. The favor of Boaz—he heard of Ruth's love, and faith in Yahweh (2:4-17)
1. His concern (2:4-7)
a. Piety/Love for Yahweh (v. 4)
"Now behold, Boaz came from Bethlehem"
The drama of the scene is heightened by the use of the word, "behold". After Ruth providentially came to Boaz's portion of the field, "*behold*, Boaz came from Bethlehem" (emphasis added). Again, not only did Ruth come to Boaz's field but she also remained long enough to meet Boaz himself. He just "happened" to be coming to the field from Bethlehem.

"And said to the reapers, 'May the LORD be with you.'"
And they said to him, "May the LORD bless you"—the reapers' reply was

according to the standard blessing of Numbers 6:24a (see also Ps. 129:8). But Boaz's greeting, "Yahweh be with you" is somewhat unusual in its construction. And it likely indicates something of Boaz's character. He was not just giving the customary greeting, but rather a personalized greeting and blessing. The two greetings together in the original grammar form a sort of poetic structure, where "Yahweh" is both the beginning and ending word. Again, this may very well have been a literary device that the narrator used to hint at the real reason Ruth "happened" to be in the field.

Though some may want to interpret this greeting as merely perfunctory, the rest of the narrative will confirm that Boaz was both a man of faith in Yahweh and a man of love for people. This greeting is the first indicator. Thus Ruth just "happened" to be at the right place, at the right time, for a man with the right character to show her grace—which was her pursuit at the beginning of the day. Though she didn't know it quite yet, she was providentially led to a man of piety/love for God.

b. Perceptiveness/Love for people (v. 5-7)
i. The question (v. 5)
"Then Boaz said to his servant who was in charge of the reapers, 'Whose young woman is this?'"
The text reads: "And Boaz said to his young man/boy who was standing over the harvesters, 'Whose young woman/girl is this?'" Boaz was evidently an observant man. He recognized a "young maiden" that was not of his household/work force. "Surely she was under someone's realm of authority", Boaz would reason—a husband or landowner.

ii. The explanation (v. 6-7)
"The servant in charge of the reapers replied, 'She is the young Moabite woman who returned with Naomi from the land of Moab'"
"The young man standing over the harvesters" then told Boaz—"A young woman—Moabitess—she is, who came back with Naomi from the fields of Moab" (YLT). The rather awkward construction emphasized Ruth's ethnicity. That Ruth was a "Moabitess" was not lost on "the servant in charge of the reapers", and no doubt the reapers were well aware of her nationality as well. It is also implied that Naomi's heralded return was well known, and this young woman was that "Moabitess" who had returned with her.

"And she said, 'Please let me glean and gather after the reapers among the sheaves'"
The young supervisor then recounted Ruth's request to Boaz. Though some believe Ruth boldly asked to "pick up and gather" alongside the harvesters, it seems better to see this as a request to pick up and gather the remnants and leftovers from the field.

"Thus she came and has remained from the morning until now, she has been sitting in the house for a little while"
The Hebrew here is quite difficult, but the sense seems to be that after receiving permission to glean, she "remained" in Boaz's field since that morning. She may have also taken a break in the servant's shelter as the NLT renders it: "She has been hard at work ever since, except for a few minutes' rest in the shelter."

Boaz will later be revealed as Naomi and Ruth's redeemer—i.e., their human redeemer/kinsman redeemer. For now, the narrator is painting him to be a man of concern, faith and perception.

2. His compassion and continued provision in light of Ruth's faith and love (2:8-13)
a. He offered provision and protection to Ruth (v. 8-9)
i. Her responsibility (v. 8)
"Then Boaz said to Ruth, 'Listen carefully, my daughter'"
Notably, "Boaz" affectionately addressed "Ruth" with the words, "my daughter"—as Naomi had earlier that morning. "Boaz", took a kind and fatherly approach to her though she was a Moabitess. He was no doubt old enough to be her father (cf. 3:10). That Boaz was a compassionate and gracious man will be born out by the following narrative. His call to "listen" to him left Ruth with the responsibility of trusting his gracious offer.

"Do not go to glean in another field, furthermore, do not go on from this one, but stay here with my maids"
Boaz's command was literally, "do not go into another field—yes, do not cross over from this one; but now cleave with my young maidens". The word "stay" or "cleave" here is from the same root used to describe Ruth's attachment and loyalty to Naomi. Boaz was offering Ruth protection in his field, with his female servants. Ruth went out seeking grace; now grace was being offered.

ii. Her reassurance (v. 9)
"Let your eyes be on the field which they reap, and go after them"
Now stating his offer positively, Boaz was not only asking Ruth not to leave but also to stay and focus her attention on going "after" or "behind" his servant girls who were part of his work force.

"Indeed, I have commanded the servants not to touch you"
The word "servants" here is once again, "young men". Boaz would insure that his male servants would not physically harass Ruth. They would not "strike" or "smite" her in any way. Included would be the prohibition of sexual molestation (Gen. 20:6; Prov. 6:29)—which a single woman and Moabitess might encounter during the days of the judges (see the moral climate of that

era in the narrative of Judges 19:1ff).

"When you are thirsty, go to the water jars and drink from what the servants draw"
This would seem to be kindness that went well beyond even cultural norms as
Block points out: "In a cultural context in which normally foreigners would
draw for Israelites [Josh. 9:21-27], and women would draw for men (Gen.
24:10-20), Boaz's authorization of Ruth to drink from water his men had
drawn is indeed extraordinary" (Block, p. 660).

With these words, Boaz offered provision and protection for Ruth.

b. He offered prayer for Ruth's blessings because of her faith in Yahweh's mercies (v. 10-13)

i. The recognition of favor/grace (v. 10)
"Then she fell on her face, bowing to the ground and said to him"
Ruth's response to Boaz's grace and generosity was to humbly, and gratefully fall "on her face, bowing to the ground". This was the response of a woman
awed by grace. In other contexts, it would be the language of worship, or the
response of a subject for royalty.

*"Why have I found favor in your sight that you should take notice of me, since
I am a foreigner?"*
Her question reflects the perplexing nature of "grace" or "favor" freely
bestowed on a person. It had been her goal to "find favor/grace" in someone's
"sight" that morning (2:2), but now having "found" it, she was perplexed,
awed, and humbled to the core. The Hebrew terms for "take notice" and "foreigner" sound quite similar and add a bit of poetic irony to the scene from a
literary standpoint.

Culturally, she would have normally been an outcast and not "noticed" for
special favor since she was a "foreigner". In fact, the same term—"foreigner"—is often used in the book of Proverbs in identifying the "adulteress"
(Prov. 5:20; 6:24; 23:27; 27:13).

ii. The request for Yahweh's blessing in light of Ruth's faith (v. 11-12)
"All that you have done for your mother-in-law after the death of your husband has been fully reported to me"
Ruth had attached herself to Naomi—not to earn favor in anyone's eyes—but
rather out of love and faith, which were already the gift of God. Boaz was
extending grace on the basis of her faith, which was evidenced to him through
her attachment to Naomi and the abandonment of her people.

The phrase "fully reported" is a Hebrew idiom that is literally rendered,
"being reported, it has been reported". This indicates that Naomi finally did
relate to the people of Bethlehem the love, devotion and, as we will see by the
next phrase, the faith of Ruth.

"And how you left your father and your mother and the land of your birth, and came to a people that you did not previously know"
Boaz may have seen the parallels between Ruth's faith and Abraham's—the patriarch of Israel (cf. Gen. 12:1-4). The word "left" was first used in Genesis 2:24 of a husband "leaving" father and mother to "cleave" to a wife. Boaz knew that Ruth had formed a covenant type relationship with Naomi and also her people, Israel—and Israel's God as the second half of verse 12 clarifies.

Boaz didn't fully explain why he had extended favor to Ruth, but instead he initially cited the evidences of Ruth's love and faith. There were of course other reasons implied from the earlier narrative: 1) Boaz is a man of faith; 2) God was providentially working to give Ruth the desire of her heart (cf. v. 2; see Block, p. 662).

"May the LORD reward your work, and your wages be full from the LORD"
Boaz realized, however, that his own generosity and love was not divine, thus he prayed for Yahweh's blessing upon Ruth's "work" of love and faith. In fact, Boaz was calling upon "Yahweh" to be faithful to the principle of "sowing and reaping" (Gal. 6:7). God "repays" those who honor Him and His people according to Proverbs 13:21 (cf. 1 Sam. 24:19; Prov. 25:22), just as surely as He does those who dishonor Him. Proverbs 19:17 says, "One who is gracious to a poor man lends to the LORD, and He will repay him for his good deed". The term "wages" was used of Jacob's "wages" due from Laban (Gen. 29:15; 31:7). Boaz was praying for Yahweh to act according to His nature as a God of equity, order and justice. Ruth was a woman of faith and love, who manifested faith and love-driven deeds. Boaz prayed for Ruth to receive divine payment/reward based upon those love-motivated works.

The next phrase indicates that Boaz did not have in mind some kind of works-righteousness system of merit before God. Ruth's reward and wages were founded in God's mercy and grace dispensed through her trust in Yahweh, as her Savior.

"The LORD, the God of Israel, under whose wings you have come to seek refuge"
Here we see Boaz's beautiful description of Ruth's faith. Her trust was in "Yahweh"—the covenant-keeping, ever-living One. Her trust was in "the God of Israel"—the one true God. The term "seek refuge" is used as a synonym for "trust" in Psalm 118:8-9. Ruth had put her confidence in "Yahweh, the God of Israel" (cf. Deut. 32:37). See 2 Samuel 22:3 for a fuller description of its meaning. It is abandonment to God for mercy, salvation, deliverance, hope and life (cf. Ps. 2:12; 5:12; 7:1; 16:1; 17:7; 18:3, 31; 25:20; 34:22; 37:40; Nah. 1:7; Zeph. 3:12).

The reference to Yahweh's "wings" of protection alludes back to

Deuteronomy 32:11 (see also Ps. 17:8; 36:7; 57:1; 61:4; 63:7; 91:4). The same root is used in 3:9, there translated "covering". Amazingly, Boaz would eventually be the divine answer to his own prayer here.

iii. The recognition of favor/grace (v. 13)

"I have found favor in your sight, my lord, for you have comforted me and indeed have spoken kindly to your maidservant"

Rather than merely a statement of fact, the expression, "I have found favor in your sight" is an expression of thankfulness—i.e., "You are gracious, my lord, because you have comforted me and spoken unto the heart of your maidservant" (cf. Block, p. 664). She acknowledged Boaz as her earthly "master" and then confirmed that she has been "comforted". His provision had brought "rest" to her. Not only that, Boaz had spoken to her heart. Either he expressed her heart in saying she had come to take refuge under Yahweh's wings, or his words were compassionate and ministered to her. Both would be true.

Here Ruth called herself Boaz's "maidservant". The term she used was not the one Boaz employed in verse eight—"maid". The word here speaks of the lowest slave in the social structure (cf. Block, p. 665).

"Though I am not like one of your maidservants"

With this qualifier, Ruth was humbly admitting that in reality she was lower than the lowest of Boaz's slaves. This isn't poor self-esteem or false humility. It is a picture of a woman who had grasped some of the amazing nature of grace. Boaz had been gracious to her—a Moabite woman in Israel. She responded by thanking him and confessing that she was his slave, though not even qualified to be a slave.

Boaz had revealed his *concern* and *compassion* to this woman of humble faith.

3. His communion and gracious protection (2:14-17)

a. The fellowship with Boaz and his people (v. 14)

"At mealtime Boaz said to her, 'Come here, that you may eat of the bread and dip your piece of bread in the vinegar'"

Boaz didn't just exhibit extraordinary grace/favor to Ruth, he actually had fellowship with her. His words weren't just showing favor to a lowly foreigner, but he invited her to eat with him and his workers. This was lavish grace in the culture of that day. For a pious Jew to fellowship/commune over a meal with a Moabitess would have been, no doubt, quite uncommon. That he said, "come here", implies that Ruth had respectfully and humbly kept her distance and did not presume upon his grace.

The "vinegar" was likely a sour wine sauce used to moisten the bread and make it more palatable. He didn't merely give her a crust of bread; instead he provided a tasty meal.

"So she sat beside the reapers; and he served her roasted grain, and she ate and was satisfied"

Ruth was privileged to sit "beside the reapers". Boaz himself "served her roasted grain" (1 Sam. 17:17; 25:18; 2 Sam. 17:28 for "roasted grain"). The statement that "she ate and was satisfied" is significant. Ruth was a destitute widow, and a Moabitess. This was likely her first full/satisfying meal she had eaten in some time. The destitute did not have soup kitchens in those days. She would have lived off of leftovers and scraps. Boaz's provision was gracious, satisfying and abundant as the next phrase indicates.

"And had some left"

The portion that Boaz handed Ruth was so abundant that even after she had eaten to satisfaction she had some "remaining". Later that evening, she would give this excess to Naomi (cf. v. 18).

b. The further favor extended (v. 15-17)
i. Grace gave her privilege, though undeserved (v. 15)

"When she rose to glean, Boaz commanded his servants, saying, 'Let her glean even among the sheaves . . .'"

The poor who might "glean" or "gather scraps" could only do so after the harvesters were done with that portion of the field. Here, however, "Boaz" himself personally commanded his "young men" to allow Ruth to gather among the fallen grain before the harvesters were finished (Morris, p. 279).

"And do not insult her"

Likely, such a bold gleaner would be run off, struck or severely rebuked for coming too close. But Boaz commanded that she not be "humiliated", "hurt", or "shamed" in any way. He gave her an uncommon and undeserved favor.

ii. Grace gave her purposed blessing (v. 16)

"Also you shall purposely pull out for her from the bundles and leave that she may glean, and do not rebuke her"

"Moreover, plundering you shall plunder for her from out of the bundles and abandon it that she may pick it up" was Boaz's further charge. She was not just given a sack of winnowed grain to take home. Ruth would have the responsibility to glean and work. But in God's grace, through Boaz, Ruth's provision would be supplied and abundant—and amazingly, without "rebuke". The term "rebuke" also speaks of "insult". "One can well imagine the abuse that persons like Ruth [a woman, a Moabitess, and destitute], who arrive at the field uninvited or unengaged, might receive from those 'upstanding' citizens who have been properly hired by the land owner to harvest the crops. Now Boaz lets his workers know that they are to have no part in such action toward Ruth" (Block, p. 669).

iii. Grace gave her plenty (v. 17)

"So she gleaned in the field until evening. Then she beat out what she had gleaned, and it was about an ephah of barley"

Ruth worked all day "until evening". Afterwards she "beat out" her gleanings—i.e., separated the grain from the chaff. Amazingly, she had "about an ephah of barley". Most scholars place that unit of measurement between 30 and 50 pounds—about three-fifths of a bushel. "To put it more vividly in our culture, the bag she brought home was the size of a colossal bag of dog food!" (Duguid, p. 161). Scholars estimate that two women could likely live for several weeks on such a quantity of grain.

God's providential grace through Boaz gave Ruth privilege though undeserved; grace gave her purposed blessing; and grace gave her abundance.

We've seen that even in the difficulties and despair of life, God's sovereign grace and hidden providence were working—through the *family of Elimelech* (he had an influential relative named Boaz); His providence was revealed in the *field of Boaz*; and through the *favor of Boaz*.

D. The favor of Yahweh recognized through the faith of Naomi (2:18-23)
1. The favor of Yahweh recognized by faith (2:18-22)
a. The report of Boaz's provision (v. 18-19)

"She took it up and went into the city, and her mother-in-law saw what she had gleaned"

It must have been quite a sight as the Moabite girl carried perhaps a fifty pound sack or shawl filled with grain "into the city" of Bethlehem. Naomi's response in verse 19 indicates that Naomi was awed by what she "saw" when Ruth came in with the grain.

"She also took out and gave Naomi what she had left after she was satisfied"
Ruth also gave "Naomi" the roasted barley left over from lunch (cf. v. 14).

"Where did you glean today and where did you work? May he who took notice of you be blessed"
Naomi's rapid fire questioning indicates extreme excitement over Ruth's unthinkable success. The double use of the term "where" is interesting in the Hebrew, in that the term ephah and "where"—*ephoh* sound quite similar. Before Ruth could answer Naomi's questions, Naomi prayed for the blessing of the one "who took notice" of Ruth. The word "took notice" is from the same root that Ruth used in verse 10.

"The name of the man with whom I worked today is Boaz"
Ruth was finally able to answer, but instead of answering *"where"* she worked, "she told her mother-in-law *with whom* she had worked"—with "Boaz". Ruth rightly understood that the location wasn't the issue so much as the gracious man, "Boaz".

b. The request for Yahweh's blessing upon him (v. 20a)
"May he be blessed of the LORD"
Upon hearing of Boaz, Naomi prayed that he would be "blessed of Yahweh". She requested that Yahweh's favor and peace be upon Boaz for the great generosity that he had shown.

"The LORD who has not withdrawn his kindness to the living and to the dead"
The pronoun "who" here can refer to either Boaz or Yahweh syntactically. Three factors indicate that Naomi was acknowledging that it was "Yahweh who [had] not withdrawn his *hesed* [loyal love, mercy and grace] to the living and to the dead". First, "Boaz" did not extend loyal love "to the dead"—i.e., Naomi's family who died in Moab. Second, in the last half of verse 20, the term, "the man" is used—but would not be necessary if she were merely continuing to speak of Boaz. Rather she had been referring to Yahweh's lovingkindness, but then spoke of Boaz as "the man". And third, an analogous grammatical construction is used in Genesis 24:27, which obviously refers to Yahweh (Block, p. 673).

Naomi had earlier urged Ruth to "forsake/leave" her (cf. 1:16), but instead she "left/forsook" her father and mother and the land of her birth (2:11). In God's gracious providence, Boaz commanded that stalks of grain be "forsaken/left" for Ruth to gather (2:16). Because of that, and now seeing evidence of God's providential care, Naomi declared her faith that Yahweh had not "forsaken" His loyal love, mercy and grace—*hesed*—to her and her family. In fact, her mention of "the dead" here may indicate that she actually knew that God was faithful and loyal in love even through the loss of her husband and two sons who died in exile, so to speak. "This speech represents a total turnaround from her despairing and accusatory words in 1:20-21" (Block, p. 673).

She saw Yahweh's kindness in conjunction with His providence as the next phrase indicates.

c. The recognition that Boaz is a kinsman redeemer (v. 20b)
"The man is our relative, he is one of our closest relatives"
Naomi then said, "A near one to us is the man—from our kinsman-redeemers is he". A "kinsman-redeemer"—here translated, "closest relatives"—was a close relative who could redeem/buy back a family member sold into slavery (Lev. 25:47-49); he could redeem/buy back land sold by a family member to eliminate debt (Lev. 25:23-28); and he could redeem/buy back the family lineage through levirate marriage (Deut. 25:5-10) (cf. *The MacArthur Study Bible* electronic edition). As well, he could avenge the murder of a close relative—thus he was a kinsman-avenger (Num. 35:12, 19-27); he could "receive restitution money on behalf of a deceased victim of a crime (Num. 5:8); and

... [he could] ensure that justice [was] served in a lawsuit involving a relative (Job 19:25; Ps 119:154; Jer 50:34)" (Block, p. 674). See Hebrews 2:14-18 for Christ's relationship to us.

In God's sovereign plan, Naomi and Ruth had a human redeemer to rescue them, protect them, and insure justice for them. He was a man of influence; a man of faith; and a man of generous compassion. No wonder Naomi prayed for Yahweh's blessing upon him then recognized the steadfast love and compassion of the One she had previously thought had cursed her.

d. The report of Boaz's protection and continued provision (v. 21)
"Then Ruth the Moabitess said"
Naomi had used the first person plural pronoun "our"—the man is from among "our" kinsmen-redeemers. But the narrator here wants to remind us that "Ruth" was still "the Moabitess"—emphasizing the scope of Yahweh's redeeming love and gracious providence. Even this hated "Moabitess" had a redeemer as she had come to the God of Israel for refuge under His wings. But perhaps "Ruth", as a "Moabitess", was unfamiliar with all the possible benefits of having a kinsman-redeemer.

"Furthermore, he said to me, 'You should stay close to my servants until they have finished all my harvest'"
The term "furthermore" likely expresses Ruth's excitement concerning the prospects of further provision. She reported that beyond all that Boaz had done, he told her to "cleave" (cf. v. 8) to his crew "until they have finished *all* [his] harvest" (emphasis added).

e. The recognition of goodness (v. 22)
"Naomi said to Ruth her daughter-in-law"
Notably, here "Ruth" is designated as Naomi's "daughter-in-law". Perhaps the significance is that in the context of the verse, Naomi was looking out for Ruth's welfare and showed familial concern for "her daughter-in-law". In the next phrase, however, she addresses "Ruth" as "my daughter"—again showing affection and relationship.

"It is good, my daughter, that you go out with his maids, so that others do not fall upon you in another field"
The verb "fall upon" can mean merely "encounter", but it can also speak of a hostile encounter/attack. It seems likely here that Naomi also knew of the dangers that a single Moabitess might "encounter" in "another field", owned or operated by men of not-so-noble character as Boaz. Naomi confirmed that Boaz's plan of protection for Ruth was "good".

Naomi recognized the favor of Yahweh, as her faith seemed to be strengthened in seeing His good providence at work.

2. The favor of Yahweh remained upon the women (2:23)

"So she stayed close by the maids of Boaz in order to glean until the end of the barley harvest and the wheat harvest"

Just as Boaz had instructed (2:8, 21) and Naomi had confirmed, Ruth "attached herself/cleaved" to Boaz's *"maids...until the end of the barley harvest"—"and the wheat harvest"*. This would have taken about seven weeks, from late April to early June.

In the context of Israel's feasts, Naomi and Ruth returned around the time of Passover, and then Ruth worked the harvests that would end at the Feast of Weeks/Pentecost (cf. Lev. 23:15-16; Deut. 16:7-11). Again, the hidden hand of God's providence had guided the women to the right place, and time, and sustained them through the harvest. It is interesting that they came back to the Promised Land, and made their exodus from Moab at the time when the Exodus and deliverance of Israel was remembered. And they came under God's protection and provision even through the day of Pentecost—the Gentile Ruth would know God's goodness on the day of Pentecost.

"And she lived with her mother-in-law"

The word "lived" means "to dwell". Ruth was faithful to her pledge of 1:16. She did not go back on her word.

As well, the entire verse serves as a summary of their lives for those two months. Ruth gleaned in Boaz's field by day, and "dwelled with her mother-in-law" by night and on the Sabbath's, no doubt. So the narrative ends beautifully, but not without its questions. What about Boaz as *goel*—redeemer—as Naomi had mentioned? So they were abundantly supplied for at least seven weeks, but what about their protection and provision for the long term? What was Naomi thinking during this time? Chapter three would reveal the answers to these questions.

For now, chapter two was meant to highlight the sovereign grace of God in providentially providing and protecting the destitute women who came to Him for shelter. Yahweh did so via providence, primarily through the kindness of a man of love and faith. God does that. Even though He is sovereignly working in both the "good" and "bad" circumstances of life, it seems He delights in using His people (those who trust Him) to reflect His character and extend His love.

Conclusion

We have seen four points that highlight God's providential protection and provision of those who seek refuge under His wings. 1) He was providentially working decades before in preparing *the family of Elimelech*. Noami's husband would have a relative and friend who could and would offer provision and protection to the destitute women. 2) He was providentially directing Ruth's path that morning, as she "happened" to find herself in *the field of Boaz*. 3) He had sovereignly prepared Boaz's character to be a man of faith and love; thus His providence granted Naomi and Ruth *the favor of Boaz*. 4) Finally, Naomi finally recognized God's providence, and thus *the favor of Yahweh* as she looked with eyes of faith.

Are we seeing God's sovereignty with eyes of bitterness or faith? The eyes of faith embrace the goodness of God and trust that He has not abandoned His loyal love to us. We need to begin to look at our circumstances with eyes of faith. We need to live by the conviction that He is good and in control, and we can trust Him—even when it hurts.

As well, are we—like Boaz—people of piety and perception? Are we filled with God's compassion and concern for others? Are we instruments in His sovereign hand to bless others in need? What do I mean by this? Duguid has summarized it well:

> Do we welcome outsiders like Ruth, the non-kosher people, the people who do not naturally fit in our community, the way that Boaz did? It is doubtful whether many rich men in Bethlehem would have looked over the laborers harvesting their fields, instantly picked out a single foreigner, and identified her as someone new. So also, perhaps, many of us scan the rows of people in our church and completely miss all of the Ruths in our congregation because we are only looking to make friends with people who are like us. We cast an eye over our neighborhood or community and completely overlook those who are outcasts and strangers, the immigrants and the homeless, the poor and the needy. We have eyes but do not easily see what Boaz saw, because we are not looking for the poor and the outcast.
>
> . . . Do we have a similar heart of compassion for those who seem to have little or nothing to offer us in return? (Duguid, p. 161).

Or are we people consumed with our own lives, our own projects, our own families, or our own group?

God is providentially working in history and in every individual life. Are we walking with Him in faith and love, so as to be used as instruments/vessels of His glory? That means having a living relationship with Him. Do you talk with Him regularly? Do you hear from Him in His Word regularly?

Praise the One who causes all things to work together for good, for those who love Him and are called according to His purpose (cf. Rom 8:28)!

Expository Sermon:
God in a Barley Field

Ruth 2:1-23

by Brad Brandt

Do you like the game-show *Jeopardy*? As you probably know, it's a game in which answers are provided for contestants who must then provide the corresponding questions. Let's try it. I'll give you a couple of definitions of words taken from the *Living Webster Dictionary* and you determine which word is appropriate for each definition. The correct answers are provided at the end of the chapter, p. 78.

Definition: *"Something which seems to go beyond the known laws of nature and is held to be the act of a supernatural being"*
Question: What is a _____?

Definition: *"The care and supervision of God over His creatures"*
Question: What is _____?

When you read the Bible you soon discover that God works in both ways. At times He does *miracles*—like parting the Red Sea, sending manna from the sky, raising a dead man to life, making a leper clean, and so on. But for every page on which you see God working a miracle you will find several pages on which there is *no miracle*. That's not to say God isn't working, for He is. He is always at work behind the scenes, guiding, directing, moving, arranging, preparing events and people to accomplish His wise, good, and eternal plan. In other words, on every page we'll see, if we'll look for it, God's *providence*.

What about now? Did you see any miracles this week, any act that went beyond the known laws of nature that God alone could accomplish? Perhaps. But did you see God's providence? His providence occurred in all of our lives, but again, we must have eyes to see it.

We often associate God with church buildings. How about barley fields? In Ruth 2 we see God at work in a barley field. We must see Him there, just like we must learn to see Him in the 'barley fields' of our lives—on the ball court, in the lunch room, on the job floor, and in the back yard. God is at work everywhere. That's why we can trust Him.

In the previous chapter we saw God working in a series of losses in the life of a woman named Naomi. In Ruth 1, a famine hit Israel as a wakeup call from the Lord to turn His wayward people back to Himself. One family decided to leave the promised land in search for food. Elimelech, his wife Naomi, and their sons Mahlon and Kilion moved to Moab. While there, Elimelech died. Naomi's sons both married Moabite women and then tragically both sons died. In one decade, Naomi lost her home, her husband, and her sons.

Yet God was at work, even in her losses. Naomi heard there was food back in Israel so she decided to return. Her daughters-in-law both tried to follow her. She convinced Orpah to remain in Moab, but she could not shake Ruth who gave this impassioned plea: "Don't urge me to leave you or to turn back from you. Where you go I will go, and where you stay I will stay. Your people will be my people and *your God my God* (1:16)."

That was Ruth chapter one. God was at work in a series of *losses*. Naomi lost her home, her husband, and her sons. But she gained something. Indeed, all Israel gained something that would play a significant role in the coming of the Messiah. *Ruth.*

That brings us to Ruth chapter two. In contrast to the losses in chapter one, in chapter two we see God's providence is a series of *gains*. God always takes care of His people, always. In Ruth 2 we see His care demonstrated in three ways in the life of Ruth through the person of Boaz.

I. The Lord directed Ruth to Boaz (1-3).

Verse 1—"Now Naomi had a relative on her husband's side, from the clan of Elimelech, a man of standing, whose name was Boaz." The writer of this short story, some feel it is Samuel but we don't know for sure, tells us this important piece of information to prepare us for what will happen later. The author is a great story teller. But his aim isn't to entertain. It's to teach us about God, namely this...

A. God has a plan for His people.

Ruth is about to meet Boaz but before she does, the writer introduces the reader to him. The name 'Boaz' means 'in Him is strength.' Interestingly, Ruth's first husband, Mahlon, had a name that meant 'weakling.' What a contrast!

We're told that Boaz is related to Naomi on Elimelech's side. That's significant as we'll see later in the book. We're also told Boaz was an important man, just how important we'll also soon see.

It's vital to remember that nothing ever just *happens*, not in God's universe. God is in control. God is directing every situation down to the very details. God has a plan for His people.

"That leads to fatalism, doesn't it?" No, not if we keep the biblical balance represented in Ruth. On the one hand God truly has a plan for His people. On the other hand...

B. God uses the decisions of His people to accomplish that plan.

In this case He used a decision made by Ruth. Verse 2—"And Ruth the Moabitess said to Naomi, 'Let me go to the fields and pick up the leftover grain behind anyone in whose eyes I find favor.' Naomi said to her, 'Go ahead, my daughter.'" Please note that...

1. Ruth was looking for food.

It's hard for us to fathom how vulnerable the widows Ruth and Naomi were. There was no social security in Israel. There were, however, God-given stipulations that provided for them. Gleaning was a right of widows, as God instructed in the Law (Deut. 24:19). A farmer was to leave the edge of his field unharvested to provide for widows.

We need a little background concerning grain farming in Israel to make sense of the story.

Harvesting grain involved the following steps (NIV Study Bible, p. 363):

1. Cutting the ripened standing grain with hand sickles, usually done by men
2. Binding the grain into sheaves, usually done by women
3. Gleaning, that is, gathering stalks of grain left behind
4. Transporting the sheaves to the threshing floor, often by donkey and sometimes by cart
5. Threshing, that is, loosening the grain from the straw, usually done by the treading of cattle, but sometimes by toothed threshing sledges or the wheels of carts
6. Winnowing, done by tossing the grain into the air with winnowing forks so that the wind, which usually came up for a few hours in the afternoon, blew away the straw and chaff, leaving the grain at the winnower's feet
7. Sifting the grain to remove any residual foreign matter
8. Bagging for transportation and storage

So Ruth decided to go looking for some grain. The KJV uses the word 'corn' which is the British equivalent of 'grain.' The particular grain Ruth is after is barley (1:22). The barley harvest began in late April.

Ruth didn't live on a farm. In fact, in that day no one did. People lived within the city walls for protection, but their farmland was located outside the city. Ruth intended to leave Bethlehem and look for food in a nearby barley field.

In verse 2 Ruth is referred to as 'the Moabitess,' one of five times in the book we're told that she is a *foreigner*, an *outsider*. That, too, is significant for it shows that God can use anyone to fulfill His amazing plan.

Verse 3—"So she went out and began to glean in the fields behind the harvesters. As it turned out, she found herself working in a field belonging to

Boaz, who was from the clan of Elimelech." Remember, Ruth was looking for food, but the Lord had something else in mind…

2. The Lord intended to give her something far greater.
It was a 'God-moment.' The NIV says, "As it turned out." The KJV uses the phrase, "Her hap was to light on a part of the field belonging to Boaz." The Hebrew phrase literally reads, "her hap happened," or "her chance chanced," or "she happened to happen on" (Huey, p. 527). From Ruth's perspective she just "happened" to end up in a field owned by Boaz. But this was no happenstance. God was at work, a fact that will become quite apparent by the time the story is done.

It's the same in your life and mine…

When I was eleven years old my dad just *happened* to take a new job, and we just *happened* to move to a town where there just *happened* to be a Bible-believing church where I just *happened* to hear the good news of Jesus Christ and just *happened* to believe in Him. Later a family just *happened* to move to that same farm town that just *happened* to have a teenage girl my age who just *happened* to accept my invitation to come to a youth group event who later just *happened* to accept my proposal to become my wife and life partner.

Think about how your hap *happened* in life. Where you were born, the people you've met, the experiences you've known, none of that just *happened*. Indeed, the Sovereign Lord has been at work in every detail, in every *hap*!

You decided to come to church today. That's your *hap*! Maybe you came to satisfy a family member, or to hear a song, or meet a friend. Maybe you are searching. Whatever the reason *you* had, know this. God uses the decisions of His people to accomplish His plan. He is up to something in your life today.

So ends scene #1. The Lord directed Ruth to Boaz. In scene #2…

II. The Lord provided for Ruth through Boaz (4-16).
Keep in mind Ruth is after food but God has a bigger agenda for her and through Ruth for the accomplishment of His redemptive plan for the world. And He intends to use Boaz to bring it about. Boaz gave Ruth five things in this scene…

A. Boaz gave her the assurance of the Lord's presence (4).
Verse 4—"Just then Boaz arrived from Bethlehem and greeted the harvesters, 'The LORD be with you!' 'The LORD bless you!' they called back."

That's an interesting greeting. Remember this story is taking place during the time of the Judges (see 1:1). What was happening at that time? Not much good! The last verse of Judges declares in Judges 21:25, "In those days Israel had no king; everyone did as he saw fit." What happens to society when everybody does what they think is right and does their own thing? Read Judges and you'll find out. Religion is marketed. Sex is degraded. Justice is perverted. Marriage and the family begin to disintegrate. That's what happened during the time of the judges.

But so did this. There was a man that went to work and greeted his workers by saying, "The LORD be with you!" This is a godly man, a rarity it would seem from reading the book of Judges, but God has His own in any age. I can't help but see a contrast here...

1. For some people God is real only in church.

Their Christianity shows up only on Sunday. Ask them if they love Jesus and they'll tell you...*on Sunday*. Ask them for evidence and they'll point to what they do...*on Sunday...at church*. That's reality for some people. God is real only in church. Conversely...

2. For others God is real wherever they go.

"The LORD be with you!" Where did Boaz say this? In a barley field with his employees. Boaz took the Lord to work with him. Some people talk about God at work but their work doesn't match their talk and it turns people off.

That wasn't the case with Boaz. He backed up his words by the way he treated his workers, as we'll soon see. And so his employees respond, "The LORD bless you!" Amazing. People are thinking about the Lord where they work!

Think of the impact this had on a newcomer to the faith like Ruth. By his actions, Boaz gave Ruth the assurance of the Lord's presence. Wow! Israel's God goes to work with them!

It didn't take long for Boaz to notice a new face in his work crew. Verse 5—"Boaz asked the foreman of his harvesters, 'Whose young woman is that?'" That's quite a question, not *who is that young woman, but whose young woman is that*? In other words, who does she belong to? Does she have a master? How about a husband? Does she belong to anyone? There seems to be more behind Boaz's question than, "Who gives that woman a W-2 at the end of the year?"

Verses 6-7—"The foreman replied, 'She is the Moabitess who came back from Moab with Naomi. She said, 'Please let me glean and gather among the sheaves behind the harvesters.' She went into the field and has worked steadily from morning till now, except for a short rest in the shelter.'"

Note the reputation Ruth is building for herself. The foreman says she is *polite* and *respectful* (she said 'please'), *hard-working* ("she has worked steadily from morning till now"), and *loyal to her mother-in-law* ("she came back from

Moab with Naomi"). Know this, you build a reputation by how you live. It takes time to build a good reputation, but sadly it can be lost in a moment of folly. Thankfully, by God's grace it can be restored.

Let me reiterate what caught this foreman's eye. Ruth *worked steadily*. There's something very attractive about being a *hard worker*. People notice, even when we don't think they're watching. As believers we ought to be the best workers on the job, not to gain attention for ourselves but for our Lord. We find this truth in the New Testament as well:

> "Teach slaves to be subject to their masters in everything, to try to please them, not to talk back to them, and not to steal from them, but to show that they can be fully trusted, so that in every way they will make the teaching about God our Savior attractive."
> —Titus 2:9-10

> "In the same way, let your light shine before men, that they may see your good deeds and praise your Father in heaven."
> —Matthew 5:16

Ruth's hard work and reputation made an impression on Boaz. Not surprisingly, he responded by giving her something else.

B. Boaz gave her a safe place to work (5-9).
Verse 8a—"So Boaz said to Ruth, 'My daughter, listen to me.'" His words 'my daughter' seem to indicate that Boaz was considerably older than Ruth (Goslinga suggests he was a middle aged man). Be that as it may, he has a proposal for Ruth…

Verses 8b-9—"Don't go and glean in another field and don't go away from here. Stay here with my servant girls. Watch the field where the men are harvesting, and follow along after the girls. I have told the men not to touch you. And whenever you are thirsty, go and get a drink from the water jars the men have filled."

Remember, Ruth left the house that morning looking for food, but God is giving her much more than she anticipated! A man has come into her life who, in spite of her background, offers to be her provider and protector.

Verse 10—"At this, she bowed down with her face to the ground [a gesture that shows reverence, honor, and appreciation]. She exclaimed, 'Why have I found such favor in your eyes that you notice me—a foreigner?'" We live in a day of entitlements where it's common for a person to think he *deserves* for people (and even God) to meet his needs. We *expect* good things to happen to us. Ruth didn't, but she truly appreciated the blessings.

Notice how she refers to herself. Why do you notice me—a *foreigner*?

Goslinga observes, "There is a minor play on words here in that the Hebrew terms translated 'notice me' and 'foreigner' resemble each other; a rough English equivalent would be 'respect a reject'" (Goslinga, pp. 531-2). Ruth can't escape the fact that she is different but that doesn't matter. In the end the fact that she is different, a *foreigner*, will result in even greater glory to God because people will say, "God works even through foreigners to accomplish His purposes!"

So much so that when we come to the genealogy of Jesus in Matthew 1, we see in addition to the listing of a host of men who were in Jesus' ancestry the names of three special women. Guess who one of them is? Matthew 1:5— "Boaz the father of Obed, whose mother was Ruth."

Boaz gave Ruth the assurance of the Lord's presence and a safe place to work. Notice his third gift…

C. Boaz gave her a blessing for her godly reputation (10-13).

Verse 11—"Boaz replied, 'I've been told all about what you have done…'" Word gets around! People notice good deeds. They make an impression. Here's what impressed Boaz…

Verse 11—"I've been told all about what you have done for your mother-in-law since the death of your husband—how you left your father and mother and your homeland and came to live with a people you did not know before."

I learn three things about Boaz and his assessment of Ruth from those words…

1. He saw beyond her past (10).

It's true that Ruth was a foreigner, a Moabitess. She used to worship Chemosh, the god of the Moabites. Boaz knew that. But that's the point. It was in her past.

2. He saw what God was doing in and through her in the present (11-12).

Boaz mentions that Ruth's parents were still living. He knows that she could have gone back to them but chose instead to go with Naomi. That decision revealed that something was more important to Ruth than her family and the familiarity of her homeland, namely Naomi and before Naomi's God, the true God of Israel. Ruth had come to know Naomi's God and she wanted to know Him better! That's why she left Moab.

There may be a connection in Boaz's mind to Abraham who also left his homeland and relatives in obedience to God's command. Ruth, like Abraham, went out not knowing where she would end up.

Ruth had put her whole trust in Yahweh. That's why she moved to Israel. And that's why Boaz verbalizes two prayer requests for Ruth in verse 12, "May the

LORD repay you for what you have done. May you be richly rewarded by the LORD, the God of Israel, under whose wings you have come to take refuge." The imagery speaks of a tiny bird snuggling under the wings of its mother for safety. It speaks of God as Protector. In coming to Israel Ruth was coming under Yahweh's wings, and that news thrilled Boaz!

Let that sink in. God chose Israel to be a means of spreading the truth about Himself to the world, and Israel was to rejoice in that honor. Sadly, Israel began to hoard the Lord. By contrast, how refreshing to see the response of Boaz! He is thrilled that a foreigner has come to believe in the true God of Israel. It brings him joy—and he says so—that Ruth has come under the wings of Yahweh. That's the way it was supposed to be in Israel.

And in the church. Does it thrill you when someone comes to know the salvation of your Lord? How do you respond when a new person comes to your church? Do you take the initiative to meet them? Do you tell them, "I'm so glad you have come here today, to get to know the living God with us! What can I do to help you? Would you like to sit with me, and maybe come to my house for dinner?" The Lord doesn't bless us so we can keep His goodness to ourselves. He blesses us so that we might in turn bless others, all to His glory.

Note the effect Boaz's words had on Ruth…

3. He gave her hope for the future (13).
Verse 13—"'May I continue to find favor in your eyes, my lord,' she said. 'You have given me comfort and have spoken kindly to your servant—though I do not have the standing of one of your servant girls.'"

Some would say that Ruth had low self-esteem. That's not true. She's a very secure person. Her security is in the Lord. That's why she made the huge decision to leave her homeland. No, she doesn't have a poor self-esteem. She just consistently puts the Lord and others ahead of herself, as the Savior would later do and call us to do.

Boaz isn't done giving yet…

D. Boaz gave her a meal (14).
"At mealtime Boaz said to her, 'Come over here. Have some bread and dip it in the wine vinegar.' When she sat down with the harvesters, he offered her some *roasted grain*. She ate all she wanted and had some left over.'"

By Jesus' time the Jews refused to eat with Gentiles. But here Boaz initiates this interaction with Ruth. He invites her to eat with him. He gives her food, specifically some roasted grain.

W. M. Thompson describes the roasted grain: "A quantity of the best ears, not too ripe, are plucked with the stalks attached. These are tied into small parcels, a blazing fire is kindled with dry grass and thorn bushes, and the cornheads are held in it until the chaff is mostly burned off. The grain is thus sufficiently roasted to be eaten, and it is a favorite article all over the country" (Morris, p. 278).

Do you see what's happening? Boaz doesn't see Ruth as a foreigner any longer. You don't offer hospitality to a foreigner, but to a *friend*. He is a godly man (and single) and she is a godly woman (and single). Boaz is initiating a *friendship*. Will it go further? You'll have to wait and see. But know this. Here's where a good male-female relationship begins, with *friendship*. Keep that in mind, young people. And keep that in mind those of you who've been married for years. Is your spouse your best friend? God created marriage for *companionship* (Gen. 2:18).

Boaz still isn't finished, however. Notice verses 15-16, "As she got up to glean, Boaz gave orders to his men, 'Even if she gathers among the sheaves, don't embarrass her. Rather, pull out some stalks for her from the bundles and leave them for her to pick up, and don't rebuke her.'" In other words…

E. Boaz gave her a surplus of food for the future (15-16).
You can't help but admire Boaz. What a godly, giving man! He told his men to let Ruth gather grain among the sheaves which meant she could glean not only where the harvest was finished but also where the workers were presently cutting and binding the stalks into sheaves.

One commentator I read suggested it was love at first sight. I'm not sure about that, but something's brewing! Boaz keeps giving and giving to Ruth. What does she think about him? We don't know yet. So ends scene 2.

Keep in mind the story of Ruth is really a story about the Lord. What have we learned about the Lord thus far? First, the Lord directed Ruth to Boaz; thus, He *directs* His people. Next, the Lord provided for Ruth through Boaz; thus, He *provides for* His people.

III. The Lord prepared Ruth for Boaz (17-23).
Here's how He did it. Watch the sequence of events unfold.

A. Naomi blessed Boaz (17-19).
Verse 17—"So Ruth gleaned in the field until evening. Then she threshed the barley she had gathered, and it amounted to about an ephah." Huey suggests that a typical ration was one to two pounds of grain per day, meaning Ruth gathered enough to last Naomi and her for weeks (Huey, p. 532).

Verse 18—"She carried it back to town, and her mother-in-law saw how much she had gathered. Ruth also brought out and gave her what she had left over after she had eaten enough." Please note that Ruth, in contrast to what so often happens today in America, didn't waste her leftover food from lunch. She appreciates God's provision, and shares it, too.

Verse 19a—"Her mother-in-law asked her, 'Where did you glean today? Where did you work? Blessed be the man who took notice of you!'" At this point Naomi blesses but still doesn't know the identity of the kind man who showered Ruth with blessings that day. She's in for quite a shock…

Verse 19b—"Then Ruth told her mother-in-law about the one at whose place she had been working. 'The name of the man I worked with today is Boaz,' she said."

Upon hearing the name Boaz, Naomi can't contain her joy. Verse 20—"'The LORD bless him!' Naomi said to her daughter-in-law. 'He has not stopped showing his kindness to the living and the dead.' She added, 'That man is our close relative; he is one of our kinsman-redeemers.'" Note that…

B. Naomi asked the Lord to bless Boaz (20).
The Lord is so real to Naomi that when tragedy struck in chapter one she affirmed the Lord's control, and now when blessings come in chapter two she likewise attributes it to the Lord. She also reveals a couple of important insights about Boaz.

1. She reveals he is a kinsman-redeemer.
What's that? In Israel God owned the land. As God's covenant people the Israelites were the caretakers of God's land. In the book of Joshua God divided and parceled out the land according to tribes, clans, and families. The land given to a family was to stay in that family. But what would happen if a man died without children to keep the land in the family? God addressed that possibility (see Deut. 25:5-10). Some other extended family member could keep the family tree alive. That person was called a *kinsman redeemer*.

Naomi tells Ruth that Boaz is one of their kinsman redeemers. One of them? You mean there are others? Yes. We'll meet another in chapter four. But for now, it's Boaz. And suffice it to say that as far as Naomi is concerned…

2. She sees in him hope for the future.
Naomi's reference to 'the dead,' referring to their deceased spouses, indicates that her wheels are turning with a developing plan. In the final verses…

C. Naomi encouraged Ruth to stay near Boaz (21-23).
"Then Ruth the Moabitess said, 'He even said to me, "Stay with my workers until they finish harvesting all my grain."' Naomi said to Ruth her daughter-in-law, 'It will be good for you, my daughter, to go with his girls, because in someone else's field you might be harmed.' So Ruth stayed close to the servant girls of Boaz to glean until the barley and wheat harvests were finished. And she lived with her mother-in-law."

That final verse sums up what Ruth did for the next three months. The two harvest seasons lasted about seven weeks, from late April to early June (Huey, p. 533). She got up daily and went to work in the fields of Boaz. And she was never alone. God was there, in the barley field and in the wheat field.

Lessons from Ruth 2: I'll mention three lessons...

1. We learn that God is a providence-working God.

David Atkinson writes, "One of the most important features of faith in God's providence is that it teaches us that even our accidents are within his care" (Atkinson, p. 59). He's right.

J. Vernon McGee observes, "No accident can happen to a child of God. He may be in a car wreck or he may be killed instantly; but for the child of God that cannot be finally defined as an accident. Nothing can come to a Christian that does not first receive the permission of God. Chance is removed from the child of God, for he is like Job of whom Satan said, 'Hast not thou made an hedge about him?'" (McGee, p. 65).

Yes, God is in control. You can trust Him.

2. We learn that God is a prayer-hearing God.

It's worth noting that every prayer in the book of Ruth is answered. In 1:9 Naomi requested that the Lord bless Ruth's household, and He did. In 2:12 Boaz requested that the Lord reward Ruth's faithfulness, and He did. In fact, He did it through the one making the prayer request, Boaz himself!

The Lord hears when His people pray. And in His time and in His perfect way, He answers!

3. We learn that God is a provision-making God.

In Ruth chapter two He provided two widows with food, but that's just the beginning. The man through whom He provided the food is also the man through whom He provided a link to the Messiah, Jesus. In a sense, we are here today because Ruth went to that barley field, met Boaz, eventually married him and had a son with him. That son became the great grandfather of King David, the ancestor of the King of kings, Jesus Christ.

And why did God go to all that trouble to send Jesus into the world? Because we are sinners who need a Savior. Jesus died on the cross for sinners, like the people living in the time of the judges and like us. He rose again and offers life eternal for those who believe in Him. Yes, our God is a providing God!

Getting Intentional About Application

by Brad Brandt

Application is vital. Getting intentional about application is also vital. If we as Bible teachers are not careful, our exposition of the Scriptures can turn into interesting history lessons that fail to equip God's people for life in the real world. By divine design, God's Word is practical. As we do the hard work of exegesis, we must keep in mind God's intended goal for the text we are handling. We are interested in touching our hearers' beliefs and behaviors.

To put it another way, biblical theology should result in practical theology. If we address what the text meant but go no further, our preaching is deficient, interesting perhaps, but still deficient. Of course, if we merely give application but fail to show the basis for that application in the text, our preaching will lack authority ("That's just the preacher's opinion," the congregation may think, and rightly so).

Once again, this Getting Intentional About Application section is an attempt to facilitate the transition from an exposition of the book of Ruth to its implementation in the lives of God's people. The following tools are certainly not the only way to accomplish this, but are merely suggestions to stimulate the creative 'applicational juices' of fellow Bible teachers!

Tool #1: A Teaching Outline

In the last chapter I suggested some potential ways to use a teaching outline. I mentioned the value of using a 'fill in the blank' approach (leaving a blank in every key point). My observation is that even young children (those old enough to read) benefit from using the outlines. One possible teaching tool for the very young is to encourage them to draw a picture of whatever comes to mind as they listen to the sermon, and then to show me after the service. I have a file for such treasures!

Here is my outline from Ruth chapter two.

From Brad's exposition:

Main Idea: God always takes care of His people, always. In Ruth 2 we see His care demonstrated in three ways in the life of Ruth through the person of Boaz.

I.   **The Lord directed Ruth to Boaz (1-3).**
  A.   **God has a plan for His people.**
  B.   **God uses the decisions of His people to accomplish that plan.**
    1. Ruth was looking for food.
    2. The Lord intended to give her something far greater.
II. **The Lord provided for Ruth through Boaz (4-16).**
  A.   **Boaz gave her the assurance of the Lord's presence (4).**

1. For some people God is real only in church.
2. For others God is real wherever they go.
B. **Boaz gave her a safe place to work (5-9).**
C. **Boaz gave her a blessing for her godly reputation (10-13).**
1. He saw beyond her past (10).
2. He saw what God was doing in and through her in the present (11-12).
3. He gave her hope for the future (13).
D. **Boaz gave her a meal (14).**
E. **Boaz gave her a surplus of food for the future (15-16).**
III. **The Lord prepared Ruth for Boaz (17-23).**
A. **Naomi blessed Boaz (17-19).**
B. **Naomi asked the Lord to bless Boaz (20).**
1. She reveals he is a kinsman-redeemer.
2. She sees in him hope for the future.
C. **Naomi encouraged Ruth to stay near Boaz (21-23).**

Lessons from Ruth 2:
1. We learn that God is a providence-working God.
2. We learn that God is a prayer-hearing God.
3. We learn that God is a provision-making God.

Tool #2: "Digging Deeper" Discussion Questions
The use of questions is a great way to teach biblical truth. It's also a wonderful way to reinforce biblical truth after the initial sermon or Bible lesson. I mentioned earlier the importance of asking two types of questions, those intended for clarification and others seeking to get at application. Here are a few suggested questions to use as follow-up with Ruth 2.

Questions for Clarification:
1. What is the difference between a miracle and providence?
2. What kind of man was Boaz? What are your initial thoughts about him based on chapter two?
3. What words describe Ruth's approach to work in this chapter?
4. It is important that we remember that the story of Ruth is part of the bigger story of redemption in the Bible. Why? What happens if we fail to connect the stories of the Bible with the redemption story of the Bible?
5. What other questions did this message raise for you?

Questions for Application:
1. In Ruth 2, God was at work in Ruth's life out in a barley field. What are some reasons that at times we fail to see God's hand in the 'ordinary' events of our lives?
2. What are some practical things we can do to learn to recognize God's providential working in our lives?
3. In Ruth 2, Ruth just "happened" to end up in a field owned by Boaz. Think of something that "happened" in your life that illustrates God's providence

(perhaps a person you just "happened" to meet that turned out to be a wonderful God-given friend, or a job opportunity you just "happened" to hear about at the right time, etc.). Then share that with the group as an occasion of thanksgiving to God.

4. In Ruth 2, God used Boaz to meet some very practical needs in the lives of two widows. Think of the widows in your local church. What needs do they have and what are some ways you can be used by God to supply those needs?

5. What are some other ways we can apply the message of Ruth chapter two to our lives?

Tool #3: A Counseling Case Study

I suggested in chapter one that the counseling case study could be used as a leadership training tool with elders/deacons. Another potential use would be in the training of Sunday School teachers, small group leaders, youth workers, and others.

Scenario: Angela is a single parent in her mid-thirties raising three children (ages twelve, eight, and six). She works nights as a nurse's aid at a local care facility and has been raising the children by herself since her ex-husband left her four years ago for another woman. Her children have attended Sunday School at your church for about two years, although she seldom comes due to her "complicated work schedule." Those were her words to you last Sunday morning when you dropped off her children at their house after church. At that time you noticed that Angela seemed quite overwhelmed with life. A broken mower was sitting in the tall grass of the side yard, the gutters were black with mildew, and a cracked garage door window caught your eye. Before leaving, you invite Angela to join her children next week in church. Her response is polite but to the point, "Thanks, but I don't have room in my life for church. Don't take me wrong. I believe in God, for sure, but it takes every ounce of my energy just to pay the bills and keep life sane for my kids."

As you drove home that day you found yourself thinking about the morning message from Ruth 2 and wondered if God hadn't just placed a providential opportunity in your life. A week later you are leading a Vacation Bible School worker's training session and decide to read the account of Ruth 2 and then share about your experience with Angela. Afterwards you ask the following...

Case Study Discussion Questions:

1. What principles do we find in Ruth 2 that can help us know how to respond to hurting people like Angela? List several.

2. Angela is one of many single parents in our world. What are some practical things we can do as a church to show the love of Christ to her and others?

3. What does Angela need from us first? What does she need from us most?

Tool #4: Counseling Assignments Utilizing Ruth 2:1-23
Suppose that in response to the loving actions of the church, Angela (from the previous case study) begins attending your church. About a month later she opens up and acknowledges, "I told you at my house that I believe in God, but I must confess I've been full of bitterness since my husband left me. I know I'm wrong and I want to change, but I don't know how. Would you help me?"

The book of Ruth could be an excellent source of hope for Angela, as it was for "Bob" in the previous chapter. If Angela agreed to meet weekly for a month, you might take her through the book of Ruth one chapter a week.

In providing care for Angela, it is important to keep in mind the instruction in Titus 2:3-4 which encourages mature women to counsel other women. With this in mind, it would be wise for a pastor to include his wife in the counseling process with Angela or to delegate her care to a godly, trained woman in the church.

The following homework assignments could be used in week two.

Week Two Reading Assignment:
1. Read Ruth chapter two three times this week. Each time you read write down your answer to the following questions:

a. What do I learn about God from this passage?

b. What do I learn about God's plan for His people from this passage?

c. What do I learn about living for God from this passage?

2. Write out Ruth 2:12 on a 3x5 card and seek to memorize it by reading it out loud three times every day. Write a paragraph about how Boaz's description of "taking refuge under the wings of the Lord" encourages you.

3. In light of what you are learning from the book of Ruth, answer the following questions (we'll discuss them at our next meeting):

a. How does my view of God need to change?

b. What am I learning about God that gives me hope?

c. What is something I need to do in light of what I am learning? Then ask the

Lord for His help and do it.

Answers to Questions at the Beginning of Chapter Two:
1. Answer: *Miracle*

2. Answer: *Providence*

CHAPTER

3

A Case for Arranged Marriages?

Ruth 3:1-18

Expositional Commentary and Outline:
The Pursuit of Redemption and the Subsequent Promise of Redemption

Expository Sermon:
A Case for Arranged Marriages?

Getting Intentional About Application

Tool #1: A Teaching Outline
Tool #2: "Digging Deeper" Discussion Questions
Tool #3: A Counseling Case Study
Tool #4: Counseling Assignments

Expositional Outline:

Ruth 3:1-18

by Rick Kress

The Book of Ruth—A Portrait of God's Loyal Love, Sovereign Redemption, and the Faith of His Believing Remnant

I. The pain of covenant faithlessness [an empty profession] (1:1-5)

II. The pity of God and the initial glimmers of faith (1:6-22)

III. The providential provision and protection of God for the destitute who live by faith (2:1-23)

IV. The pursuit of redemption and the subsequent promise of redemption (3:1-18)

    A. The plan of Naomi (3:1-5)

        1. The motive in relation to her daughter-in-law (3:1)

        2. The man apt to redeem (3:2)

        3. The mission of seeking redemption (3:3-4)

            a. Approach him respectfully (v. 3a)

            b. Approach him humbly (v. 3b)

            c. Approach him submissively, trusting him for his good favor (v. 4)

        4. The meekness/submissiveness of Ruth (3:5)

    B. The proposal of Ruth (3:6-9)

        1. The plan carried out (3:6-7)

            a. The summary (v. 6)

            b. The select details (v. 7)

        2. The plea for redemption—a proposal of marriage (3:8-9)

            a. The audience with Boaz (v. 8-9a)

            b. The amazing request (v. 9b)

    C. The promise of Boaz (3:10-18)

        1. The pleasure Ruth's proposal brought him (3:10)

        2. The promise he made to guarantee her redemption (3:11-13)

            a. The promise in general (v. 11a)

            b. The praise of Ruth's character (v. 11b)

            c. The problem of a closer relative (v. 12)

            d. The promise guaranteed (v. 13)

        3. The pledge/proof of Boaz's promise (3:14-18)

            a. The concern for her purity (v. 14)

            b. The cloak full of barley (v. 15)

            c. The collateral/assurance for Naomi (v. 16-17)

            d. The conviction of Naomi about Boaz's character and promise (v. 18)

Expositional Commentary:
The Pursuit of Redemption and the Subsequent Promise of Redemption

Ruth 3:1-18

by Rick Kress

The Bible is a divinely inspired book that reveals God's redemption of ruined and rebellious sinners, by His grace—through faith—to the praise of His glory. God delights to be gracious to those who recognize their utter helplessness and hopelessness. He delights to redeem all who would call upon Him in faith.

Ruth is a book that beautifully illustrates the redemption of two helpless and despised women. As we've seen in the previous chapters, redemption and grace shine most brilliantly when we see the darkness, pain and consequences of our sin and unfaithfulness (1:1-5). He is full of pity, compassion and mercy—even when we don't recognize it in our bitterness (1:6-22).

He providentially works in history and even the minute circumstances of our lives to bring us to the point of recognizing and desiring His gracious redemption. In this chapter we will see Naomi and Ruth recognize and seek after a human redeemer in their need—that will picture the larger reality of God's redemption.

In Ruth chapter three we see three movements in the narrative that picture the pursuit of a redeemer. In seeing this picture we should be encouraged in our Perfect Redeemer, Jesus Christ—God, who become a man, to purchase His brethren who were in bondage to sin and death.

Let's begin looking at Ruth's pursuit of a human redeemer, by faith in her divine Redeemer.

IV. The pursuit of redemption and the subsequent promise of redemption (3:1-18)
A. The plan of Naomi (3:1-5)
1. The motive in relation to her daughter-in-law (3:1)
"Then Naomi her mother-in-law said to her, 'My daughter, shall I not seek security for you, that it may be well with you?'"

It is clear here that Naomi had both affection and love for Ruth. The word "security" is related to the term translated "rest" in 1:9. Thus, Naomi became part of the answer for her own prayer of some days or weeks earlier. She understood God's sovereignty (cf. chap. 1). Yet Naomi evidently believed that it did not preclude her actively seeking Ruth's welfare. The affectionate phrase, "my daughter," is once again used. Naomi's emphasis is on Ruth's "security" or "rest" and her "good". As mentioned previously, a single woman's "security" or "rest"—i.e., permanence and stability—could be found either back in one's father's home, or with a husband. The latter is obviously what Naomi had in mind.

Verse one reveals Naomi's stated motive in relation to Ruth. Through a rhetorical question, she expressed her love for Ruth and desire for her "good" or "well-being". That would necessarily include the stability of a husband and home—not the beggarly and insecure life of a widow in those days. Duguid appropriately comments on Naomi's apparent transformation:

> What seems to have happened is that over the course of these chapters, as she experienced God's goodness and continued faithfulness (*hesed*) to her, her heart began to soften. Through the hard work of Ruth and the generosity of Boaz, she found new hope. Perhaps she even began to see that she had been too quick to blame God and to assume that when things went badly in her life it was because God was out to get her. Perhaps she began to recognize her failure to take responsibility and to repent of it. Repentance inevitably draws our attention away from ourselves and out toward others. Bitterness drives us inward in self-absorbed depression, while true repentance enables us and motivates us to start to serve other people's needs (Duguid, p. 169).

2. The man apt to redeem (3:2)

"Now is not Boaz our kinsman, with whose maids you were?"
Interestingly, Naomi used the plural pronoun, "our" in referring to "Boaz"— "Now is not Boaz *our* kinsman" (emphasis added). Ruth was part of Naomi's people. But as noted in 2:1 (though a variant form), "kinsman" means literally, "a known one"—i.e., a friend or kindred one.

"Behold, he winnows barley at the threshing floor tonight"
Naomi was aware that Boaz would be "scattering barley" or "winnowing" that evening—i.e., tossing the grain into the air to let the breeze blow the chaff away while the grain fell back to the ground. The term "behold" initially conveys the startling nature of Naomi's plan that would follow. The "threshing floor" would be a hard, likely raised area, so that the grain wouldn't mix into the dust but rather land on a hard surface, and the breeze could blow the chaff away.

Naomi revealed her plan by reminding her daughter-in-law that Boaz was their friend/kinsman, and had been already acting as protector and provider for them. He was a man perhaps apt to redeem her and grant her "security/rest".

3. The mission of seeking redemption (3:3-4)
a. Approach him respectfully (v. 3a)
"Wash yourself therefore, and anoint yourself and put on your clothes"
Naomi told Ruth literally, "Now bathe, and anoint, and put on your

wrapper/mantle"—i.e., outer garment (cf. Ex. 22:25-26 for the poor using this outer garment for a blanket at night; cf. Block, p. 683). A "bath" as well as anointing with oil would be normal first steps in preparing for marriage according to Ezekiel 16:9 (Block, p. 683). It is also interesting to note that those who are in mourning—including mourning death—would refrain from washing and anointing, and wear garments that revealed their mourning (cf. 2 Sam. 12:20; 14:2; Dan. 10:3; cf. Gen. 38:14, 19). It may be that Naomi was telling Ruth that the time for mourning her husband was over.

Whatever the exact significance, approaching Boaz about her "security" was not to be done presumptuously or flippantly.

b. Approach him humbly (v. 3b)
"And go down to the threshing floor"
Bethlehem proper likely sat on a hill at that time, and thus one would *"go down* to the threshing floor"—even though the "threshing floor" itself would normally be prominently raised on a hill for good wind access (contrast Judges 6:11).

"Do not make yourself known to the man until he has finished eating and drinking"
From a human perspective, a meal and refreshment would likely put Boaz into a more contented and refreshed mood. There would be nothing else to distract his attention or contribute to the possibility of ill temperedness. Such discretion would show humility, in that a secret approach would protect the honor of Boaz before the others who served him or with whom he ate. He would not be embarrassed or put on the spot in front of the gaze of others. He could do with her as he chose, without the constraint of what others might think.

Ruth was to approach Boaz respectfully, humbly, and...

c. Approach him submissively, trusting him for his good favor (v. 4)
"It shall be when he lies down, that you shall notice the place where he lies"
In light of what actually happened, it would seem that Naomi was telling Ruth to wait until Boaz actually fell asleep, before going to where he lay for the night (cf. v. 7-8).

"And you shall go and uncover his feet and lie down"
The phrase "uncover his feet", combined with the verb, "lie down", has led some to interpret Naomi's instructions as a proposition for an illicit act rather than a proposal for marriage. As Block has noted:

> First, the root *glh*, "to uncover," is often used in sexual contexts of "uncovering someone's nakedness" (a euphemism for exposing the genitals [footnote—Lev. 18:6-19; 20:11, 17-21; Ez. 22:10]) or of "uncovering someone's skirt" [footnote—Deut. 22:30; 27:20]. Second, the final verb, *sakab*, "to lie,"

is often used to denote sexual relations [footnote—except for Gen. 30:15-16 and 2 Sam. 11:11, the relations are always illicit (incest, homosexuality, bestiality, rape, seduction): Gen. 19:32-33; Lev. 20:11-13, 18, 20; Deut. 22:25; 27:20-23; 35:22]. Third, the noun between these verbs, *margelot*, derives from *regel*, "foot," the dual and plural of which may be used euphemistically for genitalia [footnote—Exod. 4:25; Judg. 3:24; 1 Sam. 24:3 [4]; Isa. 7:20 (all male); Deut. 28:57; Ezek. 15:25 (both female); Isa. 6:2 (heavenly creatures). Occasionally urine is called "water of the feet" (2 Kgs. 18:27 = Isa. 36:12)]. Not surprisingly, therefore, some interpret Naomi's scheme as delicate and dangerous, charged with sexual overtones (Block, p. 685).

So the narrative at this point is fraught with ambiguity, until the story unfolds and Ruth's character vindicated by Boaz's affirmation in verse 11 and actions in verse 14. As it would turn out, Ruth was literally to uncover the lower part of Boaz's body so that he would wake up without being too startled, and find her submissively at his feet.

"Then he will tell you what you shall do"
Naomi was directing Ruth to cast herself at the mercy of Boaz. She was to listen to his instructions. Boaz would decide what the best course of action would be. Naomi was trusting God to guide Boaz, and thus telling Ruth to implicitly trust God and explicitly trust Boaz's judgment at that point.

This, then, was the mission in seeking redemption. Naomi directed her daughter-in-law out of love and concern for her welfare and security. She called Ruth to approach Boaz respectfully, humbly, and submissively—trusting him for his good favor.

4. The meekness/submissiveness of Ruth (3:5)
"She said to her, 'All that you say I will do'"
Ruth promised to be faithful to Naomi's instructions. She submissively agreed to Naomi's risky plan. It involved turning away from thoughts of self, and "what if"—to trusting Yahweh, trusting Naomi, and trusting Boaz.

Thus, verses 1-5 introduce us to *the plan of Naomi*.

B. The proposal of Ruth (3:6-9)
1. The plan carried out (3:6-7)
a. The summary (v. 6)
"So she went down to the threshing floor and did according to all that her mother-in-law had commanded her"
Here we're told in summary fashion that Ruth again made good on her promise of faithfulness. She "did according to all that her mother-in-law had commanded her". She carried out Naomi's plan in approaching and seeking a kinsman-redeemer.

b. The select details (v. 7)

"When Boaz had eaten and drunk and his heart was merry"

"Boaz" ate and drank the text says, "and good was his heart". The expression speaks of contentment and gladness (Judges 18:20; 19:6, 9; 1 Kings 21:7; Ec. 7:3). Some contend that this indicates that Boaz got drunk. But there is no reason to assume this since no qualifying phrase was added (cf. 1 Sam. 25:36). The whole episode may well hint at, yet be antithetical to the narrative of Genesis 19 and the illicit, incestuous, drunken beginnings of the Moabite nation. There are subtle parallels between Lot and his daughters, and Ruth and Boaz—but Ruth's character will be vindicated, while Lot's was only further besmirched as a man of weakness, even if righteous at heart (cf. 2 Pet. 2:7-9).

"He went to lie down at the end of the heap of grain"

Though a wealthy and influential man (2:1), Boaz evidently took part in winnowing and guarding the "grain" during this portion of the harvest. It may have been several days, or perhaps weeks after Ruth and Naomi's arrival. It may be that the "heap of grain" actually gave Boaz a little privacy, away from the view of the other servants and perhaps even families who were quite likely sleeping near the threshing floor as well. But certainly the openness of the threshing floor would not lend itself to an illicit tryst in private.

"And she came secretly, and uncovered his feet and lay down"

Ruth "uncovered" Boaz's "feet" and then laid down after entering the threshing area by stealth—"secretly" (cf. Judges 4:21; 1 Sam. 18:22; 24:5). No one knew that she was there.

2. The plea for redemption—a proposal of marriage (3:8-9)

a. The audience with Boaz (v. 8-9a)

"It happened in the middle of the night"

Literally the phrase reads: "And it was, at the half of the night". Very likely Boaz did not wake up right away. It may have been some time before he felt the cold set in, or perhaps sensed someone there at his feet.

"The man was startled and bent forward; and behold, a woman was lying at his feet"

The word "startled" normally means "to tremble". It is possible that Boaz shivered, but normally the word is used in contexts of fear. Likely he became aware of someone and awoke with a frightened start. "Bent forward" speaks of "twisting". He either "bent forward" or turned in a twisting motion. Some suggest that he turned over and awoke with a start.

The term "behold" once again communicates the surprising nature of what happened—"*behold*, a woman was lying at his feet" (emphasis added).

"He said, 'Who are you?'"

The feminine pronoun is used here. He may have recognized that it was a woman lying at his feet, but did not immediately discern Ruth's identity in the darkness of the night, having just been roused from his sleep. Or it may be that the narrator here used the feminine pronoun because the audience already knows the identity of Ruth (cf. Block, p. 690, footnote 36).

Ruth now had an audience with Boaz—startled though he be.

b. The amazing request (v. 9b)
"I am Ruth your maid"
"Ruth" clearly identified herself to Boaz, as his female slave or maid. She did, however, use a different term here (*amah*) than she did in 2:13. The two terms are synonyms and both convey humility. Ruth no doubt spoke respectfully to Boaz as her superior, but this term may convey a hopeful optimism concerning the possibility of becoming more than a lowly slave. The next phrase is shocking in its implications.

"So spread your covering over your maid, for you are a close relative"
There is no indication in the earlier text that Naomi told Ruth exactly what to say or how to interact with Boaz. According to verse four, Boaz would tell Ruth what to do. It would seem then, in the context of Boaz's confusion and surprise, Ruth felt compelled to say more than just her name. Proverbs 16:1 says, "The plans of the heart belong to man, but the answer of the tongue is from the LORD". By God's sovereign grace, she made an amazing and insightful request. Literally she said, "And spread your wing over your maid, for you are a redeemer".

Earlier, as recorded in 2:12, Boaz had said that Ruth had sought refuge under the "wings" of the God of Israel, Yahweh. In other words she had come in faith to Him for grace, protection, and provision. Now she was asking Boaz to be part of Yahweh's protection and provision in her life. The expression "spread your covering" is used elsewhere in Scripture as an idiom for marriage (see especially Ez. 16:8; cf. Deut. 22:30; 27:20; Mal. 2:16; cf. Block, p. 691).

Then gloriously, Ruth identified Boaz as *goel* in the Hebrew—redeemer. Again, the relative who acted as redeemer—or kinsman-redeemer—had the following responsibilities:

> A "kinsman-redeemer"—here translated, "closest relative"—was a close relative who could redeem/buy back a family member sold into slavery (Lev. 25:47-49); he could redeem/buy back land sold by a family member to eliminate debt (Lev. 25:23-28); and he could redeem/buy back the family lineage through levirate marriage (Deut. 25:5-10) (cf. The MacArthur Study Bible electronic edition). As well, he could avenge the murder of a close relative— thus he was a kinsman-avenger (Num. 35:12, 19-27); he could "receive restitution money on behalf of a deceased victim of a crime (Num. 5:8); and . . .

[he could] ensure that justice [was] served in a lawsuit involving a relative (Job 19:25; Ps 119:154; Jer 50:34)" (Block, p. 674). See Hebrews 2:14-18 for Christ's relationship to us (from author's notes on 2:20).

Basically, Ruth was petitioning Boaz to become her security, her human redeemer, and her husband. But in humility, she did not call him "her redeemer" or "our redeemer" (cf. v. 2)—but merely, "a redeemer". He was qualified to redeem, but not necessarily obligated. As it would turn out, she was right. There was one closer relative before Boaz, according to verse 12.

So Ruth chapter three has revealed *the plans of Naomi, the proposal of Ruth*, and now . . .

C. The promise of Boaz (3:10-18)
1. The pleasure Ruth's proposal brought him (3:10)
"Then he said, 'May you be blessed of the LORD, my daughter'"
Far from entering into an illicit encounter with Ruth, Boaz rather prayed for Ruth's blessing in the name of "Yahweh"—and calls her "my daughter". He still had a protective and fatherly perspective of Ruth. Her forthright, humble, and trusting petition gave Boaz great pleasure and caused him to pray for Yahweh's blessing upon her. Verses 11-13 make it clear that Boaz understood Ruth's request to be for redemption, and not for an illicit union in the night.

It must be again acknowledged that God's hidden providence had been at work preparing the character of both Ruth and Boaz. There was no misunderstanding. There was nothing reproachable in their words or actions.

"You have shown your last kindness to be better than the first by not going after young men, whether poor or rich"
Boaz said that Ruth's "later loyalty/lovingkindness" was "better than the first". Her "first kindness" was coming with Naomi and pledging her love and loyalty to Naomi's people and Naomi's God. But now, she was living it out in an amazing and unexpected way. She was obviously seeking marriage to Boaz, for the sake of her mother-in-law. She had used the term "kinsman-redeemer" in her proposal. Boaz knew that the more "normal" or "natural" response of a woman Ruth's age would be to go "after young men"—or "choice men, whether poor or rich".

Boaz knew that Ruth was a woman of faith resulting in love. Her petition for redemption brought her redeemer—Boaz—great pleasure.

2. The promise he made to guarantee her redemption (3:11-13)
a. The promise in general (v. 11a)
"Now, my daughter, do not fear. I will do for you whatever you ask"
Ruth had taken a great risk and was in a fearful position from the human per-

spective. She had come by stealth at night to seek Boaz's hand in marriage, so to speak. But, her request of faith brought from Boaz—not disdain—rather, both a pleasure and a promise of comfort. He said, "Now, my daughter, do not fear". She was no doubt shaken by the events. But he didn't want her to be afraid. Then Boaz promised to ensure her redemption—"all that you say, I will do for you". She was his servant, but Boaz would serve her in doing whatever she asked (Block, p. 694).

b. The praise of Ruth's character (v. 11b)

"For all my people in the city know that you are a woman of excellence"
Literally the Hebrew reads, "for all the gate of my people know". The "gate" of a city would be where the town meetings would be held, and the leaders would congregate more frequently. Those that were "judges" would sit in the "gate" of the city. Those who were citizens, including the leaders and judges in Bethlehem, knew that Ruth was "a woman of excellence".

The word "excellence" was used of Boaz in 2:1. It speaks of nobility, virtue and strength—even valor. Quite interestingly, in the Hebrew Bible, Ruth follows Proverbs 31 where the "woman of excellence" is described (cf. Prov. 31:10, 29; see also Prov. 12:4). Ruth was a living model of the excellent woman. She was humble, faithful, hardworking, and loyal in her love.

> What an amazing turn of events this declaration signifies! Ruth had arrived in Bethlehem a few short weeks ago as a destitute widow, a foreigner at the mercy of the locals. And [1:22-2:23] demonstrated that this was how she perceived herself. She was the lowest of the low, with no recourse but to scavenge in the fields behind the servants of the land-owners. But because of her devotion to her mother-in-law and her willingness to abandon all for her, the townspeople knew her true character. But she did not gain this reputation by trying to be somebody, by associating with the important people. On the contrary, it was her self-effacing embodiment of Israel's lofty covenant standards, her *hesed*, her kindness and loyalty to the family of her deceased husband, especially her mother-in-law, that has won her praise of all. Boaz could have treated her as Moabite trash, scavenging in the garbage cans of Israel, and then corrupting the people with her whorish behavior; but with true *hesed* of his own, he sees her as a woman equal in status and character to himself (Block, p. 694-95).

c. The problem of a closer relative (v. 12)

"Now it is true I am a close relative; however, there is a relative closer than I"
Though Boaz's prayer, comfort and praise must have made Ruth almost euphoric in her heart, she must have been sobered by his next words—"But now truly I am a redeemer, *however*, there is a redeemer closer than I" (emphasis added). Someone had the first right of redemption in relation to

Naomi and her daughter-in-law—i.e., someone more closely related to Elimelech—perhaps a brother or cousin. Boaz obviously knew the biblical teaching on the right of redemption. And he had evidently thought about these Scriptures in regard to Naomi and Ruth—or else he was a quick thinker, having just been awakened from sleep. Perhaps Boaz had considered the possibilities, but did not initiate the redemption because there was a closer relative.

In God's sovereignty, He chose to place a potential foil into this nearly perfect story of true, biblical love. Our gracious and loving Lord does that sometimes. He desires our good, and to grow our faith in Him. He allows difficulties, tensions, and trials to come into our lives so that we will learn to trust Him. In Ruth's case, there was the problem of a "closer relative" than the virtuous and godly Boaz.

But despite the potential problem, Boaz assured Ruth in the next verse that he would see to her redemption one way or another.

d. The promise guaranteed (v. 13)

"Remain this night"

It would be unwise for Ruth to leave the protection and safety of Boaz's threshing floor in the middle of the night and try to return to the city. Thus he told her to "remain this night". But as the next phrase indicates, he was also assuring her that he would quickly deal with her request and the issue of the nearer relative.

"And when morning comes, if he will redeem you, good; let him redeem you"
Boaz knew that obedience to the law (Deut. 25:5ff)—or in this case perhaps the intent of the law, and the societal norms that don't contradict God's law—was of greater importance than his or Ruth's feelings or preferences. God's ways are always "good". But even if Boaz had to forego being Ruth's redeemer himself, he would make sure the one with the immediate right would do it. If he would buy Naomi's property back and acquire Ruth to raise up seed, then it would be "good". But he wanted to settle the matter, "when the morning comes".

"But if he does not wish to redeem you, then I will redeem you, as the LORD lives"
The word here translated "wish" is more often translated by a much stronger word—"delight". Boaz promised Ruth that she would have a redeemer the next day. If the nearer relative would do it, then that would be "fine"—but if he was "not delighted to redeem" her, then Boaz would. Emphatically he said, "I—I will redeem you, as Yahweh lives". Boaz placed himself under an oath of surety (cf. 1 Sam. 20:21).

"Lie down until morning"
The next verse makes it clear that Ruth stayed at Boaz's feet. Here then, Boaz

was telling Ruth to try and get some rest "until morning" when the matter would be settled. Though they both may have battled sleeplessness because of the events that night, Ruth could be assured by Boaz's guarantee.

3. The pledge/proof of Boaz's promise (3:14-18)
a. The concern for her purity (v. 14)
"So she lay at his feet until morning and rose before one could recognize another"
Likely the night held little or no sleep, but Ruth "lay at his feet until morning" as Boaz had commanded. But here the text says that she "rose before a man could recognize his friend". As previously mentioned, there were no doubt others nearby, but the darkness would veil exact identification.

"And he said, 'Let it not be known that the woman came to the threshing floor'"
Some speculate that perhaps he spoke to those closest to him that may have seen "the woman" at his feet—in order to ensure that gossips didn't twist the truth for their own advantage. But there is really no hint in the text that others even saw Ruth (cf. Morris, p. 294)—in fact, just the opposite (cf. v. 7b). It seems much more likely that Boaz "said" this to himself (cf. Gen. 20:11 where a similar construction is translated, "I thought").

Boaz was concerned for Ruth's reputation, as well as his own. He was a man of love and concerned for her purity.

b. The cloak full of barley (v. 15)
"Again he said, 'Give me the cloak that is on you and hold it.' So she held it, and he measured six measures of barley"
The word "cloak" here differs from the term in verse three. This was a "shawl" of some sort—an outer piece of clothing. The term "measures" is not in the Hebrew, but added to give sense to the translation. "Six" ephahs would have been at least 200 pounds—which would seem quite unlikely given that Ruth carried it into town. If the measure was an *"omer"*, then Boaz may have given Ruth about 20 pounds of grain. It may be, however, that Boaz measured out six scoops of grain and did not measure the quantity (Block, p. 698).

"And laid it on her. Then she went into the city"
After "putting" the sack of grain on Ruth—i.e., her shoulder or head—Boaz, it would seem, returned to the "city". The Hebrew uses the masculine—"*he* went into the city" as the NIV translates it more literally. It is taken for granted that Ruth returned to her mother-in-law, but it seems likely from this verse that Boaz "went into the city" to begin his preparations for Ruth's redemption. Perhaps Boaz accompanied her part of the way, while it was still dark.

c. The collateral/assurance for Naomi (v. 16-17)
"When she came to her mother-in-law, she said, 'How did it go, my daughter?'"
Again, the English translation here gives the sense, but misses some of the

vividness of the Hebrew. Literally, Naomi said, "Who are you my daughter?" Obviously Naomi recognized Ruth—and called her "my daughter". But here she was asking if she now belonged to Boaz, or was she still a Moabite widow.

"And she told her all that the man had done for her"
The events of the previous night were detailed by Ruth to her mother-in-law. What Boaz had "done" was guarantee that one way or another he would see to her redemption—and thus Naomi's.

"She said, 'These six measures of barley he gave to me,' for he said, "Do not go to your mother-in-law empty-handed"'"
As she showed Naomi the "six measures of barley", she revealed a portion of previously unknown dialogue between Boaz and Ruth. Boaz showed concern not only for Ruth, but also specifically for her "mother-in-law". Quite interestingly, the same root word here translated "empty-handed" was used by Naomi in 1:21 when she said, "I went out full, but the LORD has brought me back *empty*". Boaz was giving Naomi proof that indeed she was not "empty". Perhaps the idea of collateral on future fullness was in view. It may have been both a gift of thankfulness for leading Ruth to him and also perhaps a down payment on the bride price.

d. The conviction of Naomi about Boaz's character and promise (v. 18)

"Then she said, 'Wait, my daughter, until you know how the matter turns out; for the man will not rest until he has settled it today'"
Before Boaz's promise, Naomi had called Ruth to action in seeking a redeemer (v. 3). Now, having received his word, Naomi calls Ruth to "wait" (Block, p. 701). Again, a literal rendering of the Hebrew is interesting: "Sit my daughter, until when you will know how the word/matter will fall". Again, Proverbs 16 reveals the truth about how matters/words fall: "The plans of the heart belong to man, but the answer of the tongue is from the LORD" (Prov. 16:1); "The lot is cast into the lap, but its every decision is from the LORD" (Prov. 16:33); "The mind of man plans his way, but the LORD directs his steps" (Prov. 16:9).

Naomi's peace, as well as Ruth's at that moment, was that Boaz was a man of *hesed*—faithful, steadfast love. He wouldn't "be tranquil/rest" until the word/matter was finished that day. They could rest assured, because Boaz would not "rest" until the matter was settled—just as he had promised before the LORD.

Conclusion
The *plan of Naomi* reveals her love and concern for Ruth and faith in Boaz's character. The *proposal of Ruth* reveals sacrificial love for Naomi and trust in Boaz's kindness. The *promise of Boaz* reveals loyal love and compassion for

both Naomi and Ruth. All three exhibit biblical faith and love. Too often today love is equated with either lust or merely a sentimental feeling. But true love involves sacrifice, loyalty, commitment and faithfulness. True love sees beyond external appearance. True love is governed by the truth of God's Word. Ruth was a woman of excellence. Boaz was a man of character.

Do our plans, our proposals, and our promises reflect biblical faith and love? Is God's Word more important to us than our feelings? Are we more interested in commitment and love, than physical attractiveness and vain pursuits? Do we have a testimony that we are people of excellence because of His grace in our lives?

Ruth chapter three also reveals a picture of the helpless seeking refuge under the wings of a redeemer who could protect and provide. Have you sought your divine Redeemer? Have you approached Him respectfully, fearfully, humbly, and submissively? Have you petitioned Him to redeem you from your destitute and hopeless state? Romans 10 says, "whoever believes in Him will not be disappointed" and again, "whoever will call on the name of the Lord will be saved" (Rom. 10:11, 13 respectively). If you come to Him on those terms, seeking only grace and mercy by faith—offering nothing but your soul—He will promise/guarantee your redemption. God became a man—the Son of God, Jesus Christ. He became our kinsman, to redeem us from our slavery to sin and rebellion. He purchased those who believe—through His substitutionary death and resurrection—for His Father's purposes and glory. He gives rest, security, and a home. In doing so, He alone will be praised for eternity.

May the Lord grant us grace to press on toward the goal of Christ-likeness, that others would see redemption and the Redeemer in us.

Expository Sermon:
A Case for Arranged Marriages?

Ruth 3:1-18

by Brad Brandt

God is sovereign. What a comforting truth to know that nothing just happens! God is in absolute control of every detail that occurs in His universe. Yet it's one thing to say those words. It's another thing to see the reality of those words in action. That's what we find when we come to the book of Ruth.

About twelve centuries before Christ, a Jewish woman named Naomi moved with her husband and two sons away from their home in Bethlehem to Moab in search of food. While in Moab Naomi lost her husband and eventually her two sons as well, leaving her destitute with two Moabite daughters-in-law, Orpah and Ruth.

But as we saw previously in our study of Ruth 1, God was in control of those losses and used them to set in motion a chain of events that resulted in good, not only for Naomi but for the entire nation of Israel and even the world. Naomi moved back to her homeland with Ruth, now a believer in the God of Israel, at her side.

In chapter two God demonstrated His providential care through a series of gains. As we saw in chapter two Ruth went searching for food and came home not only with food but with a new friend, a godly man by the name of Boaz who invited her to glean alongside his servants throughout the barley and wheat harvests.

Today we come to the third chapter of Ruth where we see *providence in a predicament*. Do you believe in arranged marriages? The fact is, every marriage is arranged, by a sovereign God. To reiterate, nothing just "happens" in God's universe, not one thing, and that includes the uniting of two people in marriage.

You say, "Belief in the sovereignty of God leads to passivity, even fatalism, doesn't it?" Sadly, for some it has, but it won't if we keep this doctrine in its biblical balance. Ruth 3 shows us how.

The fact that God is in control doesn't negate human responsibility. Ruth 3 demonstrates that God works through the choices of His people to accomplish His good plan. We'll see this truth illustrated in the following three scenes.

I. Scene #1: The Wedding Plans (1-6)

Valerie Runyan shares the following humorous story: "Soon after our last child left home for college, my husband was resting next to me on the couch with his head in my lap. I carefully removed his glasses. 'You know, honey,' I said sweetly, 'without your glasses you look like the same handsome young man I married.' 'Honey,' he replied with a grin, 'without my glasses, you still look pretty good too!'" (Valerie L. Runyan, *Reader's Digest*, December, 1992.)

A good marriage is a wonderful thing! As our first scene begins, wedding plans are brewing in the mind of Naomi. Listen to verse 1, "One day Naomi her mother-in-law said to her, 'My daughter, should I not try to find a home [Heb. *manoah*, can be translated 'rest' as in 1:9] for you, where you will be well provided for?'"

In contrast with the mother-in-law jokes that abound in our day, notice the beautiful relationship that's developed between this daughter-in-law and her mother-in-law. A mutual love is seen in the first scene. First...

A. Naomi demonstrated love for Ruth (1-4).
How? She began with a question in verse 1, "Should I not try to find a home for you, where you will be well provided for?" Naomi appreciates Ruth's company but she knows that it's not in Ruth's best interest to stay with her much longer. She needs a home of her own, and Naomi takes it upon herself to do what she can to provide such a home. True love accomplishes two actions...

1. True love focuses on the needs of another person.
And then...

2. True love takes steps to meet those needs.
That's not the way it is in Hollywood, for sure. The popular notion of love in nearly every 'love story' you'll ever watch is, "I need you. I can't live without you. I want you in my life." But that's not love. Love focuses on the other person. Look at Naomi. *Shouldn't I try to find a home for you where you will be provided for?* She's not thinking about herself, but about Ruth.

Since true love involves more than thought and talk, it's not surprising to see Naomi taking action to do something to help her beloved daughter-in-law. She asks a question in verse 2, "Is not Boaz, with whose servant girls you have been, a kinsman of ours?"

Ruth has been working in the fields of Boaz now for about three months, first during the barley harvest and more recently in the wheat harvest (2:27). Naomi brings an important piece of information to Ruth's attention. *Is not Boaz a kinsman of ours?*

Why that question? Boaz was related to Naomi and consequently to Ruth, not by blood, but by marriage. According to 2:1 Boaz was kin to Elimelech,

Naomi's deceased husband and Ruth's deceased father-in-law. Naomi already informed Ruth back in 2:21 that Boaz is one of their *kinsman-redeemers*.

Next Naomi proposes a plan involving Boaz in verses 2b-4—"Tonight he will be winnowing barley on the threshing floor. Wash and perfume yourself, and put on your best clothes. Then go down to the threshing floor, but don't let him know you are there until he has finished eating and drinking. When he lies down, note the place where he is lying. Then go and uncover his feet and lie down. He will tell you what to do."

If Naomi's plan sounds strange to us it's because we don't understand two important laws God gave to Israel to help widows like Naomi and Ruth.

The first law concerns **levirate marriage**. Yahweh gave Israel this law to explain what was to happen if the man of the house died without a son to perpetuate the family name and land inheritance. Deuteronomy 25:5 explains, "If brothers are living together and one of them dies without a son, his widow must not marry outside the family. Her husband's brother shall take her and marry her and fulfill the duty of a brother-in-law to her." The law of *levirate marriage* was not intended to be a punishment, but a gracious provision for a vulnerable widow and a means whereby family love could be demonstrated.

That's in Naomi's mind. So is another law, one that pertains to the **kinsman redeemer** (the Hebrew word *goel*). We read about this law in Leviticus 25:25, "If one of your countrymen becomes poor and sells some of his property, his nearest relative is to come and *redeem* what his countryman has sold." Legally, land could not be sold permanently out of a family in Israel. Since God owned the land, and since He gave it to particular clans and families as their inheritance, God expected that land should be returned to those rightful families. In the case where a family temporarily lost control of their land (due to excessive debt or a famine, for instance), it was the responsibility of the *kinsman redeemer* to see that the land returned to the proper family (this also happened every fifty years in the Year of Jubilee; cf. Lev. 25:28).

You can tell Naomi gave some thought to this plan. *Wash and perfume yourself*, she told Ruth. *Put on your best clothes.* In any culture we know what that means. "Please notice me! I'm interested in you!" *Go to the threshing floor. Approach him after he is asleep. Uncover his feet. Lie down and wait.*

Apparently, those actions meant something in Naomi's culture different from what they would mean today. We can be sure there were no immoral connotations. As we've already seen in chapter two, Ruth is not that kind of a woman (2:11-12) and Boaz is not that kind of man (2:9).

If this sounds strange to us, think for a moment how strange our customs would seem to Naomi. After all, we have our customs too, like giving an engagement ring that will be placed on the fourth finger on the left hand (instead of in the nose as Isaac's servant did with Isaac's fiancée Rebekah in Genesis 24:47), and throwing rice at the couple at their wedding ceremony.

We may not fully understand the cultural meaning of Naomi's plan, but we can't miss the significance. With her plans Naomi demonstrated her love for Ruth. And Ruth reciprocated...

Verses 5-6—"'I will do whatever you say,' Ruth answered. So she went down to the threshing floor and did everything her mother-in-law told her to do."

B. Ruth demonstrated love for Naomi (5-6).

We see Ruth's love for Naomi in her submissive response as well as in her obedient actions. She said she would obey her mother-in-law's instructions, and she did.

Allow me to make a couple of observations about Ruth. First...

1. Ruth is not desperate for a man.

Ruth is no mindless pushover. Remember, just a few months earlier she left her mother and father, her country, her gods, and came to Israel. Think of the courage and strength that took. Think of the pressure her extended family and probably her village put on her. "You're going *where*? You're a fool, Ruth! If you leave, there's no coming back!"

But she did leave. And she left with the full realization that she might never marry again. What Jewish man would ever want her, a Gentile woman? She was prepared to be single the rest of her life. Listen to her commitment as expressed to Naomi in Ruth 1:16-17: "Don't urge me to leave you or to turn back from you. Where you go I will go, and where you stay I will stay. Your people will be my people and your God my God. Where you die I will die, and there I will be buried. May the LORD deal with me, be it ever so severely, if anything but death separates you and me."

No, Ruth is not desperate for a man. That's not what's driving Ruth. This is...

2. Ruth is determined to do all she can to see the Lord's will accomplished.

Her obedience to Naomi reflects her personal commitment to the Lord and to His revealed will. She's thinking about Naomi and her care. She's thinking about her deceased father-in-law and the Lord's instruction that a family in Israel was to have an heir. Ruth did not live for herself but for the Lord and others. That's what love is all about.

Do you know what destroys relationships? Selfishness does. Self-centered-ness does. Putting self first does. It kills marriages. It fractures parents from their teens. But it doesn't have to be that way. When there is love, and that by

God's grace, there is abundant joy in the relationship!

We saw a moment ago that the law of levirate marriage stipulated that a surviving brother was to marry the widow. But what if the surviving brother refused? Deuteronomy 25:7-10 tell what was to happen then:

> "However, if a man does not want to marry his brother's wife, she shall go to the elders at the town gate and say, 'My husband's brother refuses to carry on his brother's name in Israel. He will not fulfill the duty of a brother-in-law to me.' Then the elders of his town shall summon him and talk to him. If he persists in saying, 'I do not want to marry her,' his brother's widow shall go up to him in the presence of the elders, take off one of his sandals, spit in his face and say, 'This is what is done to the man who will not build up his brother's family line.' That man's line shall be known in Israel as The Family of the Unsandaled."

Naomi and Ruth could have done that. They could have forced the hand of their kinsman redeemer publicly at the town gate. But they didn't, choosing instead to make private contact with Boaz.

Again, that's what love does. Love always thinks about the *other* person.

Naomi demonstrated her love for Ruth. Then Ruth demonstrated her love for Naomi. And here is what made both women tick.

C. Both women demonstrated love for the Lord.

Indeed, it's love for the Lord that makes possible the kind of love we're seeing between Ruth and Naomi. Only those who know the Lord can truly love as the Lord commands. He gives the power.

Naomi and Ruth valued two things that please God. Let's learn from them…

1. God is pleased when people take marriage seriously.

Marriage is a good gift from God. That's why Naomi proposed her plan to Ruth. It's also why Ruth implemented the plan. God is pleased when His people value the institution of marriage.

2. God is pleased when people take redemption seriously.

God set up the law of the kinsman redeemer. He did so not only to provide for families in Israel that lost their land, but also to illustrate our greatest need. We all have lost something. In Adam we've lost paradise. We enter this world cut off from God. We need a Redeemer. We need to be redeemed. And God provided for us by sending His Son, Jesus, into the world. First Peter 1:18-21 explains:

> "For you know that it was not with perishable things such as silver or gold that *you were redeemed* from the empty way of life handed down to you from your forefathers, but with the precious blood of Christ, a lamb without blemish or defect. He was chosen before the creation of the world, but was

revealed in these last times for your sake. Through him you believe in God, who raised him from the dead and glorified him, and so your faith and hope are in God" (emphasis added).

If you want to please God, you must take *redemption* seriously. You must accept the Redeemer and put your trust in His redeeming work.

So ends scene one, *the wedding plans*. Now we're ready for...

II. Scene #2: The Wedding Proposal (7-15)

Two things happened in scene two...

A. Ruth entrusted herself to the kinsman redeemer (7-9).

Here's how she did it. Notice verse 7, "When Boaz had finished eating and drinking and was in good spirits, he went over to lie down at the far end of the grain pile."

J. Vernon McGee observes that the threshing floor was a public place, out in the open. Entire families gathered there to work and celebrate God's provision. Consequently, there wasn't much privacy. McGee also cites the following description of the threshing scene offered by James Patch:

> The threshing floors are constructed in the fields, preferably in an exposed position in order to get the full benefit of the winds. If there is a danger of marauders they are clustered together close to the village. The floor is a level, circular area twenty-five to forty feet in diameter, prepared by first picking out the stones, and then wetting the ground, tamping or rolling it, and finally sweeping it. A border of stones usually surrounds the floor to keep in the grain. The sheaves of grain which have been brought on the backs of men, donkeys, camels, or oxen, are heaped on this area, and the process of tramping out begins. In some localities several animals, commonly oxen or donkeys, are tied abreast and driven round and round the floor... Until the wheat is transferred to bags someone sleeps by the pile on the threshing floor (J. Vernon McGee, p. 80).

With that picture in mind, watch Boaz. He goes to the far end of the grain pile, lies down, and soon drifts off.

Verse 7 continues, "Ruth approached quietly, uncovered his feet and lay down." In the ancient Near East, it was not uncommon for immoral practices to occur at harvest time, since many of the pagan religions practiced fertility rites (Leon Morris, p. 287). But Ruth is not doing anything indiscreet and certainly nothing with immoral connotations. By her actions she is simply taking steps to put God's revealed will into practice. She is about to let Boaz know that she would be willing to accept him as the *goel*, the kinsman redeemer, to take Mahlon's place in a levirate marriage. As McGee makes clear, "Ruth could have gone before the elders of the city and demanded that he do it, and she would have been within her legal rights. But the method adopted by her, at the suggestion of Naomi, was a quiet and reticent manner of proceeding. It was so interpreted by Boaz, as we shall see" (J. Vernon McGee, p. 82).

Verses 8-9—"In the middle of the night something startled the man, and he turned and discovered a woman lying at his feet. 'Who are you?' he asked. 'I am your servant Ruth,' she said. 'Spread the corner of your garment over me, since you are a kinsman-redeemer.'"

You'll note that Ruth's request was not in Naomi's original instructions. When Ruth moved to Israel she put herself under the protective wings of Yahweh, something for which Boaz commended her in chapter two (verse 12). Now Ruth seeks to put herself under the protective care of Boaz. By her request she is letting Boaz know she is willing to marry him should he so desire. She is entrusting herself to a man qualified to be her kinsman redeemer.

It's worth noting that God Himself used that image of speech in Ezekiel 16:8, "Later I passed by, and when I looked at you and saw that you were old enough for love, *I spread the corner of my garment over you* and covered your nakedness. I gave you my solemn oath and entered into a covenant with you, declares the Sovereign LORD, and you became mine" (emphasis added).

Again, Ruth is not desperate. She is certainly not being immoral. She did what she did for two reasons.

1. She knew what God promised in His Word.
Consequently…

2. She acted upon what she knew.
Ruth is taking God at His word and acting upon it. This is about God's reputation more than Ruth's personal dream for a man. God is concerned about the care of widows. God is concerned about His land staying in the proper family in Israel. And what God is concerned about matters to Ruth.

By her actions, Ruth entrusted herself to the kinsman redeemer. Then she waited. Now the ball was in his court. His response?

B. The kinsman redeemer pledged himself to care for Ruth (10-15).
Verse 10—"'The LORD bless you, my daughter,' he replied." Boaz is a godly man and his first response is to bring the Lord into the situation.

"This kindness is greater than that which you showed earlier." He's apparently referring to the kindness she showed Naomi by coming to Israel.
"You have not run after the younger men, whether rich or poor." The implication is that Ruth *could have* married a rich younger man had she so desired. But she didn't.

What does that tell us about Ruth? Ruth didn't live by her natural desires but with a supernatural ambition. She made choices based on what was *right* rather than based on emotion or some personal whim. She could have married someone else, but then Naomi would have been left homeless and her family name would have died. Yet if she married a kinsman of Elimelech, then she would have a husband *and* Naomi would have a kinsman redeemer. Ruth is asking Boaz to marry her because he is qualified to care for both Ruth and Naomi. Again, there were other eligible bachelors for Ruth to marry, but Boaz was a *goel* who could care for Naomi and preserve the family name.

In his response Boaz gave Ruth five things…

1. Boaz gave Ruth a promise (10-11a).
Verse 11—"And now, my daughter, don't be afraid. I will do for you all you ask." Boaz is a selfless provider. He promises to take action that will result in Ruth's care even if, as we'll see in a moment, he does not have the privilege of giving that care. I will do it. That's a promise.

2. Boaz gave Ruth a compliment (11b).
"All my fellow townsmen know that you are a woman of noble character." Ruth has been in town only a few months but Boaz says in that time she earned quite a reputation in Bethlehem. He says that everybody in town knows that Ruth is a "woman of noble character." The Hebrew word (which is used of the ideal woman in Prov. 31:10) speaks of "moral worth" and can be translated "virtuous." It's worth noting that the same word was used in reference to Boaz in 2:1, there translated "a man of standing." Talk about the perfect couple! A virtuous man and a virtuous woman, a match made in heaven!

3. Boaz gave Ruth a shock (12).
"Although it is true that I am near of kin, there is a kinsman-redeemer nearer than I." In other words, *I would if I could but I can't*. The closest male relative had the right to marry a widow. Now we know why Boaz hadn't initiated this marriage proposal to Ruth. He couldn't. There was another kinsman who had first dibs. The fact that Boaz knew this indicates he has already been thinking about the subject, he's been thinking about Ruth!

4. Boaz gave Ruth assurance of her redemption (13).
"Stay here for the night, and in the morning if he wants to redeem, good; let him redeem. But if he is not willing, as surely as the LORD lives I will do it. Lie here until morning." Did you catch that? Even if Boaz doesn't get the privilege of marrying Ruth, he is going to take steps to make sure someone does. Ruth's care was his number one concern. That's real love.

The week I was preparing this message the Lord took Shirley Litteral from this world into His eternal presence after a fifteen year battle with Alzheimer's

Chapter 3: A Case for Arranged Marriages? ■

disease. Shirley and her husband, Bob, are heroes in my estimation. Bob grew up in the community where I live. The church I pastor sent them out as missionaries in the mid 1960's. The couple selflessly served nearly four decades as Bible translators in the jungles of Papua New Guinea.

Upon hearing of Shirley's home-going, I spoke with Bob on the telephone and, after sharing my condolences, said, "Thank you, Bob. You and Shirley have demonstrated for all of us who have known you that God is sufficient even for a terrible disease like Alzheimer's." And He is. By God's grace Bob selflessly cared for his beloved Shirley for fifteen years, towards the end providing total care as you would for a baby.

Just a few months prior to this Bob had sent me the book, *A Promise Kept*. The author, Robertson McQuilkin, also faced the challenges of caring for a wife with Alzheimer's. In fact, he resigned from the presidency of a college in the prime of his working career in order to care for his beloved, Muriel. He offers this explanation:

> The decision was made, in a way, 42 years ago when I promised to care for Muriel 'in sickness and in health…till death do us part.' So…as a man of my word, integrity has something to do with it. But so does fairness. She has cared for me fully and sacrificially all these years; if I cared for her the next 40 years I would not be out of her debt. Duty, however, can be grim and stoic. But there is more: I love Muriel. She is a delight to me—her childlike dependence and confidence in me, her warm love, occasional flashes of that wit I used to relish so, her happy spirit and tough resilience in the face of her continual distressing frustration. I don't *have* to care for her. I get to! It is a high honor to care for so wonderful a person (Robertson McQuilkin, *A Promise Kept*, pp. 22-23).

If married, do you love your spouse like that, with a selfless love that thinks of the other person's needs ahead of your own? That's the kind of love that Boaz exhibited for Ruth, a selfless love that thought of her good even if he was out of the picture.

5. Boaz gave Ruth a reminder of the importance of purity (14).

"So she lay at his feet until morning, but got up before anyone could be recognized; and he said, 'Don't let it be known that a woman came to the threshing floor.'"

Why did Boaz tell Ruth to stay with him, but then tell her to let no one know? The reason has to do with the high moral standards of this man. He encouraged her to remain until morning since it would be dangerous for her to leave and walk home alone in the middle of the night.

On the other hand, he made sure she left before daybreak so that their meeting on the threshing floor would remain their secret. If that information became public it might mar Ruth's reputation and his own—there is actually a provision in the Mishnah that if a man was suspected of having intercourse with a Gentile woman he could not perform levirate marriage with her (Morris, p. 293; Granted, the Mishnah was written centuries later than Ruth, but it's possible this was an unwritten custom before it became written law). Furthermore, if the nearer kinsman had any idea that Boaz was interested in marrying Ruth, he might have exploited the situation (observation by Rowley in Atkinson, p. 105).

How refreshing to see a man and woman committed to purity! Allow me to speak candidly. Sex is good, a gift from our Creator to mankind. Sex is enjoyable by God's design, a good gift to be enjoyed within the marriage relationship. It's like fire. Fire is good when it stays in the fireplace, but it becomes destructive when a burning log rolls out of the fireplace onto the family room carpet. Our society mocks purity but in so doing it cheapens sex. Sex becomes hollow when experienced before or outside of marriage. That's why true love waits until marriage. And once married, true love flees from every form of sexual immorality and chooses to use this gift as a way to serve one's spouse.

6. Boaz gave Ruth a provision (15).
"He also said, 'Bring me the shawl you are wearing and hold it out.' When she did so, he poured into it six measures of barley and put it on her. Then he went back to town."

Boaz is constantly providing for Ruth. Again, that's what love does. It looks for needs and then takes action to meet those needs.

Boaz gave Ruth "six measures" of wheat. The Hebrew text doesn't specify which measure is being used to calculate the amount. The Hebrew text simply says, "six of barley." That raises the question, "Six *what*?" In 2:17 the ephah is used, but six ephahs would amount to 24 gallons which would be way too much for Ruth to carry. If the measure was the *seah* (which was a third of an ephah), this would be about 88 pounds, "not impossible for a strong young woman," as Morris concludes (p. 294). The text says Boaz poured the grain into Ruth's shawl and then 'put it on her,' probably meaning he helped her position it for travel on her head.

This brings us to scene three. One, the wedding plans; two, the wedding proposal...

III. Scene #3: Waiting for the Wedding Day (16-18)
Verse 16—"When Ruth came to her mother-in-law, Naomi asked, 'How did it go, my daughter?' Then she told her everything Boaz had done for her...'" Let

Chapter 3: A Case for Arranged Marriages? ■

the significance of that word *everything* sink in. What a conversation that must have been!

Verse 17—"And added, 'He gave me these six measures of barley, saying, "Don't go back to your mother-in-law empty-handed."'" It's not mere coincidence that chapter one ended with the same word 'empty' telling us that Naomi came back to Bethlehem 'empty.' But now her 'empty' days are over.

Verse 18—"Then Naomi said, 'Wait, my daughter, until you find out what happens. For the man will not rest until the matter is settled today.'" Waiting is hard, but in this case, Ruth didn't have to wait long. "He'll take care of it *today*," Naomi insisted. And as we'll see in chapter four, he did! Within twenty-four hours Ruth became a bride!

Make It Personal: We learn the following lessons from Ruth 3...

1. We learn about priorities.

Because of God's grace in her life Ruth took a very simple approach to life. She put the Lord first, others next, and thought of herself last. God blessed her richly by giving her a son who was in the lineage of Messiah Jesus!

Are your priorities in order? It's so easy for us to slip here. Are there choices you need to make today to put your priorities in order, so that it's the Lord first, then others, and then self in your life as we've seen exemplified by Ruth?

2. We learn about God's purpose for marriage.

Marriage is about *serving*. Does that word describe what is happening in your home? Are you seeking day-by-day to give or to get? Men, let's learn from Boaz how to be selfless providers. And ladies, learn from Ruth how to have a godly influence on those God has called us to serve.

There's one more lesson we must glean from Ruth 3. I see it in the statement Naomi made concerning Boaz, "The man will not rest until the matter is settled." That reminds me of someone else, another Man who would not rest until the matter was settled. I have in mind another Redeemer, indeed the *final* Redeemer who said in John 5:17, "My Father is always at his work to this very day, and I, too, am working." This Redeemer had a work to do, a work of rescuing helpless sinners, and He did so as testified in His prayer in John 17:4, "I have brought you glory on earth by *completing the work* you gave me to do." This Redeemer did not stop working until He cried out from the cross, "It is finished!" (John 19:30)

D.A. Leggett comments, "In the actions of Boaz as *goel* we see foreshadowed the saving work of Jesus Christ, his later descendant. As Boaz had the right of redemption and yet clearly was under no obligation to intervene on Ruth's behalf, so it was with Christ. As Boaz, seeing the plight of the poor widows, came to their rescue because his life was governed by Yahweh and his laws, so also of the Messiah it is prophesied that his life would be governed by the law of God and that he would deal justly and equitably with the poor and with those who were oppressed (Leggett, in D. Atkinson, p. 97)." Yes, in our final lesson…

3. We learn about our need for a Redeemer.
Hebrews 4:9-10 declares, "There remains, then, a Sabbath-rest for the people of God; for anyone who enters God's rest also rests from his own work..." My friend, you are resting in the finished work of the Redeemer?

Getting Intentional About Application

by Brad Brandt

I am committed to expository preaching. By that I mean that my objective in preaching is to *expose* the biblical author's intent in my proclamation of the text of God's revealed Word. I am not authorized to impose my meaning and application upon a text, but rather am responsible to get at the writer's objective. In so doing, my people will be well nourished for God has addressed in His Word everything His sheep need for life and godliness (2 Pet. 1:3-4).

Herein lies a challenge in preaching through Ruth. Let's face it, the book of Ruth is a thrilling love story! I observed its magnetic appeal as the people of God returned on the Lord's Day week after week to find out what would happen next with this charming couple, Ruth and Boaz. But of course, this book isn't primarily about Ruth, or Boaz, or even Naomi. It's about *God*.

The author didn't write this book to entertain his readers (even though his story is spell-binding), but rather to reveal God to them (the Bible is God's self-revelation). As with any piece of narrative literature in the Bible, it is vital that we seek to convey the author's intent as we preach and apply it.

Simply put, if we approach the book of Ruth merely to find guidelines for a God-honoring dating relationship, we've missed the point (in my estimation). That wasn't the author's intent. Again, this is a book about God and His faithfulness to His covenant people and promises. As teachers we must consistently emphasize this wonderful theme in the presentation of the book of Ruth.

Having said that, does the book of Ruth also speak to issues of love and purity? Does it have anything to say to us about marriage and family? I believe it does. In the book of Ruth we see in living color wonderful illustrations of what can happen when God's covenant people take Him seriously in their lives. We might refer to these as secondary points of application.

To put it another way, we might think of Ruth's application in terms of three concentric circles (or three levels of application). In the first circle (the bull's eye, so to speak), Ruth teaches us about *God* (His providential care, His covenant faithfulness, and so on).

As we move outward to the second circle, Ruth teaches us about God's redemptive plan for *Israel* (demonstrating Israel's need, in light of the failure of the judges, for a ruler after God's own heart, David, and ultimately the Son of David).

As we continue to move outward from the center we come to the third concentric circle, the *individual* level. Having considered what Ruth has to say first about God and second His covenant people, we are now prepared to see what Ruth has to say to *individuals*. It's at this third level (and with the first two levels clearly in mind as its basis) that we can consider possible applications concerning love, marriage, family, and so forth. Paul put it this way in Romans 15:4, "For everything that was written in the past was written to teach us, so that through endurance and the encouragement of the Scriptures we might have hope" (see also 1 Cor. 10:11).

You are seeing this perspective fleshed out in the *Getting Intentional About Application* section of each chapter. As in previous chapters, here are some suggested tools to help you get at the application of Ruth chapter three.

Tool #1: A Teaching Outline
It may be helpful to discuss the process of developing a preaching outline. There is more than one way to outline a text. The *hermeneutical* outline seeks to show what the text says. It would typically use third person language (for instance, in Scene one below: A. Naomi demonstrated love for Ruth. B. Ruth demonstrated love for Naomi. C. Both women demonstrated love for the Lord.).

A *homiletical* outline seeks to communicate what the text means for the present-day audience. It may use first person language (such as, "God is pleased when *we* demonstrate love for *our* family members"), but not necessarily. It might utilize third person language to communicate timeless principles based on the text (for instance, in Scene one, part A below: 1. True love focuses on the needs of another person. 2. True love takes steps to meet those needs.).

As you may have noticed from perusing my outlines, I tend to take a blended approach, using both hermeneutical and homiletical features in the teaching outline. This is intentional. Preaching provides an opportunity to teach the congregation *how to study* a text on their own, hence the use of hermeneutical elements. I want the people to see the process I used to get from meaning to application.

But preaching must go beyond giving mere history lessons, hence the use of homiletical elements. Preaching gives me occasion to show the congregation *how to apply* a text as well. Furthermore, I want the flock to feast on the nourishing implications of the text as God intended.

With these thoughts in mind, take a look at the following teaching outline from Ruth chapter three.

From Brad's exposition:
Main Idea: The fact that God is in control doesn't negate human responsibility. Ruth 3 shows us that God works through the choices of His people to accomplish His good plan.

I. **Scene #1: The Wedding Plans (1-6)**
   A. **Naomi demonstrated love for Ruth (1-4).**
      1. True love focuses on the needs of another person.
      2. True love takes steps to meet those needs.
   B. **Ruth demonstrated love for Naomi (5-6).**
      1. Ruth is not desperate for a man.
      2. Ruth is determined to do all she can to see the Lord's will accomplished.
   C. **Both women demonstrated love for the Lord.**
      1. God is pleased when people take marriage seriously.
      2. God is pleased when people take redemption seriously.
II. **Scene #2: The Wedding Proposal (7-15)**
   A. **Ruth entrusted herself to the kinsman redeemer (7-9).**
      1. She knew what God promised in His Word.
      2. She acted upon what she knew.
   B. **The kinsman redeemer pledged himself to care for Ruth (10-15).**
      1. Boaz gave Ruth a promise (10-11a).
      2. Boaz gave Ruth a compliment (11b).
      3. Boaz gave Ruth a shock (12).
      4. Boaz gave Ruth assurance of her redemption (13).
      5. Boaz gave Ruth a reminder of the importance of purity (14).
      6. Boaz gave Ruth a provision (15).
III. **Scene #3: Waiting for the Wedding Day (16-18)**

Make It Personal: We learn the following lessons from Ruth 3...
1. We learn about priorities.
2. We learn about God's purpose for marriage.
3. We learn about our need for a Redeemer.

Tool #2: "Digging Deeper" Discussion Questions

When you are preaching God's Word, it's not easy to tell if people are grasping what you are saying. The smiles, the head nods, and the note-taking are helpful halo data, but not definitive. Giving the congregation opportunity to discuss the sermon at a later time (such as in Sunday evening small groups, or during a mid-week Bible study and prayer service) can be quite revealing. What's more, the use of carefully crafted questions can help facilitate the necessary transition from learning to living. Here are some possible questions to use as follow-up with Ruth chapter three.

Questions for Clarification:
1. What is the law of levirate marriage? Use Scripture to support your answer.
2. What is the law of the kinsman redeemer? Use Scripture to support your answer.
3. Ruth's actions at the threshing floor were more about God's reputation than her personal desire for a man. How so?
4. List several ways true love is demonstrated in Ruth chapter three.
5. How does the book of Ruth prepare us for the coming of Jesus?

Questions for Application:
1. God is a *redeeming* God. What are some practical things we can do to grow

in our appreciation for His redemption?

2. At the outset of the message reference was made to a person who says, "Belief in the sovereignty of God leads to passivity, even fatalism." Why would someone say that? How would you respond to such a person?

3. The statement was made in the message, "Marriage is about serving." What does that mean in practical terms?

4. Think about the statement, "Our society mocks purity but in so doing it cheapens sex." How does it cheapen sex? How does the example of Boaz and Ruth in chapter three encourage you?

5. What questions did this message raise for you?

Tool #3: A Counseling Case Study
The following scenario could be discussed at a training meeting for your church's care group leaders.

Scenario: Steve, a 22-year-old young man, comes to see you. You've known Steve for about three years, since he started attending your church after moving to your city from out of state. Steve, who professed faith in Christ as his Savior two years ago and demonstrated the evidence of God's transforming grace since, now seems quite distressed about something. You welcome him into your living room, thank him for coming, and invite him to share what's on his mind. He tells you he's met a wonderful Christian girl at the university where he attends, that they've been dating about a year, but that now he's perplexed. Simply put, he's fearful. He's never seen a solid marriage up close. He was raised by a single mom and doesn't even remember his dad who left when he was two.

"I'm not sure what real love is." Steve confesses. "I'll be graduating in less than a year and so will Sue. We started talking about marriage last week and it scared me to death. I think I love Sue, but how can I know for sure? I mean, how can I know we should marry? I don't want to repeat what happened to my parents. I'm just so confused." At that point Steve stops talking and looks at the floor.

Case Study Discussion Questions:
1. What would you say *first* to Steve?

2. What does Steve need *most* from you in this conversation?

3. How might you use the story of Ruth to encourage Steve in this initial conversation?

4. What other passages in God's Word might you use to help Steve initially?

Tool #4: Counseling Assignments Utilizing the Book of Ruth

Suppose that as the result of your initial meeting with Steve, he agrees to meet with you to obtain biblical counsel. You might consider using the book of Ruth to provide a basic structure for these sessions, assigning homework from Ruth and building on that homework during your sessions.

Week One Reading Assignment:

1. Read the entire book of Ruth three times this week. Each time you read it write down your answer to the following questions:

a. After the *first* time: What do I learn about *God* from the book of Ruth? Write down five observations.

b. After the *second* time: What do I learn about *God's plan for His people* from the book of Ruth? Write down five observations.

c. After the *third* time: What do I learn about *love* from the book of Ruth? Write down five observations.

Week Two Reading Assignment:

1. Read through the book of Ruth more slowly this week, one chapter per day for four days. Each time you read answer the following three questions:

a. How does my view of God need to change?

b. What am I learning that gives me hope?

c. What is something I need to *do* in light of what I am learning? Then ask the Lord for His help and do it.

2. Write out Ruth 3:11 on a 3x5 card and seek to memorize it by reading it out loud three times every day. Write a paragraph explaining what you learn about love from these words of Boaz.

CHAPTER

 4

The Romance of Redemption

Ruth 4:1-12

Expositional Commentary and Outline:
The Purchase of Redemption

Expository Sermon:
The Romance of Redemption

Getting Intentional About Application

Tool #1: A Teaching Outline
Tool #2: "Digging Deeper" Discussion Questions
Tool #3: A Counseling Case Study
Tool #4: Counseling Assignments

Expositional Outline:

Ruth 4:1-12

by Rick Kress

The Book of Ruth—A Portrait of God's Loyal Love, Sovereign Redemption, and the Faith of His Believing Remnant

I.   The pain of covenant faithlessness [an empty profession] (1:1-5)

II. The pity of God and the initial glimmers of faith (1:6-22)

III. The providential provision and protection of God for the destitute who live by faith (2:1-23)

IV. The pursuit of redemption and the subsequent promise of redemption (3:1-18)

V.   The purchase of redemption (4:1-12)

    A.   The plan and preparation of Boaz (4:1-2)

        1. The city gate (4:1a)

        2. The close relative (4:1b)

        3. The city elders (4:2)

    B.   The price that was too high for the anonymous redeemer (4:3-6)

        1. He saw the potential gain for himself and said, "I will redeem" (4:3-4)

            a. The potential gain in the purchase of the land (v. 3)

            b. The premature pledge to redeem (v. 4)

        2. He saw the price and responsibility and said, "I cannot redeem" (4:5-6)

            a. The responsibility for the Moabitess and another's inheritance (v. 5)

            b. The reversal of the premature pledge—"I cannot...I would jeopardize my own inheritance" (v. 6)

    C.   The purchase confirmed (4:7-11a)

        1. The purchase confirmed by the unwilling redeemer (4:7-8)

            a. The custom of confirmation (v. 7)

            b. The confirmation of the close relative/unwilling redeemer (v. 8)

        2. The purchase confirmed by the willing redeemer (4:9-11a)

            a. The purchase of property [the right of redemption] and the marriage of the Moabitess (v. 9-10a)

            b. The purpose of the marriage (v. 10b)

            c. The proclamation of the witnesses (11a)

    D.   The prayer of the people (4:11b-12)

        1. Fruitfulness like two women who left their family for Israel's sake (v. 11b)

        2. Faithfulness [spiritual fortune and fame] for the glory of God (v. 11c)

        3. Fellowship/participation in the Messianic Seed promise (v. 12)

Expositional Commentary:
The Purchase of Redemption

Ruth 4:1-12

by Rick Kress

Growing up, I knew some facts about the gospel—Jesus the Son of God died for sinners and rose from the grave on the third day. I accepted those facts as a sort of "fire insurance" against going to hell. I claimed to believe them—but in reality I was completely ignorant of what it really meant to believe. If the gospel is just a story that makes us feel ok about our sin and salve our conscience when we habitually and unceasingly live for ourselves—then we have no real understanding of the gospel.

God paid an infinitely high price to buy us out of slavery to sin and prospect of eternal damnation, and unspeakable and unending horror. No one else—and I mean NO ONE ELSE—would ever think of doing what He did to redeem us from our spiritual poverty and perversion.

In Ruth 4:1-12 we will see four parts of the narrative that reveal a picture of human redemption—specifically the purchase of the right of redemption. They will in some ways picture Christ's greater redemption of lost and destitute sinners.

V. The purchase of redemption (4:1-12)
A. The plan and preparation of Boaz (4:1-2)
1. The city gate (4:1a)
"Now Boaz went up to the gate and sat down there"
The syntactical structure of the sentence places emphasis on the person of "Boaz". His pursuit of Ruth and Naomi's redemption was purposeful. It didn't just happen. After going to the city (cf. 3:15) *"Boaz went up to the gate and remained there"*. He was a man of his word.

In the ancient Near East, "the gate" of a city was the place where legal transactions were made, judicial proceedings took place, and official business conducted (cf. Gen. 19:1, 9; 23:10, 18; 34:20, 24; 2 Sam. 15:2-6; Prov. 22:22; Amos 5:10, 12, 15). In an agrarian society, most everyone would pass through the gate either to go to or from the fields that were outside the city walls.

The verb "went up" serves a dual purpose perhaps. Bethlehem was likely higher than the surrounding countryside (cf. 3:3, 6); and to "go up to the gate" may have been an idiom for "go to court" (Block, p. 704). Instead of passing through the "gate", Boaz got there and "sat there". He "sat/remained" there at the "gate"—as we will see, evidently waiting for the closer relative to pass by.

2. The close relative (4:1b)

"And behold, the close relative of whom Boaz spoke was passing by"
The term "close relative" is literally "redeemer". The word, "behold", is meant to heighten the vividness of the narrative. As Boaz sat at the gate, "behold, the redeemer of whom Boaz spoke was passing by". The phrase, "of whom Boaz spoke", references the conversation of the previous night recorded in 3:12-13.

"So he said, 'Turn aside, friend, sit down here.' And he turned aside and sat down"
The word here translated "friend" is more descriptively translated, "so and so" or "such a one". It is an intentional omission. The same words (*peloni almoni*) are used in 1 Samuel 21:2 and 2 Kings 6:8, and are translated "a certain place" and "such and such a place" respectively. So the narrative says that "behold"—in God's good providence—the closer redeemer was passing by and Boaz called out to "Mr. So and So" and asked him to "turn aside" and "sit down" with him. And he did.

It is interesting to note that Boaz's name was emphasized in this verse, and the omission of this man's name is conspicuous at the end of the verse. As Block comments:

> [T]his raises an important question: Why would the narrator, who is otherwise so careful with names, keep this character anonymous? Whatever the motivation, the effect is to diminish our respect for him. To be sure, nothing overtly negative is said about him, but like Orpah, who serves as a foil for Ruth in chap. 1, this man presents a contrast to Boaz. He may be the goel, but he will shortly be dismissed as irrelevant to the central theme of the book: the preservation of the royal line of David (Block, p. 707).

3. The city elders (4:2)

"He took ten men of the elders of the city and said, 'Sit down here.' So they sat down"
These "men of age" weren't merely passing by, but Boaz intentionally "took" them to witness this transaction. Though only two or three witnesses were necessary for a legal decision (Deut. 17:6; 19:15), "ten" men were gathered together here. The significance of the "ten" is not clear. In later Judaism, "ten" would be required for a synagogue; and Jewish authorities cite that "ten" were to be present for the recital of the marriage benediction—and thus it may be assumed that Boaz was preparing for a marriage ceremony (Morris, p. 299). The antiquity of such tradition may not reach to the days of the Judges. Perhaps there was a local custom relating to redemption or marriage matters and "ten" witnesses.

What we see here then are the plans and preparations of Boaz. He was intentional about providing Ruth and Naomi with a redeemer. He purposed to make good on his promise. In like manner, but in an infinitely greater way, our heavenly Redeemer is intentional in His pursuit of our redemption and faithful to His promise.

B. The price that was too high for the anonymous redeemer (4:3-6)
1. He saw the potential gain for himself and said, "I will redeem" (4:3-4)
a. The potential gain in the purchase of the land (v. 3)

"Then he said to the closest relative, 'Naomi, who has come back from the land of Moab, has to sell the piece of land which belonged to our brother Elimelech'"

The Hebrew more naturally reads that the "piece of land which belonged to...Elimelech" had already been "sold". Scholars debate whether Naomi actually was selling the property, or if it already had been sold, and now Boaz was initiating its redemption back into the family. Duguid's comments are helpful for the pastor trying to wade through the biblical data, and cultural setting:

> Strictly speaking, as a widow, Naomi had the right neither to buy nor to sell the land outright. However, she could potentially control the right to use the land until the next Jubilee year. This is technically what is on offer in this conversation . . . It is doubtful, however, whether a detailed digression into ancient Near Eastern property rights would be helpful [at this juncture]. The simple concept of buying and selling land is probably close enough to be adequate for most people [to get the concept being communicated by the larger narrative] (Duguid, p. 181, footnote 2).

The point is that a piece of land was going to be part of the transaction. The closer "redeemer" had first right of refusal on a "piece of land which belonged to" their relative—i.e., "brother"—"Elimelech", who was now dead.

It is also interesting that Boaz started with the issue of land, rather than the marriage of Ruth. It may be, however, that Boaz wanted to be sure and communicate an "above reproach"—approach—to the marriage of Ruth. If he had first dealt with the marriage of Ruth, and the closer relative refused, and then Boaz married and acquired the land—it might appear as if he had ulterior motives in marrying Ruth. Or perhaps Boaz understood the financial strain that would be involved for the closer relative in both purchasing the land, and providing for a bride and her mother-in-law—and he wanted to communicate everything up front.

For now, Boaz was revealing the need for the redemption of the family's land (see Lev. 25:23-28). The man's response at the end of verse four indicates that he had latched on to the idea of the potential gain of purchasing the land.

b. The premature pledge to redeem (v. 4)

"So I thought to inform you, saying"
The Hebrew idiom is literally, "I—I said, I will uncover your ear". Boaz was making certain information known to the nearer redeemer—thus giving him an opportunity to partake of the blessing of service to those in need.

"Buy it before those who are sitting here, and before the elders of my people"
The verb "buy" is a call for the nearer redeemer to "acquire" the rights to the property. The acquisition would become official if declared before those who were "sitting" there watching the conversation, and "before the elders of [the] people". Interestingly, Boaz said, "the elders of *my* people" (emphasis added)—though the elders were also a part of his relative's people as well. Some suggest it is formulaic, legal language.

"If you will redeem it, redeem it; but if not, tell me that I may know; for there is no one but you to redeem it, and I am after you"
Here Boaz was clearly yielding to the closer relative's right of refusal concerning the redemption. But there is an implied eagerness to take the responsibility for himself—i.e., he would like an immediate decision, because he was eager to "redeem" and was next in line to do so.

"And he said, 'I will redeem'"
Perhaps Boaz paused for a moment, or wanted to see if he was even willing to purchase the land. It could be that the nearer redeemer did not let Boaz finish describing the more difficult details of the redemption, but interjected, "I will redeem". The grammar is emphatic: "I—I will redeem". He may have sensed Boaz's eagerness, and did not want such a golden opportunity to slip away.

Normally the nearest redeemer who redeemed the land would have use of it until he was either paid back or until the year of jubilee—when the land would revert back to the family who sold its right of use (Lev. 25:23-28). But since Elimelech had no heir, the right to the land would remain in this anonymous redeemer's immediate family from generation to generation. The prospects for gain—as he understood them at the time—seemed quite good. Yes, there would be a financial outlay for the redemption of the land, but that would be made up through not only the use of the land but also in acquiring it and effectively annexing it into his own inheritance.

He saw the potential gain for himself and said, "I will redeem".

2. He saw the price and responsibility and said, "I cannot redeem" (4:5-6)
a. The responsibility for the Moabitess and another's inheritance (v. 5)
"On the day you buy the field from the hand of Naomi, you must also acquire Ruth the Moabitess, the widow of the deceased"
Though the statutes concerning the redemption of the land (Lev. 25:25-28)

and the law of levirate marriage (cf. Deut. 25:5-10) are not exactly parallel to the case here, it seems obvious that Boaz expected the nearer relative to agree to the propriety/legality of what he was saying.

It is interesting to note that the Hebrew text uses the first person ending with the verb "acquire"—"On the day you buy the field from the hand of Naomi—also from Ruth the Moabitess, the widow of the deceased, *I* acquire in order to raise up the name of the deceased on his inheritance" (emphasis added). In fact the Revised English Bible translates the phrase, "I take over the widow, Ruth, the Moabitess" (cf. Block, p. 713, footnote 31). If this is the case, Boaz was letting the closer relative know that he may not get to keep the land in his own family forever, because Boaz would "acquire" Ruth for the purpose of raising up "the name of the deceased on his inheritance"—i.e., Boaz would seek to give Elimelech an heir through Ruth.

Because of the nearer redeemer's statement in verse six, "I cannot redeem for myself, because I would jeopardize my own inheritance," most scholars believe that an alternate reading of the Hebrew should be taken, and rendered, "On the day you acquire the field from the hand of Naomi, *you* have acquired Ruth" (emphasis added).

Whichever the case, the clear point is that this "Mr. So and So" would not necessarily be able to acquire the land permanently, since either he or Boaz would have the responsibility of raising up an heir in "the name of the deceased on his inheritance". In other words, Elimelech very well could have an heir that would be entitled to the property rights.

In effect, the redemption of the property would become more of a burden of love and compassion—self-sacrifice—rather than a means for personal gain. It would cost money to redeem the property. It would cost money and many other things (i.e., reputation, time, his whole life) to redeem Ruth, "*the Moabitess*"— Boaz was sure that Ruth's ethnic origins were clear. Verse six reveals *the reversal of the premature pledge* in light of these newly revealed factors.

"In order to raise up the name of the deceased on his inheritance"
See the principles of Deuteronomy 25:5-6 for this idea, even if the situation is not exactly parallel.

b. The reversal of the premature pledge—"I cannot . . . I would jeopardize my own inheritance" (v. 6)
"The closest relative said, 'I cannot redeem it for myself, because I would jeopardize my own inheritance'"
The "redeemer said, 'I will not be able to redeem for myself, lest I ruin my inheritance/property/possession'". The personal pronouns tell the story of this anonymous redeemer's true concern—I, myself, I and my. He was concerned

about his own welfare, property and posterity. Yet ironically, no one even knows his name today.

It would cost him to buy the field. But that could be made up in later years' profits from it. But it would also cost him to redeem Ruth, or have to buy the land and then have it potentially revert back to an heir born from Ruth. He didn't want his financial situation "jeopardized" and perhaps reputation "ruined". As well, if he did marry Ruth, and if he had only one son—then his estate would actually go to the child who would technically be of Elimelech's family. There were difficulties on every side.

"Redeem it for yourself; you may have my right of redemption, for I cannot redeem it"
The literal rendering is interesting, "Redeem for yourself—you—my redemption, because I am not able to redeem". Earlier, he had emphatically said he would redeem the land. Now he was emphatically urging Boaz to redeem it.

Though this does paint "Mr. So and So" in a somewhat negative light, it should be noted that he was not evidently bound to do this, as a brother would be according to Deuteronomy 25. And it was evident to all that Boaz was eager to take on the responsibility. Thus, in view of the price he said, "I cannot redeem".

Though an earthly picture of redemption, we see the cost and selflessness that is required of a redeemer. In an infinitely greater way, Jesus Christ sacrificed of Himself to become our Redeemer *par excellence* (Phil. 2:5-8). He had to be a kinsman, and thus became a man (Heb. 2:14ff). But He also had to satisfy the infinite cost of the demands of a good and holy God. Thus He gave up the glories of heaven for a time to come and live with us, and die for us/pay the penalty that we owed to a good and holy God—so that we could be redeemed. Redemption is deliberate and planned. It is also costly to the Redeemer—infinitely costly.

There were the plans and preparations of Boaz (4:1-2) and the price that was too high for the anonymous redeemer (4:3-6). Next, in verses 7-11...

C. The purchase confirmed (4:7-11a)
1. The purchase confirmed by the unwilling redeemer (4:7-8)
a. The custom of confirmation (v. 7)
"Now this was the custom in former times in Israel concerning the redemption and the exchange to confirm any matter"
This tells us that the author was writing to an audience that was at least a generation removed from the events of the narrative. A "custom" (though "custom" is not in the Hebrew, it gives the sense of the clause) can go out of use within a generation, but it may indicate an even longer period of time.

Chapter 4: The Romance of Redemption ■

"A man removed his sandal and gave it to another; and this was the attestation in Israel"

The narrator may well have explained this not only because it was no longer widely practiced, but to also differentiate what happened here from the stipulations in Deuteronomy 25:7-10, which describes the shaming of a brother who refuses to marry a deceased brother's wife.

He was evidently communicating that the custom of removing one's "sandal" and giving it "to another" was how deals were "confirmed" concerning "any matter", including "redemption". The sandal was "the attestation/witness/testimony in Israel". It served sort of like a handshake or signature in modern times. Many believe it was related to the idea of walking the land as a symbol of ownership (Gen. 13:17; Deut. 1:36; 11:24; Josh. 1:3; 14:9)—and now the sandal that walked the land is handed over to the new owner.

This was the custom of confirmation.

b. The confirmation of the close relative/unwilling redeemer (v. 8)
"So the closest relative said to Boaz, 'Buy for yourself.' And he removed his sandal"

The official transaction was thus confirmed. "The redeemer said to Boaz, 'Acquire for yourself.'" And evidently the closer redeemer "removed his sandal" and we would assume gave it to Boaz.

Again, though some believe this to be a modified version of the shaming of the unwilling brother spoken of in Deuteronomy 25:7-10, it would seem from the narrator's introduction in verse seven this is not the case. Rather the words and symbolic action confirmed that the right of redemption had now changed from his hand to Boaz's.

2. The purchase confirmed by the willing redeemer (4:9-11a)
a. The purchase of property [the right of redemption] and the marriage of the Moabitess (v. 9-10a)
"Then Boaz said to the elders and all the people, 'You are witnesses today . . .'"

"The elders" likely refers to the 10 witnesses that Boaz had summoned. "All the people" would indicate that a crowd had gathered around the twelve men—two of which were discussing the official rights to redeem Elimelech's estate.

After the symbolic confirmation of the exchange of rights, "Boaz" called both the official and non-official observers to "witness" what had just taken place.

"That I have bought from the hand of Naomi all that belonged to Elimelech and all that belonged to Chilion and Mahlon"

Boaz announced to the people that they were witnesses that he had "acquired" the right to redeem "all" the estate of "Elimelech" and his deceased sons,

"Chilion and Mahlon". As previously discussed, it's not likely that he "bought" the land from Naomi—but that he acquired the right to redeem it in relation to her, being now her officially recognized kinsman redeemer.

"Moreover, I have acquired Ruth the Moabitess, the widow of Mahlon, to be my wife"

It is here for the first time revealed that Ruth had been married to "Mahlon", and not Chilion. In addition to the rights to redeem Elimelech and his sons' estate, Boaz publicly announced his acquisition of the right to marry Ruth—*"the Moabitess"*. "Boaz" was himself the descendant of an outcast gentile woman, who turned to Yahweh in faith according to Matthew 1:5 (cf. Heb. 11:31; James 2:25).

b. The purpose of the marriage (v. 10b)

"In order to raise up the name of the deceased on his inheritance, so that the name of the deceased will not be cut off from his brothers or from the court of his birth place"

At first glance, looking through our culturally colored glasses, we might think that Boaz was primarily driven by emotion and feelings of desire to marry Ruth. But consistently the narrator pictures him as a purposeful and an extremely faithful man in regard to God and His Word—even the spirit of God's Word. And here he refers to a primary concern of his—the land promise and the Seed promise in Israel (Gen. 12:1-3). The coming Redeemer would come through the seed of Abraham, Isaac and Jacob—and specifically through "Judah" (Gen. 49:10), who also raised up "seed" via a levirate type of relationship—albeit less ethical in its inception (cf. Gen. 38). As well, Boaz evidently wanted to honor God by being faithful to the principles of Deuteronomy 25:6b.

Interestingly enough, the fact that "Elimelech" and "Chilion" and "Mahlon" are written in the book of Ruth testifies to the success of Boaz's expressed purpose here (cf. Ps. 34:16; 109:15; Zech. 13:2). Whereas, "Mr. So and So", by trying to preserve his heritage, is no longer remembered by name. It has been "cut off," so to speak.

The purpose of the marriage between Boaz and Ruth was ultimately to honor Yahweh in obedience to His Word. Boaz wanted to be a part of God's plan as He was keeping His promise to Abraham, Isaac and Jacob. He wanted to extend redemption to the poor and needy. Boaz wanted to be faithful to God.

"You are witnesses today"

Verses 9 and 10 are bracketed by this phrase, thus serving as an official declaration by Boaz. He was using them as legal "witness" to what had taken place symbolically, and now confirmed verbally.

c. The proclamation of the witnesses (11a)

"All the people who were in the court, and the elders, said, 'We are witnesses'"
"All the people who were in the gate, and the old men/elders said, 'Witnesses.'" "All" those present, including the "elders"—likely the quorum of 10—agreed to be legal "witnesses". Then they went on to pray for Yahweh's blessing.

D. The prayer of the people (4:11b-12)

1. Fruitfulness like two women who left their family for Israel's sake (v. 11b)

"May the LORD make the woman who is coming into your home like Rachel and Leah, both of whom built the house of Israel"
All the people present there at the gate of Bethlehem that day prayed for Yahweh to "make" Ruth "like Rachel and Leah". Those two women were the legal wives of Jacob and in effect, "built the house of Israel" (cf. Gen 30; Bilhah and Zilpah were considered secondary wives). In other words, they were the legal mothers to the twelve sons that became the twelve tribes of Israel.

Perhaps this was a typical or somewhat standard blessing in Boaz's day. Yet it is interesting to note that Rachel and Leah were also non-Abrahamites—non-Jews—who left their homes pledging allegiance to Israel and his God (cf. Gen. 31:16). The people at the gate were asking Yahweh to make Boaz fruitful—i.e., father many children—through "the woman", Ruth.

2. Faithfulness [spiritual fortune and fame] for the glory of God (v. 11c)

"And may you achieve wealth in Ephrathah and become famous in Bethlehem"
The term here translated "wealth" was used in 2:1 and 3:11. It is often rendered "virtue", "excellence", "strength/might"— even "valor". Their prayer was literally, "may you do valiantly in Ephrathah, and proclaim the Name in Bethlehem". The NASB interprets the language to speak of fortune and fame. It is thus possible that they were praying for Boaz's prosperity and the perpetuity of his family/name. But it could possibly be a prayer that he would display spiritual excellence and promote the "Name" of God in Bethlehem (cf. Young's Literal Translation)—or perhaps promote the glory of God through his own name/fame.

The prayer of the people included *fruitfulness*; *faithfulness* [spiritual fortune and fame] for the glory of God; and . . .

3. Fellowship/participation in the Messianic Seed promise (v. 12)

"Moreover, may your house be like the house of Perez whom Tamar bore to Judah"
Their final prayer included a petition that Boaz's "house" would "be like the house of Perez whom Tamar bore to Judah". The most famous levirate birth in Israel's history was the birth of Perez and his twin brother as recorded in

the narrative of Genesis 38. Ruth 4:21 indicates that Boaz was in the lineage of "Perez". Thus in the most immediate context, they were praying that Boaz's marriage to Ruth would produce offspring like Tamar did for Judah.

A careful reading of Genesis 38 intimates that more was at stake in the seed of Judah through Tamar than merely children—the righteous hope of the Seed promise to Abraham, Isaac and Jacob (cf. Gen. 38:26—"she is more righteous than I"). This becomes clearer in light of the promise of Genesis 49:10.

"Through the offspring which the LORD shall give you by this young woman" The word "offspring" is literally "seed". Again, the crowd may have most immediately had in mind the desire that Boaz become the father of a whole clan within Israel just his own clan's forefather "Perez" had. But as previously stated, for the thoughtful listener, the mention of "seed", along with the reference to Tamar and Judah would bring forth an obvious allusion to the "Seed" promises of Genesis 3:15; 4:25; 15:3; 17:19; 21:12; 22:18 [cf. Gen. 12:1-3]; 26:4.

The next passage—4:13-21—reveals that the LORD answered their prayer abundantly.

Conclusion

The human redemption that took place in the book of Ruth was meant to picture God's infinitely greater redemption of fallen sinners. As Boaz had a plan and prepared to redeem Ruth—so God is intentional in His redemption. He does not just let history happen, but is diligently bringing out His plan and purposes.

We see from today's passage that redemption is costly to the redeemer. It takes true *hesed*—sacrificial love that does not look out for one's own personal interests, but rather seeks the highest good for the one being redeemed. Philippians 2 clearly outlines the cost of redemption for our Lord Jesus Christ. Second Corinthians 8:9 says, "For you know the grace of our Lord Jesus Christ, that though He was rich, yet for your sake He became poor, so that you through His poverty might become rich". What wondrous and costly love is this—that God would become a man to die in our place and suffer the righteous wrath that we deserved as sinners! But because He did, He has a Name above every Name. If Boaz became famous for the glory of God—Jesus Christ even more so.

May we worship the One who redeemed us at a far higher price than we can ever imagine.

As well, if we are God's instruments of redemption—i.e., vessels revealing God's redemption in Christ by how we live and what we say—then are we emptying ourselves and putting on the attitude and garments of servants so that others will see Christ's glory? Or are we concerned about our heritage and name on earth? Are we intentional in our love and relationships with others? Or are we always "responding" in the moment, according to our circumstances and emotions?

If we are to have a part in God's plan of redemption, then it will cost us. In Mark 8:35-36 Jesus said: "For whoever wishes to save his life will lose it, but whoever loses his life for My sake and the gospel's will save it. For what does it profit a man to gain the whole world, and forfeit his soul?"

As we will see next time, however, if we do indeed embrace the cost of being an instrument in God's hands as we love others, He gives us the wondrous privilege of participating in His glorious plan of redemption!

Expository Sermon:
The Romance of Redemption

Ruth 4:1-12

by Brad Brandt

The week that I was preparing this message a piece of mail came across my desk with one of those "kids say the craziest things" kind of lists (Letter from W. Paul Jackson, January 2007). Apparently a group of 7-10 year olds was asked a variety of questions about marriage. One of the questions was "How do you decide who to marry?" Ten-year-old Alan said, "You got to find somebody who likes the same stuff. Like, if you like sports, she should like it that you like sports, and should keep the chips and dip coming." Ten-year-old Kristen answered, "No person really decides before they grow up who they're going to marry. God decides it all way before and you get to find out later who you're stuck with!" Another question was: "Is it better to be single or married?" Nine-year-old Anita said, "It's better for girls to be single but not for boys. Boys need someone to clean up after them."

It kind of makes you wonder where these children picked up their perspectives on marriage, doesn't it? I chuckle at Kristen's notion that *God decides it* and *you're stuck with it!* When a child says that, it's funny. Unfortunately, there are far too many adults that cling to the same way of thinking. A good dose of the book of Ruth offers all of us plenty of hope and help.

The story of Ruth is a wonderful love story. Of course, the story of Ruth, as we've been seeing thus far, is really a story about *God*, the God who works through providence to accomplish His good plan for His people.

To reset the backdrop, the book of Ruth begins during the time of the judges in Israel. Due to a famine, a Jewish man named Elimelech moved with his wife, Naomi, and their sons, Mahlon and Chilion, away from the promised land to Moab in search of food. While there, the father and his two sons died, leaving Naomi alone with her two Moabite daughters-in-law. When Naomi decided to return to Bethlehem, she urged Ruth and Orpah to stay in Moab. She convinced Orpah to do the logical thing and stay, but she couldn't shake Ruth who had become a believer in the Lord God of Israel.

After returning to Israel, Ruth went looking for food in the grain fields of Bethlehem and there met Boaz, a kinsman of her deceased husband. In our last study we watched Ruth as she carried out Naomi's plan, went to Boaz, and made it clear that she would marry her kinsman redeemer if he was so inclined. Boaz instantly expressed his willingness and eager desire to do so, but then dropped a shocking piece of news. There was a *nearer* kinsman,

Chapter 4: The Romance of Redemption ■

another man who according to the laws of levirate marriage in Israel had first dibs on Ruth. "If he is not willing, as surely as the LORD lives I will do it," Boaz told Ruth (3:13).

We have come to the climax of this delightful story. Through the actions of Boaz in Ruth 4:1-12 we see the romance of redemption in action. We also observe a beautiful illustration of four characteristics of true love.

I. True love takes action (1-4).

Before we actually look at the story itself allow me to point out what we're about to see. There's a contrast in chapter 4, a contrast between two redeemers. There's a loving redeemer named Boaz, and there's a self-focused, unnamed redeemer. Both men had the proper qualifications to help a destitute family, but only one did so. As we see Boaz in action the Scriptures are giving us a type of another Redeemer, one who exhibited perfect love for a destitute world, that being, of course, the Lord Jesus Himself.

The first thing we learn about true love from Boaz is that it *takes action*. John later would write in 1 John 3:18, "Dear children, let us not love with words or tongue but with actions and in truth." That's what Boaz did in chapter 4.

You may recall the final words in chapter 3 where Naomi said this to Ruth about Boaz: "Wait, my daughter, until you find out what happens. For the man will not rest until the matter is settled today." Naomi was right. As chapter 4 begins…

A. Boaz took steps to provide redemption (1-4a).
Three steps, to be specific…

1. He made contact with the nearer kinsman (1).
"Meanwhile Boaz went up to the town gate and sat there. When the kinsman-redeemer he had mentioned came along, Boaz said, 'Come over here, my friend, and sit down.' So he went over and sat down."

In Israel the town gate was the equivalent of our county courthouse. It's where legal business was settled. What's more, in a day before cell phones and pagers, the best way to make contact with someone was to wait at the city gate. Sooner or later everyone passed that way (Huey, p. 541).

As the story begins Boaz exhibits wisdom, tact, determination, a commitment to do things the right way, and a selfless love for Ruth, the one he hopes to marry. He makes contact with the man who is legally first in line to marry and provide protection for Ruth.

It's worth noting that the writer never gives the name of the nearer kinsman anywhere in the story. He simply identifies him by a Hebrew phrase that rhymes, *paloni almoni*. The NIV translates it 'my friend' but the AV's 'such a one' is more literal. Mr. 'So and So' would be the sense. For sure, Boaz knew his name—he was related to him—but the author of Ruth doesn't provide us with his name for a reason we'll discuss shortly.

When Boaz saw Mr. So and So, he greeted him and beckoned him to sit down on a bench at the gate. Then he demonstrated his love for Ruth by taking a second step.

2. He recruited elders (2).

"Boaz took ten of the elders of the town and said, 'Sit here,' and they did so." It's obvious Boaz has thought this through. He is setting up a court for legal proceedings. The elders (a term which comes from the Hebrew word meaning "to have a beard") held a significant place in Jewish society. They possessed clout both politically and judicially. With Mr. So and So seated and the elders in place, Boaz moved to step 3…

3. He informed the nearer kinsman about Naomi's land (3-4a).

Verse 3—"Then he said to the kinsman-redeemer, 'Naomi, who has come back from Moab, is selling the piece of land that belonged to our brother Elimelech.'" The word 'brother' seems to be used loosely here. There is rabbinic tradition, however, that says that Boaz was a nephew of Elimelech and the other man an actual brother of Elimelech, but that is merely conjecture (Goslinga, p. 543; J. Vernon McGee agrees, citing Keil and Delitzsch who confirm this view).

Although we didn't know it until now in the story, Naomi had a piece of property. It was actually Elimelech's before he died and would have been their sons' if they had lived. But since they were gone, it was now Naomi's, and since she was so poor she was selling it. One explanation is that Elimelech sold this property before taking his family to Moab, and that Naomi is now trying to exercise the family's right to redeem the land—remember, the law in Israel stipulated that land was not to be sold permanently but was to be recovered by the rightful family through the payment of the redemption price. According to this explanation, Naomi is now trying to "buy back" the family land but since she has no money, she is requesting a kinsman redeemer do it for her. In other words, she is "selling" the right of redemption (see *NIV Study Bible*, footnote on Ruth 4:3).

Boaz continues his explanation to Mr. So and So in verse 4: "I thought I should bring the matter to your attention [lit. 'I thought I should uncover your ear'] and suggest that you buy it in the presence of these seated here and in the presence of the elders of my people. If you will redeem it, do so. But if you will not, tell me, so I will know. For no one has the right to do it except you, and I am next in line."

We might wonder, "What is Boaz doing bringing up this land issue? I thought he was taking steps to marry Ruth." Just wait. It will soon be apparent. For now, allow me to restate the obvious. Boaz took steps to provide redemption, even if he ended up not being the one who provided the redemption. He would ensure Ruth and Naomi are provided for. That's what love does. Love demonstrates itself through action. Talk is often cheap, but action speaks loudly.

In contrast to Boaz who took action, notice what the nearer kinsman did.

B. The nearer kinsman said he would provide redemption (4b).

That's right, he said he would. Notice the end of verse 4, "'I will redeem it,' he said." And why did he say he would do it? Because Mr. So and So is a good businessman. It's a good deal to get this piece of property back in the family. More land means more crops. More crops mean more money. More money means more potential for the good life.

Nothing wrong with being a businessman who's got a nose for a good deal. Nothing wrong with buying land from a widow. Nothing wrong with making the most of God-given opportunities. But there's a contrast here, a day and night contrast, between two men who were qualified to redeem a piece of property. By looking at the actions of these two men we can make two simple observations.

1. It is natural to do what is good for yourself.

That's what Mr. So and So did. He assessed the situation, decided the land purchase would be good for him, and said, "Sure, I will redeem it." He did what came naturally to him, just like we so easily do. It is natural to do what is good for yourself. On the other hand...

2. It is love to do what is good for others.

And that's what Boaz did. He took steps to do what would be in the best interest of Ruth, a family that had no male descendant, and a nation whose God received honor when its citizens did the loving thing by obeying the laws He gave them.

Beloved, we live in a world that doesn't know what love is, where love is finding someone who will give you what you want—sex, a good time, image, and so on. That's not love. Love focuses *outward*. Love thinks about what is good for the *other* person and does that. For God so loved the world that He *gave His only Son*. That's love.

True love takes action. Here's a second characteristic illustrated by Boaz.

II. True love is willing to pay the price (5-6).

The contrast between Boaz and Mr. So and So continues...

A. Boaz informed the nearer kinsman of the price of redemption (5).
"Then Boaz said, 'On the day you buy the land from Naomi and from Ruth the Moabitess, you acquire the dead man's widow, in order to maintain the name of the dead with his property.'"

Boaz is a wise man. He knows that pleading for mercy from Mr. So and So won't work, that saying, "Please! I love Ruth! I want to marry Ruth, but I can't unless you help me because you are the nearest kinsman. Please let me redeem her!" won't get anywhere. But this will. The bottom line. Money talks. Boaz informs Mr. So and So of a footnote in the contract of the land purchase. "If you get the dead man's land, you also get his widow," Boaz explains. "And the child you have with her will get the land."

It was called levirate marriage, and as we learned previously, it was a God-given law in Israel to protect widows and families (Deut. 25:5-6). That piece of information gave Mr. So and So second thoughts.

Verse 6—"At this, the kinsman-redeemer said, 'Then I cannot redeem it because I might endanger my own estate. You redeem it yourself. I cannot do it.'" In other words...

B. The nearer kinsman decided the price was too high (6).
At first, the nearer kinsman was willing to buy Naomi's land, for although it would cost him some up front money, the expense would be worth it to him. His property holdings would increase. What's more, Jewish law stipulated that after Naomi and Ruth died, the land would return to the clan of Elimelech anyway. That meant the land would revert to him and his sons (and perhaps partly to Boaz). The nearer kinsman saw this as a win-win situation. Until Boaz mentioned the part about Ruth. If the nearer kinsman bought the field AND acquired Ruth, the field would belong not to his family but to the future son of Ruth.

Furthermore, this meant he would have to spend his own children's inheritance (his words indicate he already had children) to buy land that would end up belonging to Ruth's future son. That changed everything. If he married Ruth and fathered a son by her, that meant he would lose money now and the land later (Goslinga, p. 548). This was no longer a bargain, but a liability.

For the nearer kinsman it boiled down to money. He could not afford to buy the field and support a widow. Notice that...

1. He said he could not do it.
That's not really true. He could do it if he wanted to. It's just that the care of Ruth would cost him. The truth is...

2. He meant he would not do it.
Although he was qualified to be the redeemer, and furthermore had the means

to fulfill the role of redeemer, he was not willing to pay the necessary redemption price. "It might endanger my estate," he said.

I remind you we don't even know Mr. So and So's name. Do you see the irony in this? As Cassel observes, "It remains…an instructive fact that he who was so anxious for the preservation of his own inheritance, is not now even known by name" (cited in Leon Morris, p. 298).

It's possible that something else influenced the nearer kinsman's change of mind, specifically Ruth's nationality. "Ruth *the Moabitess*," Boaz stressed. The fact that Ruth was a Gentile and not a Jew seems to be a factor in the kinsman's decision. He's not quite sure about having a son with this Gentile woman. The price was too high.

Boaz knew better. He'd taken time to get to know Ruth. Granted, she was a Moabitess. That was *in her past*, and that's the point. That was in her past. She may have been born in Moab, but now she is in Israel. She no longer believed in the Moabite god of her parents, Chemosh, but in the true God, Yahweh, the Savior of Israel whom she loved and committed herself to serve until death (1:16-17). And she no longer lived as she used to in Moab, in sense-driven violation of God's Law, but she now delighted in obeying the Law of the Lord.

When the living God enters a person's life He makes them new. Aren't you glad of that fact? Second Corinthians 5:17 puts it this way, "Therefore, if anyone is in Christ, he is a new creation; the old has gone, the new has come!"

According to Mr. So and So the price was simply too high. But Boaz thought otherwise! True love is willing to pay the price!

III. True love is willing to be accountable (7-10).
The writer gives us a piece of cultural information in verse 7: "Now in earlier times in Israel, for the redemption and transfer of property to become final, one party took off his sandal and gave it to the other. This was the method of legalizing transactions in Israel." In other words, there were no sales receipts. A sandal did the trick.

Verse 8 states, "So the kinsman-redeemer said to Boaz, 'Buy it yourself.' And he removed his sandal." In Psalm 60:8 God says, "Moab is my washbasin, upon Edom I toss my sandal; over Philistia I shout in triumph." Here Mr. So and So removed his sandal to make it official that he was not going to fulfill the duty of the kinsman redeemer. By giving it to Boaz…

A. The nearer kinsman gave up his right to redemption (7-8).
Can't you see this fellow walking home that day wearing one sandal? He wasn't a bad guy. He didn't do anything illegal. He assessed the situation and did the rational thing.

Nonetheless, the contrast is striking. Mr. So and So was willing to take, but Boaz was willing to give. Mr. So and So was concerned about himself and endangering his estate, but Boaz was selfless and concerned about the care of two widows. Mr. So and So did the logical thing, but Boaz did the loving thing. Whereas Mr. So and So gave up his right to redemption…

B. Boaz made a public commitment to be a faithful redeemer (9-10).

Verses 9-10—"Then Boaz announced to the elders and all the people [in a time when few written records were kept it was important to have witnesses who could attest that a transaction was legal], 'Today you are witnesses that I have bought from Naomi all the property of Elimelech, Kilion and Mahlon. I have also acquired Ruth the Moabitess, Mahlon's widow, as my wife, in order to maintain the name of the dead with his property, so that his name will not disappear from among his family or from the town records. Today you are witnesses!'"

The author makes it clear that Boaz made two public commitments that day…

1. He promised to be a good husband to Ruth.
And…

2. He promised to maintain the name of the dead.
He actually mentions Ruth's first husband by name, Mahlon. A lesser man might avoid the subject, but Boaz talks openly about the first husband of the woman he intends to marry. And he talks openly about her past. Note the words, 'Ruth the Moabitess' again. There's no derogatory intent in Boaz's words. He's simply stating a fact. Some say that love is blind, but Boaz wasn't blind. He knew exactly who he was marrying. He knew about Ruth's past and her new life in the present.

Huey comments about the author's repeated reference to 'Ruth the Moabitess' in the book: "He may have wanted to suggest that if a mere human being could love an outcast, redeem her, and bring her into fellowship with himself, God could love all the outcasts of the world, redeem them, and bring them into fellowship with himself" (Huey, p. 544).

Goslinga observes, "Boaz here stood revealed as a great and selfless man, a splendid contrast to the petty, self-seeking figure of the nearest kinsman redeemer" (Goslinga, p. 549). The nearer kinsman operated by the philosophy, "What's the least I can do? How little is enough?" By contrast, Boaz models true love, "What's the most I can do to implement God's good law for the good of others?" (Goslinga, p. 550)

May I say a word to those who are contemplating marriage? Marriage is a huge commitment and not to be entered into lightly. You would do well to receive godly counsel *before* entering marriage to ensure you have come to grips with the truth about the person you are marrying. Do you know who the person really is, their past, their character in the present, their aspirations for the future?

Warren Wiersbe tells the painful story about John Wesley's marriage:

> While crossing a bridge in London, John Wesley stumbled and sprained his ankle. Some friends carried him to the house of Mrs. Mary Vazielle on Threadneedle Street. She was a widow with several children. She cared for Wesley and his response to her concern was to ask her to marry him. If we were writing fiction we might say that the sprained ankle was God's providential way to bring those people together. But the marriage was a disaster, and Mary finally left John.
>
> Had Wesley consulted with his brother Charles, and asked for the prayers of the brethren, he might have avoided that unfortunate situation. Mary was accustomed to her quiet home, and it was difficult for her to travel with her husband and stay in uncomfortable inns. It is unfortunate that Mary was not content just to ignore John's ministry; she actually opposed it. She gave certain personal letters to his enemies and even made additions to them that made them worse! Once she even pulled her husband around on the floor by his hair! "I felt as though I could have knocked the soul out of her!" one of Wesley's friends said. Wesley concluded that his unhappy marriage encouraged him to work harder and not complain about missing the comforts of a home. Certainly it encouraged him to be away from home more! (W. Wiersbe, *Wycliffe Handbook of Preaching and Preachers*, Moody Press, 1984, p. 246)

How tragic! And how refreshing to see the way Boaz approached marriage! He didn't marry out of a whim, nor due to infatuation as so often is the case today. He faced reality concerning Ruth and made a commitment to love her. True love takes action. True love is willing to pay the price. True love is willing to be accountable. Finally...

IV. True love receives God's blessing (11-12).

In response to Boaz's public commitment, the people at the gate called upon Yahweh and asked Him for three blessings...

A. The people asked the Lord to bless Ruth (11a).

Verse 11a—"Then the elders and all those at the gate said, 'We are witnesses. May the LORD make the woman who is coming into your home like Rachel and Leah, who together built up the house of Israel.'" Notice that the people affirm that *the Lord* is the giver of children, that He is the One who gave children to Rachel and Leah, the wives of Jacob, children through which the Lord formed the nation of Israel. Note also the people's view of the purpose of marriage, to have children and thereby populate the promised land. In stark contrast, think about how many people view marriage today. They marry seeking *personal gratification*. "The purpose of marriage is *to satisfy me*," they believe. No wonder so many marriages fail.

B. The people asked the Lord to bless Boaz. (11b)

Verse 11b—"May you have standing in Ephrathah and be famous in Bethlehem." God loves to give honor to those who honor Him. "Do that!" the people are saying. "Give honor to this man who has shown himself to be a man of honor!"

C. The people asked the Lord to bless their offspring. (12)

Verse 12—"Through the offspring the LORD gives you by this young woman, may your family be like that of Perez, whom Tamar bore to Judah." Since the first son would legally be reckoned as Mahlon's, the people ask the Lord to give Boaz many more children who would legally be his. Again, the people affirm that children come from the Lord. They mention Tamar, an ancestress of Boaz who had a levirate son fathered by Judah. "Do for Boaz and Ruth what you did for Judah and Tamar. Give them offspring!"

Answer this. Did the Lord grant this prayer request the people offered that day? Indeed, He did! In three ways…

1. The prayer was immediately answered through Obed (17).

Verse 13—"So Boaz took Ruth and she became his wife. Then he went to her, and the LORD enabled her to conceive, and she gave birth to a son." Verse 17—"And they named him Obed." God answered the prayer! But He wasn't finished…

2. The prayer was eventually answered through David (22).

Verse 17 continues, "And they named him Obed. He was the father of Jesse, the father of David." As a result of the moral and spiritual decline during the period of the judges, it became obvious that Israel needed a godly leader to bring them back to the Lord. The Lord was preparing that man long before he was born. King David, the man God Himself later called "a man after my own heart" (Acts 13:22) was the great-grandson of Boaz and Ruth.

There was another, even greater fulfillment to this prayer request. The kinsman redeemer Boaz foreshadowed another Redeemer, the final one. Job announced in Job 19:25, "I know that my Redeemer lives, and that in the end he will stand upon the earth." Boaz rescued two helpless widows. The final Redeemer rescued a helpless humanity!

Here's how He did it. The Son of God agreed to come to earth as a man. He came to make a redemption payment as Paul explains in Galatians 4:4-5, "But when the time had fully come, God sent his Son, born of a woman, born under law, to redeem those under law, that we might receive the full rights of sons." In order to redeem man, God became a man. There could have been no redemption if the Son of God had not become our kinsman. So that's what He did. God the Son entered the world as a man through the virgin birth in the person of Jesus Christ. And while on the earth, the perfect God-man willing-ly paid the redemption price for sinners. The cost? His own life. Jesus shed His blood and died on the cross. On the third day God verified His acceptance of the payment price by raising His Son from the dead.

In the book of Ruth, the nearer kinsman *could have* but chose not to redeem. In contrast, Kinsman Jesus, like Boaz, not only *could have* but willingly and joyfully *chose* to redeem! Of this Redeemer Hebrews 12:2 states, "…Who for the joy set before him endured the cross, scorning its shame, and sat down at the right hand of the throne of God."

It's one thing to be *able* to do something, but that's not enough. For a task to be accomplished the one who is able must additionally be *willing* to do so. And Jesus was!

No wonder Paul praised Him in Ephesians 1:7: "In him we have *redemption* through his blood, the forgiveness of sins, in accordance with the riches of God's grace."

The theme of redemption is one of the great themes in the Bible. Redemption means "to purchase by paying a price" (J. Vernon McGee, p. 167). Boaz redeemed some land and two helpless widows by paying some money. But Jesus redeemed a multitude of undeserving sinners by spilling His own blood.

Did you realize that this is the theme of heaven's song? It is according to Revelation 5:9: "And they sang a new song: 'You are worthy to take the scroll and to open its seals, because you were slain, and with your blood you pur-chased men [KJV 'have *redeemed* us'] for God from every tribe and language and people and nation.'" Yes…

3. The prayer was ultimately answered through Jesus.
The question is, have you done what Ruth did? Have you asked the Kinsman Redeemer to redeem you, and have you come to rest in His saving care? If by God's grace you have, then you can sing the following…

> Redeemed, how I love to proclaim it!
> Redeemed by the blood of the Lamb;
> Redeemed thro' His infinite mercy,
> His child and forever I am.
> Redeemed, and so happy in Jesus,
> No language my rapture can tell;
> I know that the light of His presence

With me doth continually dwell.

I think of my blessed Redeemer,
I think of Him all the day long:
I sing, for I cannot be silent;
His love is the theme of my song.

Redeemed, redeemed,
Redeemed by the blood of the Lamb;
Redeemed, how I love to proclaim it!
His child and forever I am.
(Fanny Crosby, "Redeemed")

Getting Intentional About Application

by Brad Brandt

When I began my studies as a freshman in college, I was a pre-med major intending to become a medical missionary some day. My wife often says in jest, "When we were dating I thought I was going to marry a doctor, not a pastor." God's ways are intriguing.

The fact is, I've never set a broken bone in my life (I switched majors my sophomore year to pre-seminary Bible). Yet ironically, as a pastor I set bones all the time, spiritual bones, that is. I have in mind Paul's exhortation in Galatians 6:1, "Brothers, if someone is caught in a sin, you who are spiritual should *restore* [Greek, *katartizo*, used elsewhere of mending torn nets and also of setting broken bones so they function again] him gently. But watch yourself, or you also may be tempted."

It's been well said that a pastor is a doctor of the soul. In many ways I view pastoral ministry in a small community as being—to borrow terminology from the medical world—a General Practitioner. Rather than specializing on one particular facet of soul work, I am privileged to equip the saints in a variety of ways. I preach the Word publicly, counsel the Word privately, apply the Word personally to the hurting in hospitals and homes, and evangelize with the Word expectantly with those whom God brings into my life. Of course, my God-given calling isn't to do the work of the ministry for the saints, but to equip the saints to do the ministry (Eph. 4:11-12).

That's why *Getting Intentional About Application* is so important. My people need more than sermons, as vital as good, expositional sermons are. As a pastor my calling is to engage in a Word-centered ministry that helps God's people experience the kind of life the Great Physician intended. The aim isn't learning for learning's sake. The aim is learning for *living's* sake, all to the glory of God. It is my privilege to help God's people "in all things grow up into Him who is the Head, that is, Christ" (Eph. 4:15).

With these thoughts in mind, I offer the following tools once again for your consideration. I hope you'll gain a seed thought or two that will serve you well as you seek to administer the good medicine of God's Word to the Body of Christ.

Tool #1: A Teaching Outline

It's been well said, "If there is a mist in the pulpit there will be fog in the pew." I have found the use of a "main idea" (or "proposition") statement to be quite helpful at eliminating pulpit mist. Typically I develop this statement after the basic exegetical work on a text is completed, in preparation for the creation of a preaching outline. In one sentence (sometimes it stretches to two) I seek to state as clearly as possible what the message is all about. If someone called and woke me up in the middle of a Saturday night and asked, "Pastor Brad, what are you preaching tomorrow?" this 'main idea' statement should come out automatically (okay, that's a bit of an exaggeration but you get the idea; I should clarify that I've never received a midnight phone call requesting sermon information, for other requests indeed, but not sermon info!).

I typically state the "main idea" somewhere towards the beginning of the sermon, usually after an opening illustration and right before launching into the first main point. Below you will notice the main idea and sermon outline for Ruth 4:1-12.

From Brad's exposition:

Main Idea: Through the actions of Boaz in Ruth 4:1-12 we see the romance of redemption which beautifully illustrates for us four characteristics of true love.

I.   **True love takes action (1-4).**
   A.   **Boaz took steps to provide redemption (1-4a).**
      1. He made contact with the nearer kinsman (1).
      2. He recruited elders (2).
      3. He informed the nearer kinsman about Naomi's land (3-4a).
   B.   **The nearer kinsman said he would provide redemption (4b).**
      1. It is natural to do what is good for yourself.
      2. It is love to do what is good for others.
II. **True love is willing to pay the price (5-6).**
   A.   **Boaz informed the nearer kinsman of the price of redemption (5).**
   B.   **The nearer kinsman decided the price was too high (6).**
      1. He said he could not do it.
      2. He meant he would not do it.
III. **True love is willing to be accountable (7-10).**
   A.   **The nearer kinsman gave up his right to redemption (7-8).**
   B.   **Boaz made a public commitment to be a faithful redeemer (9-10).**
      1. He promised to be a good husband to Ruth.
      2. He promised to maintain the name of the dead.
IV. **True love receives God's blessing (11-12).**
   A.   **The people asked the Lord to bless Ruth (11a).**
   B.   **The people asked the Lord to bless Boaz (11b).**
   C.   **The people asked the Lord to bless their offspring (12).**
      1. The prayer was immediately answered through Obed (17).
      2. The prayer was eventually answered through David (22).
      3. The prayer was ultimately answered through Jesus.

Tool #2: "Digging Deeper" Discussion Questions

I appreciate a person who can ask good questions. I've noticed that the use of well crafted questions in the delivery of a sermon facilitates a real connection between a preacher and a congregation. While preaching I try to ask the kinds of questions the text raised for me while interacting with the Scriptures earlier in my study. The rest of the sermon then seeks to answer those questions.

Good questions are also invaluable as we seek to help God's people apply God's Word to their lives. Parents could use the "digging deeper" questions with their children over Sunday dinner. Sunday School (or Adult Bible Fellowship) classes could interact with them as a follow-up to the Ruth sermons. Other possible uses were mentioned in previous chapters. Here are some suggested questions to get started with Ruth 4:1-12.

Questions for Clarification:
1. In what ways were Boaz and the nearer kinsman *similar*?
2. In what ways were Boaz and the nearer kinsman *different*?
3. Why did the nearer kinsman change his mind about redeeming Naomi's property?
4. What does this story teach us about our Redeemer, Jesus Christ?
5. What are some other passages in God's Word that teach us about the subject of *redemption*? Find at least five other passages, read them, and summarize in a sentence one insight they each give us.

Questions for Application:
1. What are some practical things we can do to grow in our appreciation for the work of *redemption* that Christ accomplished?
2. What did you learn about love in this study that was helpful?
3. What counsel should we give to someone if they say they don't *feel* love any longer for their spouse? Use Scripture to support your answer.
4. What practical things can we do to grow in our ability to demonstrate the kind of love Boaz exhibited in the book of Ruth?
5. What is one specific step you believe God would want you to take this week, by His grace, in light of what you have learned from Ruth 4?

Tool #3: A Counseling Case Study
The following case study is written for use in small groups after the congregation has heard a message from Ruth 4:1-12. The group leader should read the scenario and then facilitate interaction by means of the discussion questions. Group members should be encouraged to support their answers by using Scripture (e.g. "In light of what verse 2 says, I think…").

Scenario: Angela (a fictitious character) has met "Mr. Right." That's what she has been telling your small group at church for the past two Sundays. She met Larry just four months ago at the school where they both teach. Angela, who became a believer three years ago while in college, is a 23-year-old, first year elementary school teacher. Larry, age 22 and also in his first year of teaching, is an only child who still lives at home. Angela says she "led him to the Lord" shortly after they met.

"When's the wedding?" someone asks Angela just before the beginning of this week's small group meeting.

"Three weeks from Saturday!" she responds. "We're going to have a quaint ceremony at Larry's parent's lodge. You're all invited!"

"Whoa! Three weeks?" someone in the crowd chimes in—it was more of a statement than a question. "That's a pretty quick romance, isn't it?"

Angela insists it's because "God brought us together" and "It was love at first sight" and "We just know we're right for each other."

No one says anything else about the wedding until the small group meeting ends that night. As people are leaving, Angela approaches you (the group leader) and asks, "Can I ask you something? Why do I get the feeling that not everybody here is as excited as I am about me getting married? I want to know."

Case Study Discussion Questions:
1. Angela's view of love seems more influenced by Hollywood than the Bible. How so?

2. What are some questions that Angela may need to address? Take some time to frame those questions now.

3. Supposing you are the group leader that Angela approaches, how would you respond to her? How might you use the story of Ruth in the conversation?

Tool #4: Counseling Assignments Utilizing Ruth 4:1-12
Suppose Angela demonstrated a teachable spirit in the above scenario and expressed a willingness to meet the following week for counseling. The book of Ruth could serve you well as an excellent place to begin with Angela as you seek to help her honor God in her life. You might ask her to complete the following assignments and then go over them with her at the beginning of the counseling session (if you are a man I would encourage you to include your wife in the session).

Assignments to be Completed Before This Week's Counseling Appointment:
1. Read through the book of Ruth, one chapter per day for four days. Each time you read answer the following three questions (two or three sentences per answer):

a. What did I learn about *God* from this chapter?

b. What did I learn about *love* from this chapter?

c. What did I learn about *decision-making* from this chapter?

d. What did I learn about *marriage* from this chapter?

2. After you finish reading through the book of Ruth, write down your observations about the following individuals...

How would you describe Naomi?

How would you describe Ruth?

How would you describe Orpah?

How would you describe Boaz?

3. What questions did your reading of the book of Ruth raise for you? Write them down and we'll discuss them at our meeting.

Note to Counselor: If Larry is willing to participate with Angela in this counseling session with you, have him complete the same assignment. You may want to talk with him personally prior to the session to introduce yourself (if you don't already know Larry) and to explain the purpose of the assignment.

CHAPTER

 **5**

Watching God Bring Good Out of Bad

Ruth 4:13-22

Expositional Commentary and Outline:
The Prize of Redemption—Participation in God's Plan of Redemption

Expository Sermon:
Watching God Bring Good Out of Bad

Getting Intentional About Application

Tool #1: A Teaching Outline
Tool #2: "Digging Deeper" Discussion Questions
Tool #3: A Counseling Case Study
Tool #4: Counseling Assignments

Expositional Outline:

Ruth 4:13-22

by Rick Kress

The Book of Ruth—A Portrait of God's Loyal Love, Sovereign Redemption, and the Faith of His Believing Remnant

I. The pain of covenant faithlessness [an empty profession] (1:1-5)
II. The pity of God and the initial glimmers of faith (1:6-22)
III. The providential provision and protection of God for the destitute who live by faith (2:1-23)
IV. The pursuit of redemption, and the subsequent promise of redemption (3:1-18)
V. The purchase of redemption (4:1-12)
VI. The prize of redemption—participation in God's plan of redemption (4:13-22)
   A. The son born to Boaz and Ruth—and his significance to Naomi (4:13-17)
      1. The birth of a son in the sovereignty of God—a reoccurring event in Israel's sacred history (4:13)
         a. The obedience of Boaz and Ruth/human responsibility
         b. The overriding hand of God/divine sovereignty
      2. The blessing of Yahweh [and perhaps a prayer for the boy] (4:14)
         a. The praise of Yahweh
         b. The prayer that his [the boy's] or His [Yahweh's] name be proclaimed in Israel [both would be true in relation to the other]
      3. The blessings of Naomi (4:15-17)
         a. The prayer for longevity (v. 15a)
         b. The praise of Ruth's love for Naomi (v. 15b)
         c. The participation in the son's upbringing (v. 16)
         d. The personal name of the son—Obed, meaning "one who serves" (v. 17)
         e. The progeny of the son (v. 17c)
   B. The sovereign significance of that son in God's plan of redemption (4:18-22)
      1. The "generations" of Perez (v. 18a)
      2. The genealogy of David (v. 18b-22)
         a. Perez
         b. Hezron
         c. Ram
         d. Amminadab
         e. Nahshon
         f. Salmon
         g. Boaz
         h. Obed
         i. Jesse
         j. David

Expositional Commentary:
The Prize of Redemption—Participation in God's
Plan of Redemption

Ruth 4:13-22

by Rick Kress

Human illustrations always fall short in describing divine truths, but they may still convey at least a descriptive element from the lesser to the greater. That being said, perhaps today's message is best introduced with this illustration. Salvation is like a parade of beautifully restored classic automobiles. Each car was found in its own place—some in the local dump or junkyard; some were abandoned and rusted in a field; others were hidden in a garage but for lack of use were broken down. But the master restorer came and wonderfully renewed and actually made these old junkers better than new. That, in and of it itself, would be wonderful. But then he takes them all and puts them on display in a parade. As the cars pass by, people are able to admire the restorative prowess and skill of the restorer. These old cars are not renewed for themselves—but rather to play a role in a larger display of glory.

In Ruth 4:13-22 we'll see two main points that reveal the wonderful privilege that believers can have as they live a life of faith and love.

Let's begin looking at the first point in this final passage of the book of Ruth.

VI. The prize of redemption—participation in God's plan of redemption (4:13-22)
A. The son born to Boaz and Ruth—and his significance to Naomi (4:13-17)
1. The birth of a son in the sovereignty of God—a reoccurring event in Israel's sacred history (4:13)
a. The obedience of Boaz and Ruth/human responsibility

"So Boaz took Ruth, and she became his wife, and he went in to her"

The word "took" as an expression of marriage is seen in other notable marriages such as Abram's marriage to Sarai (Gen. 11:29) and Isaac's marriage to Rebekah (Gen. 24:67; cf. 25:1; Ex. 2:1; 6:20, 23; Deut. 20:7). "Boaz married Ruth, and she became his wife". Ruth had first acknowledged herself to be a "foreigner" in 2:10 and then lower than Boaz's lowest slave in 2:13. In 3:9 she identified herself as his "maidservant". But here the narrator says, "she became his *wife*" (emphasis added). What amazing grace, and an amazing turn of events from the human perspective.

The phrase "he went in to her" is a euphemism for sexual relations. Boaz's stated purpose for marriage was to obey the spirit of the law of redemption in regard to the wife of a brother—and raise up seed for that brother (4:5b; cf.

Deut. 25:5-6). In other words, he wanted to obey God by trying to give the deceased relative's widow a child. Here then we see the obedience of Boaz and Ruth. No doubt it would be the natural consummation of the marital relationship—but still it should be noted that they indeed did their part in trying to "raise up the name of the deceased" (4:5).

b. The overriding hand of God/divine sovereignty
"And the LORD enabled her to conceive, and she gave birth to a son"
A literal rendering of this sentence would be: "And Yahweh gave to her conception, and she bore a son". This pregnancy was a "gift" of God as are all children (Ps. 127:3). But it should be remembered that Ruth had been barren, very possibly through 10 years of marriage (cf. 1:4-5). Much like such notable women in the Scriptures as Sara (Gen. 11:30; 16:1; 21:1-2), Rebekah (Gen. 25:21), and Rachel and Leah (Gen. 29:31; 30:2, 17, 22)—it was Yahweh who enabled Ruth to "conceive" (cf. 1 Sam. 1:5, 19-20; Luke 1:7, 24).

In addition, we see the sovereign hand of God in that "she gave birth *to a son*" (emphasis added). He could become heir to the family name and property, as well as support the family in the future. But even beyond that, in the future—as we'll see in the genealogy at the end of the chapter—he could become a forefather to the future king/King (see also Gen. 3:15 for the "seed" promise that was the hope of every Israelite woman). The birth of a male child after years of barrenness would have alerted the original audience that God was up to something of significance concerning His unique plan and program, which would result in the redemption of fallen sinners. The genealogy at the end of the chapter would confirm that suspicion, as it culminated in the birth of "David"—Israel's greatest king, save the Lord Jesus Christ. Notably then, the crowd's prayer of verses 11-12 was finding initial fulfillment here.

So with a very succinct statement here in verse 13, the narrator highlights how God used the submissive obedience of two believing individuals to bring about His sovereign purpose and advance His plan of redemption.

2. The blessing of Yahweh [and perhaps a prayer for the boy] (4:14)
a. The praise of Yahweh
"Then the women said to Naomi, 'Blessed is the LORD who has not left you without a redeemer today'"
The birth of this special and somewhat miraculous son brought praise from "the women" of Bethlehem. The phrase "blessed be Yahweh" is an acknowledgment of His innate goodness and the goodness of His actions toward men. He blesses man with His good purposes and man blesses Him for who He is and what He had done. Specifically here, "the women" praise Yahweh in relation to "Naomi" who had come back to Bethlehem with a very different out-

look on Yahweh's sovereignty the year before—see especially 1:20-21.

The reference to Naomi's "redeemer" could potentially refer to Boaz, or Yahweh Himself, but in context seems to refer to the son born to Ruth and Boaz (see especially the pronouns that culminate in the last phrase of v. 15— "given birth to him"). He was now the closest relative to Naomi. He would eventually serve as her security and the heir of the family name and property.

The point is that Yahweh was praised because of His sovereign goodness and mercy toward Naomi in providing for her.

b. The prayer that his [the boy's] or His [Yahweh's] name be proclaimed in Israel [both would be true in relation to the other]

"And may his name become famous in Israel"

Using a similar phrase as the prayer of verse 11, here the women prayed— "may his name be proclaimed in Israel". Because of the pronoun "his" at the end of v. 15, it would seem that this is most likely a prayer that Naomi's grandson become a man of significance "in Israel". In verse 11, the phrase is more ambiguous—"proclaim the name in Bethlehem"—and may have been either a reference to Boaz or Yahweh. Here, however, as just stated, it seems best to understand this as a prayer that the boy would become a man of significance "in Israel". Again, little did they know at the time that indeed he would be the forefather of king David (cf. v. 17).

3. The blessings of Naomi (4:15-17)

a. The prayer for longevity (v. 15a)

"May he also be to you a restorer of life and a sustainer of your old age"

Literally the women said, "He will be a restorer of soul and a provider for your gray hair"—or "may he be a restorer of soul and a provider for your gray hair" depending on the interpretation of the grammatical form of the main verb. The point is that the women were praying for and reminding Naomi of her blessings. This grandson would give "comfort" to the formerly bitter one (again cf. 1:20-21; see also Lam. 1:16). He would be her "provider" in her old age. The New Living Translation seems to have caught the spirit here: "May he restore your youth and care for you in your old age".

b. The praise of Ruth's love for Naomi (v. 15b)

"For your daughter-in-law, who loves you and is better to you than seven sons, has given birth to him"

It is notable that Naomi and her grandson are the main characters in this final scene rather than Ruth—though indeed Naomi's "daughter-in-law" is highly praised at the climax of this blessing. The women do not reference Ruth as "the Moabitess" but rather as Naomi's "daughter-in-law". Naomi was now obviously the object of Yahweh's favor in that she had a redeemer-grandson, who was born from a "daughter-in-law who loves [Naomi] and is better in regard to [Naomi] than seven sons".

Biblically speaking, the term "love" speaks of a sacrificial commitment to help and serve another for their good and God's glory. Ruth clearly pledged and lived out that type of sacrificial commitment to Naomi's welfare (cf. 1:16-17; and really the entire book). As Block comments:

> In fact, more than anyone else in the history of Israel, Ruth embodies the fundamental principle of the nation's ethic: "You shall love your God with all your heart" (Deut 6:5) "and your neighbor as yourself" (Lev 19:18). In Lev 19:34 Moses instructs the Israelites to love the stranger as they love themselves. Ironically, it is this stranger from Moab who shows the Israelites what this means (Block, p. 729).

Later in Israel's history, Jonathan, son of Saul, would have that same type of love for David (cf. 2 Sam. 1:26).

The phrase "seven sons" seems to be used in contexts that communicate great blessing from God (1 Sam. 2:5; Job 1:2; 42:13; cf. 1 Sam. 1:18 for a similar overall phrase but the use of 10 instead of 7). But here the women of Bethlehem acknowledged and reminded Naomi that her one "daughter-in-law" was better than the perfect number of "sons". Ruth's character would no doubt influence the character of the one to whom she had "given birth". He would thus reflect his mother's character and be a restorer of life and a sustainer in her old age.

In reciting the blessings of Naomi, there was the implicit prayer for longevity; the praise of Ruth; and now . . .

c. The participation in the son's upbringing (v. 16)

"Then Naomi took the child and laid him in her lap, and became his nurse"
The term here translated "lap" is sometimes translated "bosom", but it is "never used of the breast at which a child nurses" (Block, p. 730). The masculine form of the term here rendered "nurse" is used of Mordecai's role to Esther in Esther 2:7 and of the guardians of Ahab's sons in 2 Kings 10:1, 5 (cf. Num. 11:12; Is. 49:23 for the masculine form as well) (Huey, p. 546). Semi-literally, Naomi became the child's "faithful one".

Naomi came back empty according to her testimony in 1:20-21, but now she was a faithful nanny/grandma to this boy. This too was part of her blessings.

d. The personal name of the son—Obed, meaning "one who serves" (v. 17)

"The neighbor women gave him a name, saying, 'A son has been born to Naomi!' So they named him Obed"
The naming of a child by "women" other than a mother is unique here in the

Old Testament (Block, p. 730). Instead of "the women" of verse 14, here it was "the neighbors" (feminine) who "gave [the child] a name". Perhaps these "neighbor women" were more closely acquainted with Naomi or trusted by her. Though the "son" was born to Ruth by Boaz, the "neighbor women" saw the great blessing to Naomi. Thus they said, "A son has been born to Naomi!" They named the boy "Obed", which means "servant" or "one who serves"— evidently because he would "serve" Naomi in her old age and "serve" as her son in some senses.

e. The progeny of the son (v. 17c)
"He is the father of Jesse, the father of David"
Here the narrator adds an interpretive and historical note to the preceding story. The story of Naomi, Ruth and Boaz was not only about God's grace and redemption of a small family; it was on an account of seemingly small events that would forever alter history. Obed would become the grandfather of "David" i.e., Israel's most famous and most beloved king prior to Jesus Christ. This would be the answer to the crowd's prayer in 4:11—both Boaz and Yahweh's names would be heralded because of progeny of this sovereignly given son named Obed. This too would be part of Naomi's eternal blessing. In heaven she will be able to praise the glory of His grace, faithfulness and matchless wisdom—as should we.

Ruth ends with *the son born to Ruth and Boaz—and his significance to Naomi.* But the following appendix/genealogy that closes the book underscores *the sovereign significance of that son in God's plan of redemption.*

B. The sovereign significance of that son in God's plan of redemption (4:18-22)
1. The "generations" of Perez (v. 18a)
"Now these are the generations of Perez"
The following genealogy officially traces the claim set for in verse 17—that Obed was the father of Jesse, the father of David. The Hebrew word here translated "generations" is *toledoth*. The original audience would have no doubt been immediately reminded of the various genealogical listings in the book of Genesis that began with the same word. In fact, the term *toledoth* serves as the primary literary marker within Genesis (cf. Gen. 2:4; 5:1; 6:9; 10:1; 11:10, 27; 25:12, 19; 36:1, 9; 37:2; see also Num. 3:1; 1 Chron. 1:29). A different form of the word was also used in the genealogical lists of Numbers chapter one. First Chronicles 2:1-15 gives an extended genealogy that parallels this one but without the actual term *toledoth*.

The use of the term *toledoth* in Genesis always designated a significant movement in God's program of redemption. Save the first reference of "the generations of the heavens and earth" in Genesis 2:4, the rest of the uses of toledoth signaled either the continuance of the "Seed" promise of Genesis 3:15 or the narrowing of that promise. In other words, the genealogies of Adam to Noah (Gen. 5); Noah to Shem (Gen. 6:9); Shem to Terah and his son Abram (Gen. 11); Abram/Abraham to Isaac and Isaac to Jacob (Gen. 25:19; 37:2)—all revealed that the Seed promise of worldwide blessing would come through Israel. The genealogies of Ishmael and Esau (Gen. 25:12; 36:1, 9) reveal that the promised "Seed/Redeemer" would *not* come through their lineage or the nations that come from them.

This *toledoth* here at the end of the book of Ruth, then, would signal to the believing remnant that something significant in God's program of redemption was being revealed—and quite likely it involved the narrowing of the "Redeemer-Seed" promise that would lead to the world's blessing and redemption. The final "genealogy" in Genesis was of Jacob and his twelve sons (Gen. 37:2). At the end of Jacob's life, as recorded in Genesis 49:8-12, he prophesied that the Ruler would come from the tribe of Judah (cf. 1 Chron. 5:2). Judah had three sons whose progeny would populate the tribe of Judah according to Genesis 46:12. According to Numbers 26:19-21, the "sons of Perez" became the leading/dominant clan within the tribe of Judah. The believing student of these Scriptures would then wonder if the Ruler/Redeemer-Seed would then be from that clan. This genealogy confirms that probability and leads the reader from "Perez" to "David"—who would be then be graced with the divine promise of a "Seed"/Son who would rule God's house forever (cf. 2 Sam. 7:12-13; 1 Chron. 17:11-14).

2. The genealogy of David (v. 18b-22)
a. Perez
"To Perez"
As previously seen, "Perez" was born from the most notorious levirate type of union in the Scriptures—the one between Judah and his daughter-in-law, Tamar (Gen. 38; cf. note on Ruth 4:10b). See particularly 4:12 concerning the prayer about the house of Perez. And as just mentioned, the "sons of Perez" became the dominant clan in Judah (Num. 26:19-21), and evidently both Elimelech and Boaz descended from "Perez". Why did the author begin with "Perez", rather than Judah? One explanation may be that there could have been concern about the promised "seed" being fulfilled through a Moabitess. But beginning with the genealogy of Perez would have been an equally shocking reminder of God's grace and confounding wisdom in furthering His promise (I'm indebted to Scott Morris in Sunday evening discussion for this insight).

There are ten names in this genealogy recorded at the end of the book of Ruth. This fact, combined with certain chronological difficulties, has lead most scholars to believe that there are names left out—but that the most prominent members were included to show the genealogical link between Judah's son Perez, and David.

b. Hezron
"To Perez was born Hezron"
According to Genesis 46:6-12, "Hezron" was born in Canaan, but traveled with his great-grandfather Jacob and the rest of the family to Egypt to sojourn under Joseph's leadership there. See also Numbers 26:21; 1 Chronicles 2:5, 9, 18, 21, 24-25; 4:1; Matthew 1:3; and Luke 3:33.

c. Ram
"And to Hezron was born Ram"
In 1 Chronicles 2:9, "Ram" is listed as one of Hezron's "sons", which could refer to either a son or descendant. Later, in 1 Chronicles 2:25, a "Ram" is listed as Hezron's grandson—the firstborn of Hezron's firstborn—but this may have been another Ram in light of 1 Chronicles 2:10, 27. Matthew 1:3 calls him "Aram" in the Greek, and Luke 3:33 refers to him as "Arni". The names are close enough to assume that they are the same individual with alternate spellings, taking into account the translation variables.

d. Amminadab
"And to Ram, Amminadab"
"Amminadab" became Aaron's father-in-law according to Exodus 6:23, when his daughter married the future high priest of Israel, and brother of Moses. This relationship and his having fathered "Nahshon" are the two most notable designations of him in the Scriptures (cf. Num. 1:7; 2:3; 7:12; 10:14; 1 Chron. 2:10).

e. Nahshon
"And to Amminadab was born Nahshon"
First Chronicles 2:10 says that "Nahshon" was the leader/prince of the sons of Judah during the time after the Exodus. He was Aaron's brother-in-law (Ex. 6:23). He led Judah and its army according to Numbers 2:3-4; 10:14. He assisted Moses with the census (Num. 1:7). He presented the dedicatory offering for the altar on behalf of the tribe of Judah (Num. 7:12, 17). See also Matthew 1:4 and Luke 3:32.

f. Salmon
"And to Nahshon, Salmon"
"Salmon" is called "Salma" in 1 Chronicles 2:11 (cf. 1 Chron. 2:51, 54). See also Matthew 1:5 and Luke 3:32 [there called "Sala"].

g. Boaz
"And to Salmon was born Boaz"
Matthew 1:5 records that "Salmon" evidently married "Rahab" the Canaanite harlot who came to faith in Yahweh before the conquest of Jericho (cf. Josh.

2:1-7; 6:17-25; Heb. 11:31; James 2:25). "Boaz" came either from that union directly, or was descended from it. See also 1 Chronicles 2:11-12; Matthew 1:5; and Luke 3:32.

h. Obed
"And to Boaz, Obed"
Interestingly enough, though Boaz's intention was to obey the spirit of God's law and raise up seed for his deceased kin (cf. 4:10), Elimelech and Mahlon, God's inspired Word records "Boaz" as the father of "Obed" instead of either Elimelech or Mahlon. God honors those who are willing to lose their life for His sake. See also 1 Chronicles 2:12; Matthew 1:5; and Luke 3:32.

i. Jesse
"And to Obed was born Jesse"
Again, whether or not "Jesse" was the direct son of "Obed" or was a grandson or great grandson is not clear. But the lineage was traced from "Obed" to "Jesse". First Samuel 16:1 calls him "Jesse the Bethlehemite". First Samuel 17:12 says, "David was the son of the Ephrathite of Bethlehem in Judah, whose name was Jesse, and he had eight sons. And Jesse was old in the days of Saul, advanced in years among men". See also 1 Chronicles 2:12; Matthew 1:5; and Luke 3:32 (cf. Is. 11:1, 10).

j. David
"And to Jesse, David"
"David" was Israel's greatest king and the human founder of the dynasty of Davidic kings within Israel. This reference to "David" would seem to imply that the book of Ruth in its final form was compiled after "David" became well known in Israel. The Jewish audience after David would also recognize that the promised Ruler of the Seed of Israel through Judah would be a descendant of "David" (2 Sam. 7; 1 Chron. 17).

This genealogy that closes the book of Ruth serves as an indicator to the believing student of Scripture that God was indeed at work in moving forward His plan and program of redemption—even in the chaotic and heinous "days of the judges" (1:1). He was doing so by keeping the nation alive through various human judges/deliverers in Israel—faults and all. Yet in His infinite grace and wisdom, God was advancing the "Seed" promise—the line of the coming Redeemer—through faithful/believing individuals who were sacrificing themselves for others in love, in order to honor God through obedience to His Word. This is the *prize of redemption*—participation in the Lord's sovereign and wonderful plan of bringing glory to Himself through the salvation of sinners.

Conclusion
So we've seen *the son born to Ruth and Boaz—and his significance to Naomi,*

as well as the sovereign significance of that son in God's plan of redemption. In the end, because of God's loyal love, grace, and sovereign redemption, the pain of sin and its consequences is turned into the prize of serving God and furthering His plan of redemption in Christ.

The book of Ruth was meant to picture and reveal God's matchless and wonderful redemption and His faithfulness to continue His plan even through awful times of sin and rebellion, via a remnant of believers who possess His loyal love and faith. According to Matthew 1:1ff, the Messiah eventually came because of the loyal love and faith of an outcast Moabite woman, a wayward Israelite woman who was slowly brought back to repentance, and a kinsman redeemer who wanted above all else to honor God and obey His Word. They may not have known the extent of their involvement in God's plan, but they pressed on in faith.

Are we instruments in God's plan of redemption?

The book of Ruth should lead us to exult—rejoice exceedingly—in the wonderful, matchless grace of God in Jesus Christ. He is a redeeming God. He is sovereign. No one can thwart His purposes and plan. No one can separate His chosen from His love and redemption. Amazingly, He then uses those He redeems to further His plan of redemption. What a prize! Are we participating in that prize?

Expository Sermon:
Watching God Bring Good Out of Bad

Ruth 4:13-22

by Brad Brandt

It's a tale as old as time. Girl meets boy. Boy falls for girl. Girl lets boy know she's interested in him. Boy lets girl know he feels the same. Boy and girl marry and live happily ever after!

Someone might say, "That's not the way it is in real life. Boy and girl may meet and fall for each other, but in real life there is no happily ever after." Sad to say that's often the case. Which helps explain why many in our day have a low view of marriage.

Be assured, however, marriage isn't the problem. When God is in it, a marriage can sing! And God saw fit to include in His Word a true story to illustrate the point. We've been examining this amazing love story line by line, and now we've come to the final scene.

Let's quickly reset the stage from the previous episodes. Ruth met Boaz. Boaz fell for Ruth. Ruth let Boaz know she was interested in him. Boaz let Ruth know he felt the same. Boaz and Ruth married and lived happily ever after!

Okay, maybe that's not exactly the way the story went. We're not sure about the 'happily ever after' part, but the rest is close.

Now answer this. Who is the main character in the book of Ruth? Someone might say, "It's Ruth, isn't it??" Actually, she is *not*. Although the book bears her name (at least in our English Bibles), Ruth is not the main character. Nor is Boaz. Nor is Naomi. Who then is? Let there be no doubt about it. The main character in the book of Ruth is *God*.

We must always keep this in mind when we study the Bible. When God gave us the Bible He never intended for it to be merely a collection of inspirational stories filled with role models for living. The Bible is first and foremost *His self-disclosure*. That is, in giving us the Bible God is *revealing Himself* to us.

God wants us to know Him. We can learn some things about Him by looking at general revelation (creation)—that He is powerful and wise and caring. But if we're really going to know God, we need more than general revelation. We need *special* revelation. That's what the Bible is, a book that reveals God to us, a book that ultimately reveals the Person of God's Son to us, Jesus Christ, a Person we must know and believe in if we are to truly know God.

So what do we learn about God from the book of Ruth? We discover a very simple yet very encouraging truth. We learn that God specializes in bringing *good results out of what appear to be bad circumstances.* That's good to know if you happen to have what appear to be bad circumstances in your life! The book of Ruth makes it clear that God is at work in our lives even when it doesn't feel to us like He is at work.

Allow me to restate the premise. God is able to bring good results out of what appear to be bad circumstances. A skeptic might say, "I'd like to see some proof to substantiate that premise." Okay, here it is. God brings good out of bad in two ways in the book of Ruth and specifically in Ruth 4:13-22.

I. God can bring good out of bad for a family (13-17).

As we've seen, the story begins with the spotlight on one very ordinary family that lived in Israel during the time of the judges (about twelve centuries before Christ). It was the family of a woman named Naomi. Naomi's family (which consisted of Naomi, her husband Elimelech, and their two sons Mahlon and Kilion) made a decision to do something that was a bad thing, bad in the sense that it resulted in some very unpleasant outcomes. Yet as we see at the end of the story, God turned that which was *bad* into an amazingly good thing. To fully appreciate this truth we need to go back again to the beginning of the story.

Chapter 1, verse 1—"In the days when the judges ruled, there was a famine in the land, and a man from Bethlehem in Judah, together with his wife and two sons, went to live for a while in the country of Moab." Note the decision. A family decided to move to Moab. Was that a good decision? No.

A. A family's move to Moab was a bad thing.
It ended up being bad in three ways.

1. Naomi's family left the promised land.
They lived in Bethlehem which means "house of bread," but they left Bethlehem and went to Moab looking for bread. Why did they leave? A famine hit.

You say, "That sounds like a legitimate reason to leave." But wait. God sent this famine just like He said He would in Deuteronomy 28:23-24. God had given Israel the promised land and had promised to meet their needs IF they would trust and obey Him. This famine was a God-sent wake-up call to His wayward people. The proper response was not relocation but repentance. The fact that Naomi's family moved to Moab seems to indicate a lack of trust in the Lord. That's a bad thing. And so is this…

2. Naomi's sons married non-believers.
Moabite women, to be precise. That's what happens when you move your family to Moab. Your Hebrew boys meet Moabite girls. Kilion married Orpah.

Mahlon married Ruth. Both young ladies were raised in families that worshipped false gods, the chief being Chemosh (1:15). The fact that Naomi's sons married Moabite young ladies seems to indicate that they married nonbelievers (we know that Orpah went back to her 'gods' in 1:15). That's a bad thing. And so is this…

3. Naomi lost her husband and sons.
Her husband, Elimelech, died first, leaving her to raise her sons alone. Then Mahlon and Kilion died. All three of her men died and left her all alone, a widow in a foreign land. That's a bad thing.

There's a contrast in the book of Ruth between *emptiness* and *fullness*. This contrast is exemplified in the words Naomi spoke after she returned from Moab to Bethlehem in 1:21: "I went away *full*, but the LORD brought me back *empty*" (emphasis added).

I think we can make a pretty solid case that the move to Moab was a bad thing, at least bad in the sense that it resulted in some great losses for Naomi and her family. But on the other hand…

B. A family's move to Moab became a good thing (13-17).
Think your way through the book and you'll see seven demonstrations of goodness that resulted all because Naomi's family moved to Moab. In other words, if the family had not moved to Moab the following would not have occurred, not from a human perspective anyway.

1. Ruth gained salvation.
Mahlon married Ruth—although not a forbidden decision it certainly was not a wise decision for a Hebrew boy to marry a Moabite girl. But through it all God worked to bring salvation to Ruth so that she could testify to her mother-in-law in Ruth 1:16: "Don't urge me to leave you or to turn back from you. Where you go I will go, and where you stay I will stay. Your people will be my people and your God my God." Because Naomi's family moved to Moab a pagan girl named Ruth gained salvation. That's a good thing! So is this…

2. Boaz gained a godly wife (13a).
The two met in a barley field in chapter two. Ruth, following Naomi's instructions, made known to Boaz her willingness to marry him in chapter three, and Boaz reciprocated in chapter four, fulfilling the role of kinsman redeemer. In contrast to Mr. *Paloni Almoni*, the nearer kinsman who considered Ruth a liability to his estate, Boaz gladly paid the necessary redemption price in the first scene of chapter four, and in so doing secured Ruth's hand in marriage.

Verse 13 states, "So Boaz took Ruth and she became his wife." If Naomi hadn't gone to Moab, Ruth would never have come to Bethlehem. But Naomi did go, and Ruth did come, and Boaz gained a godly wife! That's a good thing. As is this…

3. Boaz and Ruth gained a special son (13b).

Verse 13 continues, "Then he went to her, and the LORD enabled her to conceive, and she gave birth to a son." Why did this dear couple bear a son? The text makes it clear that *the LORD* gave the child to them. He *enabled her to conceive.*

Do you view your children that way, as gifts the Sovereign Lord has placed in your care? Sometimes I wonder when I hear things like, "We've decided to get our education first, then work for three years, and then after we've purchased our home—one with three bedrooms and a fenced in backyard—we're going to have our first of three children, three years later our second, and four years later our third child." I'm not against family planning, but I am concerned when we "plan" God right out of our lives.

If there is anything the book of Ruth makes clear it's this. God is sovereign. Nothing just happens in our lives, for in all things God is at work. That's true when Naomi loses two sons in chapter one, and when Ruth gains a son in chapter four. In 1:13 Naomi said, "The LORD's hand has gone out against me!" In 4:13 we're told of Ruth, "The LORD enabled her to conceive." God is in control when 'bad' things enter our lives—a famine, the loss of a spouse, and the death of children. He also is in charge of the 'good' things that come our way—such as the conception of a child for Ruth and Boaz.

Naomi's family moved to Moab—that doesn't seem to be a good thing. But out of that God brought about something very good—Boaz and Ruth gained a special son! There's more. Out of the losses of the Moab venture…

4. Naomi gained a special daughter-in-law, son-in-law, and grandson (14-15).

"The women said to Naomi: 'Praise be to the LORD, who this day has not left you without a kinsman-redeemer. May he become famous throughout Israel! He will renew your life and sustain you in your old age. For your daughter-in-law, who loves you and who is better to you than seven sons, has given him birth.'"

At the end of chapter one we saw the women of Bethlehem witnessing Naomi's bitter lament. Now at the end of chapter four the women gather around this new grandmother to celebrate her joy. They affirm that the Lord has given her a kinsman redeemer, not referring here to Boaz but to this baby. This newborn is now the *goel*, the *deliverer*, the one who takes away Naomi's sorrow and guarantees the future hope of her family.

Blessings from God often come in unexpected packages. At the beginning of the story Ruth seemed like a liability to Naomi, but not anymore. The women's compliment of Ruth is quite striking. In Old Testament times people placed great stress on the importance of sons, but here the women assert that Ruth is more valuable to Naomi than *seven sons*! Today's world is skeptical about the mother-in-law and daughter-in-law relationship—and the jokes abound. But God used a daughter-in-law to give hope not only to her mother-in-law, but as we'll see, to the entire nation of that mother-in-law.

Out of the painful losses of Moab Naomi gained a devoted daughter-in-law, a generous son-in-law, and a joy-giving grandchild. Those are three good things! And there's still more!

5. Israel gained a godly king (16-17).

"Then Naomi took the child, laid him in her lap and cared for him. The women living there said, 'Naomi has a son.' And they named him Obed. He was the father of Jesse, the father of David."

Obed means 'servant' (perhaps a shortened form of 'Obadiah' which means 'servant of Yahweh'). That's a strange name (to call a boy 'servant') and it's even stranger noting that the women of Bethlehem gave the child his name. Perhaps the ladies are anticipating the fact that this newborn will serve and care for Naomi in her old age.

When Obed grew up he had a son named Jesse. Jesse later grew up and had eight sons (1 Sam. 16:1-13) and the youngest was a shepherd boy, poem-writing singer and slayer of giants who delivered Israel and became their king. It's ironic that the one the ladies called 'servant' ends up being the grandfather of Israel's greatest ruler, David!

It's worth noting that David did not forget his Moabite roots, for during the time in his life when he fled from Saul, David asked the king of Moab to allow his parents to stay there for refuge (1 Sam. 22:3-4; observation by Huey, p. 547). A Hebrew family's move to Moab, is that a bad thing? Yes, but out of it God gave to Israel a godly king who made God's reputation great in the world! And that's a good thing, but there's still more! Out of a family's loss in Moab…

6. The world gained a Savior.

The book of Ruth ends with a genealogy which we'll examine momentarily. For now note where the Ruth genealogy ends, *with David*. What happened after David? We need another genealogy to answer that question. Turn to Matthew 1 and notice the names…

> **1:2** "Abraham was the father of Isaac, Isaac the father of Jacob, Jacob the father of Judah and his brothers…" [Let's skip a few names and pick it up at…]

1:5-6 "Salmon the father of Boaz, whose mother was Rahab, Boaz the father of Obed, whose mother was Ruth, Obed the father of Jesse, and Jesse the father of King David...." [Look familiar? Those are the names we see in Ruth 4. Now move to the end of the genealogy...]

1:15-16 "Eliud the father of Eleazar, Eleazar the father of Matthan, Matthan the father of Jacob, and Jacob the father of Joseph, the husband of Mary, of whom was born Jesus, who is called Christ." [Now we know what the story of Ruth is ultimately all about! Twelve centuries ahead of time God was providing a vital link that would move His plan forward another step, a step closer to Jesus! But why? Why did Jesus come? We find the answer right here in Matthew 1...]

1:21 "She [Mary] will give birth to a son, and you [Joseph] are to give him the name Jesus, because he *will save his people from their sins.*"

A family moved to Moab and experienced great loss, but out of their loss the world gained a Savior! That's not only a *good* thing but the *best* thing. It means that you and I can be saved from our sins because Jesus took the penalty for them on the cross, and you and I can enjoy eternal life because Jesus conquered the grave and lives and saves any person who will believe in Him.

But even that isn't the end. There's something else that's good that God brought out of the loss of Naomi's family. You say, "What could be better than our salvation?" You need to realize that our salvation is a means to something, something that is the highest good in the entire universe...

7. The Lord gained praise (14a).
Notice verse 14 again, "The women said to Naomi: '*Praise be to the LORD*, who this day has not left you without a kinsman-redeemer'" (emphasis added). That's why God gave Naomi a redeemer named Boaz. That's why God gave the world a Redeemer named Jesus. That's why God does everything that He does, so that He might receive what He alone rightfully deserves. *Praise!*

Verse 14 may well be the key verse of the book. Who brought this family through the pain they endured? Who then provided the redeemer, Boaz? Who blessed this couple with a child? The answer to each question is *God!*

Now ponder this question, are you giving God what He deserves? Did your lips give Him heartfelt praise when you woke up this morning, and did your life give Him deserving praise this past week for His redeeming love? He is worthy, my friend! He is worthy for many reasons and here is the one that confronts us in the book of Ruth. He specializes in bringing *good results out of what appear to be bad circumstances.* He can do it for a family, as He did with Naomi's. He can do it with your family, too, so trust Him fully.

But perhaps you're still not convinced of the premise. Perhaps you're struggling to believe that God can bring *good out of bad*, thinking, "You don't know how bad things are in my life!" Be encouraged. The book of Ruth concludes with yet more evidence of the premise in verses 18-22:

> "This, then, is the family line of Perez: Perez was the father of Hezron, Hezron the father of Ram, Ram the father of Amminadab, Amminadab the father of Nahshon, Nahshon the father of Salmon, Salmon the father of Boaz, Boaz the father of Obed, Obed the father of Jesse, and Jesse the father of David."

You say, "What kind of evidence is that? All I see is a bunch of strange names!" Then let's look again because in that peculiar list we discover something else about God.

II. God can bring good out of bad for a nation (18-22).

It's interesting that Mahlon is not mentioned in the lineage, considering that in a levirate marriage such as Boaz had with Ruth, the first child was to keep alive the family name of the deceased husband, in this case Mahlon. But in this genealogy, Boaz is identified as the father of Obed.

For that matter, why does the book of Ruth end with a genealogy? We can't be sure because the author doesn't specify. But we know there is purpose for all Scripture is inspired and profitable (2 Tim. 3:16-17). I would offer the conjecture that the purpose here is to teach us something about God and how God works. This genealogy makes it clear that God works through two types of people as He accomplishes His redemptive plan.

A. God works through undeserving people.

The author mentions ten names covering a span of around 650 years from Perez to David. Many commentators feel that names have been omitted from the list, suggesting it took more than ten generations to cover the span of 650 years, and that suggestion is possible. For instance, here Ram appears as the son of Hezron, whereas in 1 Chronicles 2:25, 27 Ram is listed as the son of Jerahmeel and the *grandson* of Hezron. The Hebrew word translated "father of" is flexible and is meant to show a connection but not necessarily a literal father-son link.

The ten names in Ruth 4 can be organized into two groups of five. The first five names (Perez to Nahshon) were men who lived during the time Israel was in Egypt and then in the desert journey after Egypt. The second five names (Salmon to David) all lived in the land of Canaan.

Again, there were probably other names in David's ancestry, but these ten are sufficient to show a vital connection. In other words, the point of the author is to show the link between Judah (by his son Perez) and David. He wants us to know that David is from the tribe and line of Judah.

But why? The answer is *grace*. God works through *undeserving people*. This list mentions only *fathers*, but every time a child is born there is also a *mother*. Think about the kind of mothers God used in this link between Judah and David. The list begins with Perez so let's start there. What was true of her?

1. The mother of Perez had sex with her father-in-law.

The sordid story appears in Genesis 38. Judah married a Canaanite woman who bore him three sons—Er, Onan, and Shelah. When Er became of age Judah gave him a wife by the name of Tamar. But Er was a wicked man and the Lord put him to death childless. Judah proceeded to give Tamar to his second son, Onan, so he could have a son to carry on his brother's name. But Onan refused, so the Lord put him to death. Judah had one more son, Shelah, who was eligible to take the widowed Tamar. But Judah refused to give Shelah to Tamar, fearing he would die, too.

When Tamar realized Judah had no intent to allow her to marry Shelah, she took matters into her own hands. She disguised herself and dressed up as a prostitute, and enticed Judah, her own father-in-law, to have sex with her. She conceived twin boys, the oldest named Perez. That illegitimate son, Perez, became the link through which the messianic line continued.

Is there significance to the fact that ten generations are listed in Ruth 4 from Perez to David? Consider this stipulation of the Law recorded in Deuteronomy 23:2, "No one born of a forbidden marriage nor any of his descendants may enter the assembly of the LORD, even down to the tenth generation."

According to M. R. DeHaan, ancient rabbis interpreted it to mean that no descendant of an illegitimate child would sit upon the throne of Israel until the tenth generation (*The Romance of Redemption*, p. 179). God never violates His own word.

The point of the story isn't to commend Tamar. It's to show that God works with and through undeserving people.

Let's look at another example. Verse 21 tells us who Boaz's father was, *Salmon*. Do you know who his mother was? The genealogy in Ruth 4 doesn't tell us, but the one in Matthew does. According to Matthew 1:5, Boaz's mother was Rahab. Why does Matthew record Rahab's name? Who was she?

2. The mother of Boaz was a prostitute.

Rahab, according to Hebrews 11:31, was the Canaanite harlot from Jericho who became a believer in the Lord and hid the spies.

In case you're doing the math and wondering, Rahab actually lived in Joshua's time—that's roughly 1400 B.C. Was Boaz a contemporary of Joshua? Probably not. Boaz probably lived towards the end of the period of the judges, about 250-300 years after Joshua and hence after Rahab.

"But Matthew's genealogy says Rahab was his mother, doesn't it?" The NIV does, but literally the text says Boaz was "of Rahab," indicating that he came from her. It's likely that Rahab was Boaz's 'mother' in the sense that she was his ancestress (like the Bible refers to 'our father Abraham,' in Rom. 4:12, which means 'our ancestor Abraham;' observation by J. Walvoord & R. Zuck, *The Bible Knowledge Commentary*).

Whether it's mother or great-grandmother, the point is still the same. Does Rahab deserve to be included in the genealogy that connects Judah to David, and David to Jesus? No, and that is the point. She didn't deserve it. No one deserved it! But God works through undeserving people. There's more…

3. The mother of Obed was from a pagan family.
Who's that? Ruth. Ruth didn't grow up in a God-fearing home. She was raised to worship idols. Yet the Lord saved her.

It's worth noting that in his genealogy Matthew makes reference to four women: Tamar, Rahab, Ruth, and Bathsheba (whom he simply calls the one who 'had been Uriah's wife'). And why are they there? Because of *grace*. God works through *undeserving* people.

The genealogy in Ruth 4 reveals something else about God…

B. God works through unlikely people.
Look at the final word of the book. *David.* What was true of David? Much could be said, but allow me to point out four things…

1. David was from a common family.
The book of Ruth shows us that.

2. David was the youngest of eight sons.
When Samuel came to Jesse's house to anoint one of his sons as Israel's next king, he was impressed by Eliab, the oldest son. But God told him no and explained, "Do not consider his appearance or his height, for I have rejected him. The LORD does not look at the things man looks at. Man looks at the outward appearance, but the LORD looks at the heart" (1 Sam. 16:7). David was so unlikely a candidate that he wasn't even invited to the meeting!

3. David was a sinner like us.
Who can forget his blunder with Bathsheba? He never did. What then made David a great king?

4. David was a great king because God was great to David.

It's amazing to think that God was preparing the line of David long before Israel even requested a king, years before their first king, Saul, was even alive! Yes, God specializes in bringing good out of bad. He did it for a family and even for a nation.

Lessons from Ruth: Let's reflect on three lessons.

1. Learn to see God in the ordinary events of life.

When you read the book of Ruth you don't see blazing and spectacular miracles. There is no parting of the Red Sea, no staffs turning into snakes, no children being raised from the dead. Instead, you see God working in the way He seems to prefer most, behind-the-scenes in the *ordinary events of life.*

Beloved, God is always at work, *always.* Nothing just *happens* in His universe, for indeed He orchestrates every detail to bring about His good and perfect will.

Many of us have a dwarfed view of God. We believe in a miniature, domesticated God. What we need is a *big* view of God, a view that sees Him in the ordinary events of life.

2. Learn to trust God in the perplexing events of life.

When you don't know what God is up to, be assured that He does. Even in the 'bad' times, He is up to something *good.*

That's the truth of Romans 8:28: "And we know that in all things God works for the good of those who love him, who have been called according to his purpose." In *all things* God works for the good of His people. And what is that 'good'? Verse 29 tells us. "For those God foreknew he also predestined to be conformed to the likeness of his Son, that he might be the firstborn among many brothers." God is forming a people that will resemble His Son, the Lord Jesus. That's what He is doing in the book of Ruth. He is fulfilling His plan to form a people who will share the likeness of His Son.

Without Naomi, there would be no Ruth. Without Ruth, there would be no Boaz. Without Boaz, there would be no Obed. Without Obed, there would be no David. Without David, there would be no Son of David, Jesus. Without Jesus, there would be no people for God to conform to the likeness of His Son, and that means there would be no hope for you or me.

Life is filled with perplexing events. Perhaps yours is even now. Be encouraged.

William Cowper, a friend of John Newton, the writer of *Amazing Grace*, suffered with severe bouts of depression throughout his life. At times he plummeted so low that he became suicidal. Is depression a good thing? It's certainly far from pleasant, yet God worked through it in Cowper's struggles. Cowper learned to meditate on the deep truths of God that sustained his soul. He even wrote some amazing hymns that we sing today, such as *There Is a Fountain Filled With Blood*. He also penned the following poem/hymn filled with amazing insight into the nature and ways of God.

> *God moves in a mysterious way His wonders to perform;*
> *He plants his footsteps in the sea, and rides upon the storm.*
>
> *Deep in unfathomable mines of never failing skill*
> *He treasures up his bright designs and works his sovereign will.*
>
> *Ye fearful saints, fresh courage take; the clouds ye so much dread*
> *Are big with mercy, and shall break in blessings on your head.*
>
> *Judge not the Lord by feeble sense, but trust him for his grace;*
> *Behind a frowning providence He hides a smiling face.*
>
> *His purposes will ripen fast, unfolding every hour;*
> *The bud may have a bitter taste, but sweet will be the flower.*
>
> *Blind unbelief is sure to err, and scan his work in vain;*
> *God is his own interpreter, and he will make it plain.*

The cross was the greatest tragedy of all, for on the cross the perfect Son of God was brutally killed, an utter atrocity! Yet God was there, guiding, even using that terrible deed to bring about the greatest of goods, the demonstration of His matchless grace and the salvation of helpless sinners like us.

Dear friend, we can trust God for He knows what He is doing. And that's what we must do by His gracious enablement. When life is perplexing we need to learn to *trust God*.

3. Learn to magnify God in all the events of life.

This is the message we learn from the tiny book of Ruth. God is at work, not just in the spectacular and miraculous, but in the commonplace details we're so prone to overlook. He is *the God of everyday life* and He is honored when His people consciously choose to magnify Him in all His ways.

Getting Intentional About Application

by Brad Brandt

Several years ago a young teenage girl came to our church for counseling. Her story was heartbreaking. She shared with me that her mother was in prison and she didn't know her father. As I listened to her that day I was filled with both sorrow and joyful anticipation—sorrow because of the pain she'd known, and joyful anticipation because of the hope I knew the sufficient Scriptures had to offer her.

I begin with the premise that God's Word is very practical. It offers life-transforming help to those enslaved by their own sins and to those injured by sins committed against them. Unfortunately, I at times fail to give the Scriptures' practical help and hope to people because I fail to give serious enough attention to *application*. It's so easy to assume that just because we have read and explained the Bible, we have sufficiently enabled our people to experience its wonderful fruit. This assumption falls painfully short.

To use an analogy from the farm, that's like leading a calf to the fence, filling the feedbox on the *other* side of the fence, but failing to open the gate. When we preach God's Word and proclaim the wonderful things God did for His people *back then*, but fail to show our listeners how it applies *today*, we are in essence sending the message, "There's nourishing food for hungry souls in this book, of that you can be sure. I just hope you can find the gate."

Once again, that's why *Getting Intentional About Application* is crucial. God's Word is practical and it's our privilege to show God's people just how practical it is for *their lives*. Here are some tools for the final scene in Ruth.

Tool #1: A Teaching Outline

Some object to the use of sermon outlines, suggesting that outlines remove the element of suspense from the preaching event, making it too predictable. I suppose this is true, but in my estimation the advantages of a fill-in-the-blank type of outline outweigh the disadvantages. A well-crafted outline helps people (and the preacher!) stay on track, engaged in the listening and learning process. It also gives them something tangible to take home for review and implementation purposes. Granted, the goal is life transformation to the glory of God, and not merely to fill in the blanks. But the failure to achieve life transformation isn't the fault of the outline itself, more likely a neglect of sufficient attention to concrete, practical steps of application.

Here is my sermon outline from Ruth 4:13-22.

From Brad's exposition:
Main Idea: God specializes in bringing good results out of what appear to be

bad circumstances. He does so in two ways in Ruth 4:13-22.

I.   God can bring good out of bad for a family (13-17).
- **A.   A family's move to Moab was a bad thing.**
  - 1. Naomi's family left the promised land.
  - 2. Naomi's sons married non-believers.
  - 3. Naomi lost her husband and sons.
- **B.   A family's move to Moab became a good thing (13-17).**
  - 1. Ruth gained salvation.
  - 2. Boaz gained a godly wife (13a).
  - 3. Boaz and Ruth gained a special son (13b).
  - 4. Naomi gained a special daughter-in-law, son-in-law, and grandson (14-15).
  - 5. Israel gained a godly king (16-17).
  - 6. The world gained a Savior.
  - 7. The Lord gained praise (14a).

II.   God can bring good out of bad for a nation (18-22).
- **A.   God works through undeserving people.**
  - 1. The mother of Perez had sex with her father-in-law.
  - 2. The mother of Boaz was a prostitute.
  - 3. The mother of Obed was from a pagan family.
- **B.   God works through unlikely people.**
  - 1. David was from a common family.
  - 2. David was the youngest of eight sons.
  - 3. David was a sinner like us.
  - 4. David was a great king because God was great to David.

Lessons from Ruth:
1. Learn to see God in the ordinary events of life.
2. Learn to trust God in the perplexing events of life.
3. Learn to magnify God in all the events of life.

Tool #2: "Digging Deeper" Discussion Questions

It's wonderful to proclaim and expound God's Word for God's people. It's also very helpful, having preached God's Word, to give God's people opportunity to chew on it and digest it *together*. I often glean helpful insight into the meaning and application of God's Word *from* the congregation I pastor as together we interact with a text. Once again, good questions facilitate this interaction. Here are a few to get started in reflecting on Ruth 4:13-22.

Questions for Clarification:
1. Who is the main character in the book of Ruth? Support your answer biblically.
2. What are some specific ways in which Ruth became a tremendous source of blessing to Naomi?
3. What do we learn in Ruth 4:13-22 about the God-honoring view of children? Contrast this view with common attitudes in today's society towards children.
4. What's the significance of the genealogy that ends the book of Ruth?
5. What additional questions does this passage raise for you?

Questions for Application:
1. Respond to the statement made earlier in the chapter: "Many of us have a

dwarfed view of God. We believe in a miniature God, a domesticated God. What we need is a *big* view of God." What are some evidences of a 'dwarfed view of God'?

2. To follow up on the previous question, what are some practical things we can do to develop a 'big view of God'?

3. Nothing just happens in God's universe, as the book of Ruth so powerfully illustrates. What are some practical ways this truth will affect our lives, if we truly believe it?

4. How does the ending of the book of Ruth give you hope?

5. In your opinion, what is the theme verse of the book of Ruth, and why? How does that verse encourage you?

Tool #3: A Counseling Case Study

The following scenario and discussion time could be used in an elders'/deacons' meeting for the purpose of 'pastoral care' training. One could preface the reading of the scenario with this explanation: "As you listen to the following scenario, think about the message of the book of Ruth and how you might use it to minister help and hope to a person like 'Scott.'"

Scenario: Scott is 47 years old and lives alone. He's been through two broken marriages in his life. The last one ended four years ago and sent Scott into deep despair. He contemplated suicide at the time, but as a last resort visited your church on a Sunday morning. He later acknowledged that this was the first time in his life he had heard the gospel clearly presented. Three months later God graciously opened Scott's eyes and he professed faith in Jesus as his Savior and Lord. After that Scott began to devour the Word of God, never missing a church service and consistently pouring over the Scriptures as a part of his daily routine.

Last week, Scott approached you with a burdened look on his face. He cleared his throat and shared the following, "Something's bugging me and I can't shake it. Now don't get me wrong. I'm so thankful to be a Christian. It's amazing to be forgiven and to know I'm going to spend eternity with Jesus. The hope of heaven thrills my soul."

"Mine, too!" you respond. "But I don't get it. How does thinking about heaven 'bug' you?"

"No, not heaven! It's *this life* that discourages me. As you know I was such a self-absorbed man before Christ saved me. I've got two failed marriages and a boat-load of baggage to prove it. I wish so badly that I could go back and undo my past, not just for personal reasons but for my Lord's sake. I know my sins added to His pain. But I can't go back. And I feel so second-rate in my life. I just can't shake this question, 'Can anything *good* come out of my life?'"

At that point Scott paused, looked you right in the eye and repeated in an almost pleading sort of way, "Can anything good come out of my life?"

Case Study Discussion Questions:
1. Using your own words, summarize Scott's struggle. How does he view God? How does he view himself? How does he view the Christian life?

2. What would you say *first* to Scott?

3. How might you use the story of Ruth to help Scott?

Tool #4: Counseling Assignments Utilizing Ruth 4:13-22
Suppose you offer to meet with Scott (from the previous scenario) for biblical counseling and he agrees. Once again, as in the scenarios presented in earlier chapters, the book of Ruth provides you with an excellent framework for helping someone like Scott. You might suggest meeting together to go through the book of Ruth and to discuss its implications for Scott's presenting question. Both of you could complete and be prepared to discuss the following assignments.

Week One Reading Assignment:
1. Read the entire book of Ruth three times this week. Each time you read it write down your answer to the following questions:

a. After the *first* time: What do I learn about *God* from the book of Ruth? Write down five observations.

b. After the *second* time: What do I learn about *God's plan for His people* from the book of Ruth? Write down five observations.

c. After the *third* time: What do I learn about *my question ("Can anything good come out of my life?")* from the book of Ruth? Write down five observations.

Week Two Reading Assignment:
1. Read through the book of Ruth more slowly this week, one chapter per day for four days. Each time you read answer the following three questions:

a. How does my view of God need to change?

b. What am I learning that gives me hope?

c. What is something I need to *do* in light of what I am learning (then ask the Lord for His help and do it)?

A Selected Bibliography with Brief Annotations

Atkinson, David. *The Message of Ruth* in The Bible Speaks Today Series. Downers Grove: IVP, 1983.
A good reference for the expositor with helpful insights for grasping the point of the text.

Barber, Cyril J. *Ruth: A Story of God's Grace.* New Jersey: Loizeaux Brothers, 1989.
A very good exposition, helpful for both exegetical insight and devotion.

Block, Daniel I. *The New American Commentary: Judges, Ruth.* Nashville: Broadman, 1999.
An indispensable exegetical commentary for the expositor, yet there is a surprising amount of devotional help tied to the exegesis as well. Highly recommended.

Campbell, Jr. Edward F. *Ruth: A New Translation With Introduction and Commentary* in The Anchor Bible Series. Garden City, New York: Doubleday & Company, 1975.
Offers scholarly insights into the text, word meanings, and cultural significance of Ruth.

Constable, Tom. *Tom Constable's Expository Notes on the Bible.* Galaxie Software, 2003.
Very helpful for the expositor. Clear and concise notes that help synthesize the text.

Davis, John J. & Whitcomb, John C. *A Commentary on Joshua-2 Kings.* Winona Lake, IN: BMH, 2002.
Brief, but helpful in both synthesis and exegesis.

DeHaan, M. R. *The Romance of Redemption: The Love Story of Ruth and Boaz.* Grand Rapids: Zondervan, 1958.
Provides a dispensational perspective of the significance of Ruth's message.

Duguid, Iain M. *Esther & Ruth.* New Jersey: Presbyterian & Reformed, 2005.
A tremendous help to the preacher. Eminently quotable and well written. Highly recommended.

Eaton, Michael. *Preaching Through the Bible: Judges and Ruth.* England: Sovereign World, 2000.
Very brief, but of some help because of its simplicity.

Gardiner, George E. *The Romance of Ruth.* Grand Rapids: Kregel Publications, 1977.
Brief but helpful, the fruit of the author's pastoral ministry. Helpful devotional thoughts.

Goslinga, C. J. *Joshua, Judges, Ruth* in The Bible Student's Commentary. Grand Rapids: Zondervan, 1986.
Excellent resource for the Bible student and teacher, helpful explanations, and observations of textual meaning and application.

Huey, Jr. F.B. "Ruth" in *The Expositor's Bible Commentary.* ed. by Frank E. Gaebelein. Grand Rapids: Zondervan, 1992.
A solid work. Useful for the expositor.

Keil, C. F. and Delitzsch, F. *Commentary on the Old Testament in Ten Volumes: Volume II, Joshua, Judges, Ruth, I & II Samuel.* Grand Rapids: Eerdmans, 1976.
Helpful for the expositor interested in the intricacies of the Hebrew text.

Lewis, Arthur. *Judges and Ruth.* Chicago: Moody, 1979.
Brief survey.

Luter, A. Boyd. *Ruth & Esther: God Behind the Seen.* Scotland: Christian Focus, 2003.
A fine exposition. Recommended.

McGee, J. Vernon. *In A Barley Field.* Glendale, CA: G/L Regal Books, 1968.
Valuable insights provided for interpreting and applying Ruth. Good examples given for how to apply Ruth's message.

Morris, Leon. *Judges & Ruth* in Tyndale Old Testament Commentaries. Downers Grove: IVP, 1968.
Solid material here for the preacher and teacher. Recommended.

Reed, John W. "Ruth" in *The Bible Knowledge Commentary: Old Testament,* ed. John F. Walvoord and Roy B. Zuck. Wheaton: Victor Books, 1985.
Brief, yet an insightful basic explanation of the text.

Appendix: Suggested Answers for Counseling Case Studies

One of the tools I proposed for use in making practical application of the book of Ruth is the counseling case study. This commentary offered five sample scenarios for your consideration (one per chapter). Based on initial feedback from test readers, it became apparent that providing suggested answers to the case study questions might prove helpful for readers. With that in mind, I have added this appendix.

A disclaimer is in order. I do not present the following as definitive answers, but merely as helpful (hopefully) suggestions to stimulate your thinking. In our church's biblical counseling training ministry we regularly use case studies as a teaching tool with counselors in training. Typically, there will be three (sometimes more) trainers leading the group discussion. This is intentional so as to provide prospective counselors with a variety of perspectives on how to apply biblical principles to particular problems. What you are about to read is simply *one* perspective on how to apply Ruth's message to contemporary situations.

To reiterate, I do not offer my answers as *the* answers. While God's Word is inerrant and sufficient, I recognize that as a biblical counselor I am inherently neither. Nevertheless, I offer the following comments to seek to demonstrate my firm commitment that God's Word does have *real* answers for the *real* problems we encounter as we seek to help *real* people.

As you will observe, I've chosen to copy the previous scenarios below (to eliminate page flipping), and have inserted my thoughts in a conversational sort of way, one question at a time.

From Chapter One...

Scenario: Bob is a fifty-five year old member of your church. He and his wife, Sally, raised three children, all college graduates with honors. The children are now living, working, and raising their own families in other parts of the country. When the children were younger and at home Bob and Sally never missed any of their school functions (Bob coached their Little League teams, Sally was a den-mother, and so on). The couple team-taught a teen Sunday School class for the past eight years.

Nine months ago Sally died suddenly of a stroke and Bob understandably hasn't been the same since. He continues to attend church regularly but sits by himself, often cries as the hymns are sung, and leaves quickly once the service ends. He asked for a break from his Sunday School teaching the week after the funeral, and hasn't shown any desire to resume since.

You approach him after the service one Sunday, affirm your love and express your desire to help Bob. He breaks down and begins to sob, saying, "I just can't live without Sally. I need her. We did everything together. Why does God seem so distant from me?"

Case Study Discussion Questions:
1. What insights from Ruth chapter one should affect the way we view and seek to help Bob?

We're introduced to several truths in the first chapter of Ruth that help us understand how best to help Bob. The first (perhaps not in importance but in approach) is that *it's okay to grieve.* Death is not 'normal,' contrary to popular opinion. Death is the tragic consequence of Adam's sin (and ours) in God's world. We live in a sin-cursed world where people (including God's people) get sick and even die prematurely (from our perspective, that is). Naomi grieved intensely for a period of time. Bob is certainly not wrong for grieving.

Secondly, *God is sovereign.* He is in control of everything that happens in His universe, including what happens to families like Naomi's, and Bob's. The loss of her spouse and children certainly took Naomi by surprise, but it didn't surprise God. As the book of Ruth will vividly illustrate, God works all things together for His glory and the ultimate good of His people. As we seek to help Bob, we must minister that truth to him very gently, not as a flippant cliché, but as a hope-giving rock for his soul.

Thirdly, *God specializes in bringing good things out of difficult circumstances.* That's the story of the Bible and we certainly see it in Ruth. Granted, we may not know precisely what those good things will be for Bob (Naomi certainly didn't know at the end of chapter one), but the mere fact of the matter offers great hope when the loss is still raw. Romans 8:29 indicates that the primary, good outcome of "all things" (from 8:28) is the formation of a people that resemble God's Son.

Fourthly, *God's provisions may come in unexpected and easily overlooked packages.* Naomi didn't recognize at first the great blessing God had given her in the person of Ruth. God has assuredly placed grace-provisions in Bob's life, too, and it's our privilege to help him begin to identify them.

One final truth from Ruth one is this. *God has a purpose for the surviving spouse.* Bob may be thinking, "I can't live without my Sally." I remember counseling a widower once who continually said similar things long after his wife was gone. It was a major turning point in his life when he recognized that the wise God who took his wife from this world had *left him here*, indicating He had a purpose for him now as a single man.

I am not suggesting that we dump these five truths on Bob all at once. We're not called to 'dump truth' on people, but to minister it gently and in appropriate doses.

2. In light of these biblical principles from the book of Ruth, what can the church do to help Bob?

Psalm 68:6 says, "God sets the lonely in families." By God's design the church is a *family*, a network of relationships created by Christ's atoning work and sealed by the Holy Spirit. Bob's church has a wonderful opportunity to live out its identity in its response to this brother in need. How?

For starters, the church family ought to look for ways to provide Bob (and others like Bob) with expressions of fellowship. Sit down next to Bob in church. Express your appreciation for him. Let him know his tears, should they come, are welcome. Invite him to join your family for the Sunday noon meal.

In addition, give Bob opportunity to talk. Take him out for a cup of coffee and *listen*. Let him talk about Sally. Let him express his feelings, even his frustrations without chastening him. Don't be too quick to answer the *why* question (remember the trouble Job's friends got themselves into by doing that). Granted, in time he will need to do more than *talk*, but your listening will open the door for truth-sharing.

At some point you will want to talk with Bob about his Sunday School teaching. Help him think through some questions, like: Do I still have a heart for teaching teens? How can my God-given gifts best minister to the Body as a single man? It is so important to help hurting people see that God still has a ministry to accomplish both *in* and *through* them in His church.

3. Suppose you offer to meet with Bob for counseling and he agrees…

a. What would you want to accomplish in the *first session*? What passages of Scripture might you share with him that would give him hope?

In the first counseling session with any person, several objectives are essential. We need to gather data (by listening and observing), establish Christ-like involvement as a servant, begin to discern what problems the person is experiencing (from the standpoint of feelings, thinking, and behavior) and give hope by using God's sufficient Word. That's what we'll want to do with Bob, to listen intently, to ask open-ended questions that will help us discern what he needs from us, to demonstrate selfless love for him in his season of loss, and to begin ministering the hope-giving truths of the Scriptures.

Which Scriptures might we use? I regularly turn to passages like Romans 15:13, Romans 8:28-29, 1 Corinthians 10:13, Ephesians 1:3-4, and 1 Peter 1:3-9 to give hope to hurting people like Bob in the initial session.

b. What practical homework assignment(s) might you give Bob to help him?

This will depend largely on what happens during the first session. The purpose of homework is to begin applying biblical principles to particular needs in the counselee's life in order to help him please Christ and be God's kind of person (2 Cor. 5:9). The goal is not to *remove* problems, but to help him respond to problems in God honoring ways (James 1:2-4). In order to help Bob regain a sense of God's purpose for his life, I might assign the following:

1. Read the book of Ruth this week, one chapter a day. Each time you read write down: a) Something you learned about God; b) Something you learned about God's plan for His people. Be prepared to discuss these insights at our next appointment.

2. Write Romans 15:13 on a 3x5 card, read it before every meal, and be prepared to quote it word perfect at our next appointment. Also, be prepared to share how this verse affected you this week.

3. Keep a daily journal this week, including what times you got up and went to bed, how you spent your days, when you ate your meals, what activities you performed, idle times (include what you were thinking and wanting), etc.

c. Suppose you meet weekly with Bob to pray with him and provide biblical encouragement and counsel, yet in the *fifth* session he is still saying, "I *must* have Sally back. I just can't live without her." What biblical truth might you share with Bob to help him think differently? What homework might you give Bob at this point to transform his thinking?

I touched on this in question one above. Bob needs help grasping the truth that *God has a purpose for the surviving spouse*, that God intends to use him now (at least for a season) as a single man. As the question indicates, this is a *fifth* session topic, not a first session topic, and as the scenario states, the discussion is taking place nine months after his wife died. This truth needs to be administered gently, understandingly, and compassionately.

As far as homework goes, I have found the book *Trusting God: Even When Life Hurts* (NavPress), by Jerry Bridges, to be a wonderful resource for helping individuals like Bob. I would assign a chapter a week, encouraging him to underline what he considers to be the ten most meaningful sentences in each chapter, and be prepared to discuss them at our next appointment.

From Chapter Two...

Scenario: Angela is a single parent in her mid-thirties raising three children (ages twelve, eight, and six). She works nights as a nurse's aid at a local care facility and has been raising the children by herself since her ex-husband left her four years ago for another woman. Her children have attended Sunday School at your church for about two years, although she seldom comes, due to her "complicated work schedule." Those were her words to you last Sunday morning when you dropped off her children at their house after church. At that time you noticed that Angela seemed quite overwhelmed with life. A broken mower was sitting in the tall grass of the side yard, the gutters were black with mildew, and a cracked garage door window caught your eye. Before leaving, you invite Angela to join her children next week in church. Her response is polite but to the point, "Thanks, but I don't have room in my life for church. Don't take me wrong. I believe in God, for sure, but it takes every ounce of my energy just to pay the bills and keep life sane for my kids."

As you drove home that day you found yourself thinking about the morning message from Ruth 2 and wondered if God hadn't just placed a providential opportunity in your life. A week later you are leading a Vacation Bible School worker's training session and decide to read the account of Ruth 2 and then share about your experience with Angela. Afterwards you ask the following...

Case Study Discussion Questions:
1. What principles do we find in Ruth 2 that can help us know how to respond to hurting people like Angela? List several.

Principle #1—*Nothing just 'happens' in life.* The doctrine of 'providence' as seen in the book of Ruth has tremendous implications for our daily lives. There are no 'chance' meetings. Ruth didn't just 'happen' to end up in a field owned by Boaz, for God was at work. Likewise, when the Lord allows our path to cross the path of a person in need (as in this scenario involving Angela), we need to see the situation for what it is, a *divine appointment.*

Principle #2—*Real faith shows up in the real world.* As we observed in Ruth two, Boaz demonstrated the reality of God in his life by the way he approached his work (he took God to work with him). Even Boaz's employees recognized this. He didn't just *tell* the people around him that the Lord was important to him. He *showed* them by his treatment of them, his work ethic, and so on. It's great to invite Angela to church where she can *hear* about Christ, but in this scenario we have an opportunity to *show* her Christ. How? By performing actions that will meet pressing needs in her life (for example, mowing her grass, cleaning her gutters, and fixing her garage window). Are these needs her *greatest* need in life? We know they are not (we'll have more to say about that in question three below). But Angela's physical needs provide a present opportunity for us to show the reality of living faith which God may use to open subsequent opportunities to present the object of our faith (the gospel message). Related to this is...

Principle #3—*Real faith works.* The Bible clearly teaches that salvation is by grace alone through faith alone, and not by works (Eph. 2:8-9). But while our works are not the *basis* of our salvation, they are the *fruit* of it (Eph. 2:10). The Bible does not support the so-called 'social gospel' (simply stated, the notion that in some measure salvation is by our works), but it does present a gospel that produces social concerns (a salvation that works). Boaz didn't just call himself a believer in Yahweh. His actions demonstrated his profession. He put God's Law into practice in the treatment he gave a Moabite widow. We have a similar opportunity with Angela.

Principle #4—*God is a providing God, and since we are His children there ought to be a family resemblance.* He provided for our needs (and still does). Consequently, we should prepare ourselves to demonstrate the same family trait when our Father places needy people in our lives. Ruth learned about Yahweh's generous nature by experiencing generosity from His follower, Boaz. Likewise, people like Angela are learning what God is like by observing our actions.

2. Angela is one of many single parents in our world. What are some practical things we can do as a church to show the love of Christ to her and others?

First of all, *pastors need to preach and teach God's Word.* You say, "What does *that* have to do with meeting the needs of single parents?" And the answer to that good question is, a lot! Ephesians 4:11-12 indicates that the pastor's God-given assignment is to "prepare God's people for works of service." I like to think of my pastoral role as a player-coach. Yes, I'm in the game (a player) but my primary responsibility is to prepare the rest of the team to play the game (a coach). As I consistently proclaim God's sufficient Word to the saints, the Spirit of God uses His Word to equip the Body of Christ to function in Christ-like ways in obedience to the Head. As a pastor it encourages my heart greatly to see what happens when God's Word is taught and God's people take seriously their call to 'do the work of the ministry.'

There are many 'works of service' the Body can perform in ministering to single parents. If a woman is raising children alone (as in Angela's case), there may be needs for house and vehicle maintenance, childcare, transportation of children to school events, and so on. She may need parenting counsel and perhaps male role models if she has a son. She needs the encouragement of listening ears and faithful prayer support.

Paul offers a piece of valuable counsel in Galatians 6:10, "Therefore, as we have opportunity, let us do good to all people, especially to those who belong to the family of believers." We find here a helpful guide when it comes to benevolence. When it comes to good deeds, we're to start with our fellow family members in God's household. Then if we're able, we're to go beyond the church family and do good to all people. In other words, the order is local church first, then community (and beyond).

3. What does Angela need from us *first*? What does she need from us *most*?

What Angela needs *most of all* is what every person needs, and that is *to know Jesus Christ*. She says she believes in "God" (nearly everyone in our Bible-belt community would say that), but we realize that belief in a generic "God" can save no one. Jesus clearly asserted that He alone is the way, the truth, and the life (John 14:6). So Angela needs for us to introduce her to the Lord Jesus.

But how best can we do that? Look again at Angela. She is overwhelmed with life. *Survival* is her mode of operation. We know she needs Christ, but she probably doesn't. All she sees is the immediate. The eternal will have to wait, so she thinks.

What Angela needs from us *first* is to see Christ. We have an opportunity to make Christ attractive to her by our willingness to get involved in her life (in ways we suggested in question 2). As Jesus instructed in Matthew 5:16, "Let your light shine before men, that they may see your good deeds and praise your Father in heaven."

From Chapter Three…

Scenario: Steve, a 22-year-old young man, comes to see you. You've known Steve for about three years, since he started attending your church after moving to your city from out of state. Steve, who professed faith in Christ as his Savior two years ago and demonstrated the evidence of God's transforming grace since, now seems quite distressed about something. You welcome him into your living room, thank him for coming, and invite him to share what's on his mind. He tells you he's met a wonderful Christian girl at the university where he attends, that they've been dating about a year, but that now he's perplexed. Simply put, he's fearful. He's never seen a solid marriage up close. He was raised by a single mom and doesn't even remember his dad who left when he was two.

"I'm not sure what real love is," Steve confesses. "I'll be graduating in less than a year and so will Sue. We started talking about marriage last week and it scared me to death. I think I love Sue, but how can I know for sure, I mean, how can I know we should marry? I don't want to repeat what happened to my parents. I'm just so confused." At that point Steve stops talking and looks at the floor.

Case Study Discussion Questions:
1. What would you say *first* to Steve?

"Steve, I'm so glad you came to see me and shared this with me!" That's probably what I'd say *first*, or something to that effect. Steve needs encouragement. His coming to see me affords me the wonderful privilege to help him develop a biblical understanding of love and marriage, and more generally a growing understanding of the goodness, wisdom, and grace of God. It's often tough for a young person to humble himself and seek godly counsel when facing important decisions (for that matter, it's not easy for a person *regardless* of age!).

"God is so good, Steve! He has given us everything we need for living the kind of life that pleases Him. I'd love to spend some time with you right now as we seek to discern what would please Him in your life. The first way I can help you is by *listening*. Would it be okay if I asked you a few questions?"

Data gathering is vital for effective biblical counseling. Proverbs 18:13 says, "He who answers before listening—that is his folly and his shame." One of the quickest ways to insure giving *bad* counsel is to give counsel too quickly. Asking good questions, followed by attentive listening and processing of the information shared, is non-negotiable. Without it, says Proverbs 18:13, folly will result.

Some questions I might pose for Steve would be (not necessarily in this order):

—"Tell me about Sue. What's she like?"
—"What do you *think* love is?"
—"How did the subject of marriage happen to come up last week?"
—"What makes you think you might *repeat* what happened to your folks?"
—"What specifically about marriage scares you so much?"

2. What does Steve need *most* from you in this conversation?

He needs my encouragement to think and act biblically as he makes decisions concerning his relationship with Sue. I can assure him that God's Word has sufficient answers for all the problems of life (2 Pet. 1:3-4), and I would be honored to help him find God-honoring answers to his questions. Of course, we wouldn't want to tackle all the pertinent questions that very night, but we could establish a good starting point by addressing the issue of his *fear*.

The Scriptures teach that true love casts out fear (1 John 4:18). As we learn what true love is and then put that knowledge into practice by putting on love for God and others, fear's power diminishes. Thankfully, true love 'comes from God' (1 John 4:7). We love because He first loved us. In fact, if we know Christ the ability to love is guaranteed by the Holy Spirit who lives in us. Galatians 5:22 indicates that the fruit of the Spirit is *love*. In His amazing grace, God enables us as His children to do what we could not do naturally on our own. He *supernaturally* enables us to reflect His love by the ministry of His Spirit.

There is much more we'll probably want to share with Steve (as we continue to gather data and grow in our understanding of what he is thinking), but this foundational truth is significant. It's wonderful to know that our ability to live the kind of life that pleases God is not limited by our past, but depends upon His abounding grace.

3. How might you use the story of Ruth to encourage Steve in this initial conversation?

I love to use biblical stories in counseling situations. Certainly, the story of Ruth is an attention-grabbing and hope-giving account. Steve is concerned that his past (his lack of seeing a God-honoring model of marriage by his parents) may limit his ability to experience a God-honoring, fulfilling marriage. It will be a joy to share with him what God mercifully did in and through Ruth's life. Ruth certainly had no God-honoring model to learn from either (her parents worshipped a pagan deity), but God's grace was sufficient for her.

Indeed, God chose to incorporate her into the very lineage of His Son. Furthermore, the theme of God's providence as illustrated in the book of Ruth can provide Steve with reason for great hope. God has a proven track record of redeeming sinners who didn't even know His Word, let alone have role models of it, and turn them into marvelous trophies of His grace!

4. What other passages in God's Word might you use to help Steve initially?

In order to give this brother hope about God's good plan for his life I might share one of the following promise-giving texts:

Jeremiah 29:11 "'For I know the plans I have for you,' declares the LORD, 'plans to prosper you and not to harm you, plans to give you hope and a future.'"

Exodus 15:13 "In your unfailing love you will lead the people you have redeemed. In your strength you will guide them to your holy dwelling."

Though these Old Testament verses were originally given to Israel as God's chosen Nation, by way of application they reveal God's heart towards believers today.

From Chapter Four...

Scenario: Angela (a fictitious character) has met "Mr. Right." That's what she has been telling your small group at church for the past two Sundays. She met Larry just four months ago at the school where they both teach. Angela, who became a believer three years ago while in college, is a 23 year old, first year elementary school teacher. Larry, age 22 and also in his first year of teaching, is an only child who still lives at home. Angela says she "led him to the Lord" shortly after they met.

"When's the wedding?" someone asks Angela just before the beginning of this week's small group meeting.

"Three weeks from Saturday!" she responds. "We're going to have a quaint ceremony at Larry's parent's lodge. You're all invited!"

"Whoa! Three weeks?" someone in the crowd chimes in—it was more of a statement than a question. "That's a pretty quick romance, isn't it?"

Angela insists it's because "God brought us together" and "It was love at first sight" and "We just know we're right for each other."

No one says anything else about the wedding until the small group meeting ends that night. As people are leaving, Angela approaches you (the group leader) and asks, "Can I ask you something? Why do I get the feeling that not everybody here is as excited as I am about me getting married? I want to know."

Case Study Discussion Questions:
1. Angela's view of love seems more influenced by Hollywood than the Bible. How so?

In the typical Hollywood movie, love occurs within a two hour block of time. Two characters meet, get to know each other a little bit (maybe), begin to have feelings for each other, and then boldly assert they can't live without each other. I'm not knocking quick romance, but I would question whether 'love' is the best term to describe such instant attraction.

The notion of "falling in love" certainly falls far short of the biblical concept of love. As demonstrated by Boaz in Ruth chapter four, true love exhibits some very tangible characteristics: it takes action (Boaz initiated the redemption payment), is willing to pay the necessary price (Boaz calculated and delighted in paying the cost of the redemption), is willing to be accountable (Boaz made a *public* commitment), and consequently receives God's blessing. The idea that one can "fall in love" guts love of its volitional depth. Emotions are wonderful but they must flow out of a person's volition and action, as God Himself exemplified, "For God so *loved* the world that He gave His one and only Son (John 3:16)." Biblically understood, love is fundamentally a decision to take sacrificial action to meet the needs of another person motivated by a desire to please God.

When Angela says it was "love at first sight," what she means is that she *felt* an immediate attraction to Larry when she met him. Again, her understanding of love is *feeling-based*. The truth about feelings is that they can leave just as quickly as they came. True love, however, is unchanging. As Paul put it in 1 Corinthians 13:7-8, "It always protects, always trusts, always hopes, always perseveres. Love never fails."

2. What are some questions that Angela may need to address? Take some time to frame those questions now.

For Angela, the will of God is a personal, individual matter, something God makes known *to me*. The Scriptures caution against this and emphasize the importance of seeking godly counsel. Here are a few questions Angela ought to consider (and we might encourage her to explore) as she seeks to discern God's good purposes for her life:

—What insight does Proverbs 15:22 ("Plans fail for lack of counsel, but with many advisers they succeed") give concerning decision making?
—Does my understanding of love square with the Bible's explanation (for instance, in 1 Corinthians 13 & 1 John 4:7-21)?
—Do I have a biblical basis for concluding that the wedding is truly the will of God?
—Why did I become upset when I sensed that others didn't seem to share my excitement about my wedding plans?

3. Supposing you are the group leader that Angela approaches, how would you respond to her? How might you use the story of Ruth in the conversation?

It's vital to remember that a true friend doesn't merely tell you what you *want* to hear (that's flattery), but what you *need* to hear in order to please God. Furthermore, a mark of maturity in the Body of Christ, according to Ephesians 4:15, is when we learn to "speak the truth in love" with one another. In this scenario, Angela has opened the door by asking for honest input.

For starters, I would thank her for her coming to me, communicate my appreciation for her as a sister in Christ, and express my intent to seek the glory of our Savior and her good in this important decision. I would emphasize that marriage is a wonderful gift given by our gracious and good God, and that by His design it is a picture of Christ's relationship with His bride, the Church (Eph. 5:23, 25). The latter truth underscores the importance of exercising great discernment before entering marriage, since marriage isn't just about *me*, but is an opportunity to exalt Christ.

I would remind Angela that God in His wisdom has given us wonderful examples in His Word of how real people honored Him in the past as they considered marriage. I would encourage her to read the book of Ruth, asking her to pay particular attention to what we learn about *love* from the actions of Ruth and Boaz. I would then let her know that my wife and I would like to meet with her soon to discuss what she gleaned from reading Ruth (see question one above for particulars), as well as to pray with her as she seeks God's good purposes for her life.

From Chapter Five…

Scenario: Scott is 47 years old and lives alone. He's been through two broken marriages in his life, the last one ended four years ago and sent Scott into deep despair. He contemplated suicide at the time, but as a last resort visited your church on a Sunday morning. He later acknowledged that this was the first time in his life he had heard the gospel clearly presented. Three months later God graciously opened Scott's eyes and he professed faith in Jesus as his Savior and Lord. After that Scott began to devour the Word of God, never missing a church service and consistently pouring over the Scriptures as a part of his daily routine.

Last week, Scott approached you with a burdened look on his face. He cleared his throat and shared the following, "Something's bugging me and I can't shake it. Now don't get me wrong. I'm so thankful to be a Christian. It's amazing to be forgiven and to know you're going to spend eternity with Jesus. The hope of heaven thrills my soul."

"Mine, too!" you respond. "But I don't get it. How does thinking about heaven 'bug' you?"

"No, not heaven! It's *this life* that discourages me. As you know I was such a self-absorbed man before Christ saved me. I've got two failed marriages and a boat-load of baggage to prove it. I wish so badly that I could go back and undo my past, not just for personal reasons but for my Lord's sake. I know my sins added to His pain. But I can't go back. And I feel so second-rate in my life. I just can't shake this question. Can anything *good* come out of my life?"

At that point Scott paused, looked you right in the eye and repeated in an almost pleading sort of way, "Can anything good come out of my life?"

Case Study Discussion Questions:
1. Using your own words, summarize Scott's struggle. How does he view God? How does he view himself? How does he view the Christian life?

Many today would insist that Scott has a 'low self esteem' and that what he needs is help restoring his damaged psyche. Some would even attempt to use the Scriptures to support this premise, for instance suggesting that God's Law is summed up in *three* commands in Matthew 22:37-39: "Love the Lord your God...and love your neighbors as yourself." The three commands, they say, are *love God, love neighbor, and love yourself.* Some would go so far as to assert that heeding the third command is essential to fulfilling the first two. "You can't love God and others until you first learn to *love yourself,*" the reasoning goes.

The counsel is faulty for a variety of reasons. First, Jesus clearly stated in the text at hand that the Law hangs on *two* commandments (Matt. 22:4). In fact, He assumes that man's tendency is to be self-focused, even self-absorbed. The Law calls us to *love God* and to *love neighbor* with the same tendency we already have to focus on ourselves. Indeed, elsewhere Jesus calls us not to *love* self, but to *deny* self (Matt. 16:24), even to *hate* self (Luke 14:26). To suggest to a person who struggles with so-called 'low self esteem' that he needs to *love himself more* will only lead him deeper into the bondage of sinful introspection (for further help on the subject, I recommend Jay Adams' helpful book, *The Biblical View of Self-Esteem, Self-Love, and Self-Image*, Harvest House Publishers).

Scott doesn't need help adjusting a supposed 'low self esteem.' Granted, he is thinking wrongly about himself, but more fundamentally, he is thinking wrongly *about God*. Scott's view of God, which comes through loudly and clearly in his comments, is skewed. He certainly is not alone in his unbiblical notions about the Maker.

Scott would readily agree that God is holy which necessitates that He banish sin from His presence. Scott would likewise admit that God is just and consequently cannot overlook sin but must judge it. Scott rightly sees God as a God who must deal firmly with sin. What Scott fails to grasp, however, is the wonderful sufficiency of the gospel. In His grace, God did take care of Scott's sin problem. His Son died as a substitute, exhausting the fullness of God's just wrath in the place of the sinner (1 John 2:1-2; Rom. 3:21-26). What's more, God mercifully gives the justified sinner the merit of His perfect Son's righteousness (2 Cor. 5:21).

Scott misunderstands the sufficiency of God's grace. God's grace is greater than the sinner's sin (Rom. 5:20 "Where sin increased, grace increased all the more"). Scott is refusing to believe God who has stated, "There is no condemnation for those who are in Christ Jesus (Rom. 8:1).

How does Scott view himself? He sees himself as a child of God, but a distant one. He is convinced that God's condemnation continues to rest on him (contrary to Romans 8:1). He believes that he must endure a second-rate life due to the greatness of his sinful past. He fails to grasp the sufficiency of Christ's atoning work in his behalf. He needs to grow in his understanding of God's grace of which Paul, the chief of sinners, would say, "The grace of our Lord was poured out on me abundantly, along with the faith and love that are in Christ Jesus (1 Tim. 2:14)."

Scott's view of the Christian life follows suit. He believes that God's grace is sufficient to take him to heaven some day, but is *insufficient* for present living. His unspoken implication is that God works only through *deserving* people, people who don't have 'too bad' of a past. Again, the wonderful news of the glorious gospel is that because of and through Christ, God has a *first rate* plan for all of His children. He intends to bring glory to Himself through their lives (1 Tim. 1:15-17).

2. What would you say *first* to Scott?

Scott's question reveals the depth of Scott's pain. Can anything good come out of my life? I wonder how many people sitting in churches today hold to similar notions. As explained in the previous answer, there is tremendous hope for Scott (and others like him). The solution isn't to downplay Scott's assessment by saying, "Surely, you're overreacting, Scott. I'm sure you did some good things in your past. Focus on that. Then you'll feel better about yourself." Not only does such counsel understate the severity of sin, it also misses the point. God's agenda isn't that His children feel good *about themselves*. His agenda is that His children exalt *His wonderful Son*!

With that in mind the first thing I would want to say to Scott would be something like, "Scott, I am so glad you shared your feelings with me and asked me that important question! I believe there is great hope for you, a hope that rests not in what you have or have not done, but in *what God has said*. God's Word has so much to say about the question you're wrestling with! Would you be interested in looking at this priceless truth with me?"

If Scott agreed to do so, I would open the Scriptures and begin to unpack the important truths explained above in question 1. What a thrill it is to share with burdened people like Scott the hope-giving message of the gospel! The gospel message not only gives sinners the hope of heaven but also gives children of God the hope of first-rate living prior to heaven (I am indebted to Jerry Bridges for his helpful emphasis that Christians need to *preach the gospel to themselves every day*; see Jerry Bridges, *Transforming Grace*).

3. How might you use the story of Ruth to help Scott?

The final verses of Ruth 4 would be an excellent passage to discuss with Scott.

I might begin by asking, "Scott, when you look at that genealogy (in Ruth 4:18-22), what do you see?" His likely response might be, "A bunch of names! Why? What should I see?" I would then help him see that this is no mere 'bunch of names,' but a God-inspired record of the fact that God specializes in working through undeserving sinners to accomplish His purposes.

At that point I might back up and begin to walk through the book of Ruth with Scott. The story of the book of Ruth reveals in living color that God works through unlikely people to fulfill His redemptive plan, all to His glory. I would encourage Scott to reread this story, asking him to pay particular attention to God's dealings with and through the character Ruth. There was certainly nothing in Ruth's past that could merit God's favor. To the contrary, she was a pagan idolater, yet God in His grace rescued her, transformed her, and incorporated her into the wonderful redemption story that ultimately resulted in the coming of Jesus Christ.